Marketing Communications
2005–2006

The Chartered
Institute of Marketing

Marketing Communications 2005–2006

Graham Hughes and Chris Fill

ELSEVIER
BUTTERWORTH
HEINEMANN

AMSTERDAM BOSTON HEIDELBERG LONDON NEW YORK OXFORD
PARIS SAN DIEGO SAN FRANCISCO SINGAPORE SYDNEY TOKYO

Elsevier Butterworth-Heinemann
Linacre House, Jordan Hill, Oxford OX2 8DP
30 Corporate Drive, Burlington, MA 01803

First published 2005

British Library Cataloguing in Publication Data
A catalogue record for this book is available from the British Library

Library of Congress Cataloguing in Publication Data
A catalogue record for this book is available from the Library of Congress

ISBN 0 7506 6648 X

For information on all Elsevier Butterworth-Heinemann publications
visit our website at http://books.elsevier.com

Typeset by Integra Software Services Pvt. Ltd, Pondicherry, India
www.integra-india.com
Printed and bound in Italy

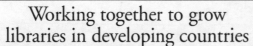

Contents

Preface
welcome to the CIM coursebooks

Welcome to the coursebook for the CIM Professional Diploma module in Marketing Communications. The syllabus is designed to build on the knowledge of the theories underpinning marketing communications and the effective application of communications tools such as advertising, PR, sales promotion, personal selling, direct and interactive methods and sponsorship. These are the major tools at the disposal of the communications practitioner although it is recognized that there are many facets to the ways in which messages reach their intended targets. There is a focus on the importance of co-ordination in achieving effectiveness, which involves examining the ways in which communications tools interrelate.

Structure

The coursebook has been structured in a way that means as you work through the units you are building the knowledge in the right order so that you have a strong command of the subject and, of course, are better placed to pass the assessments set. You should work through the units in numerical order and complete as many of the activities as possible.

The syllabus for the Marketing Communications module is provided at the end of the book for your reference, and in each unit you are referred to the syllabus references being covered. All the syllabus topics are covered, but not specifically in the order laid out in the module syllabus. This approach is intended to make your learning process easier and build incrementally.

Support

This coursebook has been written so that you can develop an understanding of the subject quickly, have easy reference to all the topics that you need to know about and be able to work through a series of activities to assist your understanding of the subject. It has been deliberately kept slim and manageable, designed to provide you a programme of learning about Marketing Communications.

However, this is not textbook, it is a coursebook designed to help you learn and understand. We strongly recommend that you do not rely on the coursebook alone for your studies. References should be made to one of the essential textbooks recommended by the CIM and for this particular module the textbook is:

Chris Fill (2005) *Marketing Communications: Engagement, Strategies and Tactics*, 4th edition, Harlow: Pearson Education.

This book provides the depth of analysis that is required in a postgraduate course and will enable you to appreciate why certain actions are recommended as well as the 'how-to' aspect. Therefore, please use the two learning resources in tandem.

In addition to these books you are encouraged to read the weekly trade papers, in particular, *Marketing, Marketing Week, Campaign, PR Week* and *Precision Marketing.* We have included references to numerous websites that will support points being made. You should also use MarketingOnline, the online learning resource provided by Butterworth-Heinemann. If you are able to use all of these resources, then we are confident that you will not only be successful in the assessment, but enjoy learning about this fast-changing subject.

Good luck with your studies.

Graham Hughes and Chris Fill

Authors' acknowledgements

We would like to thank all those who have given their time, skills, knowledge and patience to the development of this coursebook.

In particular, we would like to thank our families for their understanding and patience during the writing period, the 'lost' weekends and evenings!

An introduction from the academic development advisor

In the last two years we have seen some significant changes to CIM Marketing qualifications. The changes have been introduced on a year-on-year basis, with Certificate changes implemented in 2002, and the Professional Diploma in Marketing being launched in 2003. The Professional Postgraduate Diploma in Marketing was launched in 2004. The new qualifications are based on the CIM professional Marketing Standards developed through research with employers.

As a result, the authoring team, Elsevier Butterworth-Heinemann and I have all aimed to rigorously revise and update the coursebook series to make sure that every title is the best possible study aid and accurately reflects the latest CIM syllabus. This has been further enhanced through independent reviews carried out by CIM.

We have aimed to develop the assessment support to include some additional support for the assignment route as well as the examination, so we hope you will find this helpful.

There are a number of new authors and indeed Senior Examiners in the series who have been commissioned for their CIM course teaching and examining experience, as well as their research into specific curriculum-related areas and their wide general knowledge of the latest thinking in marketing.

We are certain that you will find these coursebooks highly beneficial in terms of the content and assessment opportunities and a study tool that will prepare you for both CIM examinations and continuous/integrative assessment opportunities. They will guide you in a logical and structured way through the detail of the syllabus, providing you with the required underpinning knowledge, understanding and application of theory.

The editorial team and authors wish you every success as you embark upon your studies.

Karen Beamish
Academic Development Advisor

Professional Postgraduate
Diploma in Marketing

Professional Diploma
in Marketing

Professional Certificate
in Marketing

Introductory Certificate
in Marketing

Study note © CIM 2005

How to use these coursebooks

Everyone who has contributed to this series has been careful to structure the books with the exams in mind. Each unit, therefore, covers an essential part of the syllabus. You need to work through the complete coursebook systematically to ensure that you have covered everything you need to know.

This coursebook is divided into units each containing a selection of the following standard elements:

- ○ *Learning objectives* – Tell you what you will be expected to know, having read the unit.
- ○ *Syllabus references* – Outline what part of the syllabus is covered in the module.
- ○ *Study guides* – Tell you how long the unit is and how long its activities take to do.
- ○ *Questions* – Are designed to give you practice – they will be similar to those you get in the exam.
- ○ *Answers* (at the end of the book) – Give you a suggested format for answering exam questions. *Remember* there is no such thing as a model answer – you should use these examples only as guidelines.
- ○ *Activities* – Give you a chance to put what you have learned into practice.
- ○ *Debriefings* (at the end of the book) – Shed light on the methodologies involved in the activities.
- ○ *Hints and tips* – Are tips from the senior examiner, examiner or author and are designed to help you avoid common mistakes made by previous candidates and give you guidance on improving your knowledge base.
- ○ *Insights* – Encourage you to contextualize your academic knowledge by reference to real-life experience.
- ○ *Key definitions* – Highlight and explain the key points relevant to that module.
- ○ *Definitions* – May be used for words you must know to pass the exam.
- ○ *Summaries* – Cover what you should have picked up from reading the unit.
- ○ *Further study* – Provides details of recommended reading in addition to the coursebook.

While you will find that each section of the syllabus has been covered within this text, you might find that the order of some of the topics has been changed. This is because it sometimes makes more sense to put certain topics together when you are studying, even though they might appear in different sections of the syllabus itself. If you are following the reading and other activities, you coverage of the syllabus will be just fine, but do not forget to follow up with trade press reading!

About MarketingOnline

Elsevier Butterworth-Heinemann offers purchasers of the coursebooks free access to MarketingOnline (www.marketingonline.co.uk), our premier online support engine for the CIM marketing courses. On this site you can benefit from:

○ Fully customizable electronic versions of the coursebooks enabling you to annotate, cut and paste sections of text to create your own tailored learning notes.
○ The capacity to search the coursebook online for instant access to definitions and key concepts.
○ Useful links to e-marketing articles provided by Dave Chaffey, Director of Marketing Insights Ltd and a leading UK e-marketing consultant, trainer and author.
○ A glossary providing a comprehensive dictionary of marketing terms.
○ A frequently asked questions (FAQs) section providing guidance and advice on common problems or queries.

Using MarketingOnline

Logging on

Before you can access MarketingOnline you will first need to get a password. Please go to www.marketingonline.co.uk and click on the registration button where you will then find registration instruction for coursebook purchasers. Once you have got your password, you will need to log on using the onscreen instructions. This will give you access to the various functions of the site.

MarketingOnline provides a range of functions, as outlined in the previous section, which can easily be accessed from the site after you have logged on to the system. Please note the following guidelines detailing how to access the main features:

1. *The coursebook* – Buttons corresponding to the three levels of the CIM marketing qualification are situated on the home page. Select your level and you will be presented with the coursebook title for each module of that level. Click on the desired coursebook to access the full online text (divided up by chapter). On each page of text you have the option to add an electronic bookmark or annotation by following the onscreen instructions. You can also freely cut and paste text into a blank word document to create your own learning notes.
2. *e-Marketing articles* – To access the links to relevant e-marketing articles, simply click on the link under the text 'E-marketing Essentials: useful links from Marketing Insights'.
3. *Glossary* – A link to the glossary is provided in the top right-hand corner of each page enabling access to this resource at any time.

If you have specific queries about using MarketingOnline, then you should consult our fully searchable FAQs section, accessible through the appropriate link in the top right-hand corner of any page of the site. Please also note the a *full user guide* can be downloaded by clicking on the link on the opening page of the website.

unit 1
introduction to marketing communications

Learning objectives

For many businesses, marketing communications represent the focal point of their marketing activities, and in some cases the two areas are synonymous. The roles of advertising, sales promotion, public relations, personal selling and other promotional tools are significant in achieving marketing success. The advent of new technologies has been changing the nature of communications activities, information gathering and purchasing which are being made increasingly easier via the Internet. However, many basic principles concerning how communications work remain sound. These include the ways in which individuals and groups influence different dimensions of purchase decision-making behaviour.

After completion of this section you will be able to:

o   Understand the importance of marketing communications in achieving marketing success

o   Explain some of the theories that underpin marketing communications

o   Demonstrate how communications work in influencing purchase decision-making

o   Describe the roles that individuals and groups play in making communications effective

o   Understand the purchase decision-making process and the factors that influence its operation

o   Explain the different types of appeal used in marketing communications and the concept of likeability

o   Understand the issues concerning ethics and corporate social responsibility and their impact on marketing communications.

Syllabus references include: 1.1, 1.2, 1.3, 1.5, 2.8.

Key definition

Marketing communications are a management process through which an organization enters into a dialogue with its various audiences. Based upon an understanding of the audiences' communications environment, an organization develops and presents messages for its identified stakeholder groups, and evaluates and acts upon the responses received. The objective of the process is to (re)position by influencing the perception and understanding of the organization and/or its products and services, with a view to generating attitudinal and behavioural responses. (Fill, 2002)

Introduction to the coursebook

Marketing communications play an increasingly significant role in achieving overall marketing success. In large part, this is due to many organizations developing a relationship building approach to how they deal with customers on a long-term basis. This coursebook is structured in a way that identifies the key principles which underpin marketing communications and demonstrates how these principles are applied in many different types of situation, using the tools of marketing communications. In broad terms, there are a number of issues that influence marketing communications strategies and activities:

- Need for a co-ordinated approach in implementing communications campaigns
- Continuing advances in media and communications technologies
- Media fragmentation – new opportunities for communications channels
- Influence of ethics and corporate social responsibility
- Availability of detailed customer information and database technology
- More demanding and better informed customers
- Need for better evaluation and effectiveness measurement.

These issues will be discussed, some in a number of places, in this coursebook. The coursebook provides coverage of the whole syllabus for this module. Syllabus references are highlighted at the start of each unit where they are specifically addressed, although there will be areas of the syllabus which are dealt with in more than one unit (Table 1.1). The coursebook is only one of the tools that you will use in order to develop your understanding and knowledge of the subject. References are made to other sources including the essential textbooks recommended by CIM. Make sure you read as widely as possible around the topics discussed, making full use of those indicators contained in each unit for Further study, and Hints and tips. A number of activities will involve you in looking at the websites of different types of organizations, these will further aid the development of your knowledge and understanding of key issues.

Table 1.1 Learning outcomes and unit/syllabus guide

Learning outcomes	Study units/syllabus reference
Explain the role of marketing communications and advise how personal influences might be used to develop promotional effectiveness	Unit 1 – Syllabus 1.1–1.3
Explain how the tools of the promotional mix can be co-ordinated in order to communicate effectively with customers and a range of stakeholders	Unit 2 and Unit 8 – Syllabus 2.1–2.5, 2.16
Devise a basic media plan based on specific campaign requirements using both online and offline media	Unit 7 – Syllabus 2.6–2.7
Develop marketing communications and brand support activities based on an understanding of the salient characteristics of the target audience	Unit 1 and Unit 2 – Syllabus 1.3–1.5, 2.2–2.4
Explain the main elements, activities and linkages associated with the formulation and implementation of a marketing communications plan	Unit 6 – Syllabus 2.13
Recommend a suitable marketing communications budget	Unit 6 – Syllabus 2.14
Explain the importance of developing long-term relationships with customers, channel members, agencies and other stakeholders and transfer such knowledge to the development of marketing communications activities	Unit 4 and Unit 5 – Syllabus 3.1–3.5, 4.1–4.7
Suggest suitable methods to influence the relationships an organization has with its customers, any marketing channel partners and other stakeholders, using marketing communications	Unit 2, and Unit 4 and Unit 5 – Syllabus 4.1–4.7
Use the vocabulary of the marketing communications industry and be able to communicate effectively with other marketing practitioners	Unit 3 – Syllabus 4.4–4.7
All learning outcomes are designed in order that you can apply marketing communications in practice in a range of different situational contexts	The learning outcomes are relatively broad in nature and as such the syllabus references above are indicative only. At the start of each unit, the syllabus references are more specific to the topics covered

The communications process

It is not surprising that with all this 'noise' (Figure 1.2) surrounding us, the task of marketing communications has become increasingly difficult. For any message to get through, it must break through the surrounding noise and grab hold of the potential consumers' attention. To understand the complex process of marketing communications, we have to recognize that each and every one of us have to use some form of filtering system in order to extract the information we need from everything that surrounds it.

Activity 1.1

Spend 10 minutes or so thinking about the kinds of marketing communications messages you can recall 'receiving' over the last 24 hours. Can you identify what kinds of information this has included and what responses you have made?

If you found the above difficult in terms of remembering what you had received, over the next 24 hours make a record of your exposure to marketing communications and your response to this.

We can look at a simple model of communication which describes the various stages. At its simplest level, we can describe the model as having three elements. The first is the sender of the message. The second is the message itself, and the third is the recipient of the message. This could be depicted as shown in Figure 1.1. Unfortunately, this model oversimplifies the nature of the process. It makes no allowance for the fact that the message may not be understood or even received by the recipient; nor does it take into consideration the means by which the message is transmitted to the receiver.

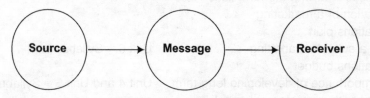

Figure 1.1 A simple model of the communication process

A better understanding of the process is provided by the more detailed model shown in Figure 1.2.

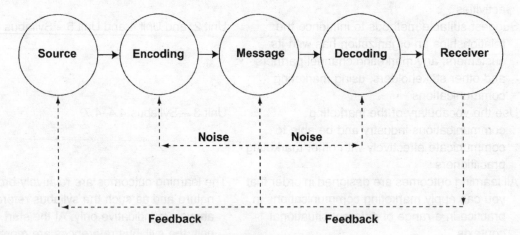

Figure 1.2 A linear model of the communication process
Source: After Shannon and Weaver (1962)

Sender – The sender is the source of the message, that is the organization – they ascertain the need to communicate with the customer and will then through the encoding process, identify the appropriate basis of communication.

Encoder – Encoding the actual message, its content and the intended meaning into a symbolic format that can be transmitted and understood by the target audience; symbolic format being appropriate words, pictures, images or music that the customer might identify with and be attracted by.

Channel – The method by which the message is communicated, for example TV, radio, the Internet.

Decoding – The customer actually understands the symbolic format that was transmitted, that is associating with the symbols, words or images used.

Receiver – The target audience – the customer, the organization or the audience for which the message was intended.

Feedback – The response the receiver makes – their communication back to the actual source of the message.

Noise – Background noise, interference, distortion of the message, its content and meaning, making it difficult for the receiver to interpret, understand and respond to the message accordingly – overcoming noise is of the essence in order to gain successful feedback.

Even with this extended model there are a number of complexities that occur that may make the process ineffective. Importantly, we must recognize that the message is only one of many which the intended receiver will be required to deal with in a relatively short period of time. To understand that, think of yourself reading a newspaper or a magazine. The advertiser who wants to tell you something about their product must compete for your attention not only with the variety of other advertisements included in that issue, but also with the diversity of articles for which you bought the publication in the first place. The resultant noise may well interfere with the effective communication of the message. The reader may not spend enough time reading the advertisement, and may only glean enough information to form an impression of the intended message. The intended receivers will not necessarily be devoting all their attention to this particular media. They may be, at the same time, watching TV or listening to the radio. There will be advertisements in the magazine from other firms, many of them direct competitors. The amount of information we receive and more significantly retain, will vary greatly.

In addition, there is all the 'surrounding noise' with which we have to deal. Few of us have the opportunity to consider an advertisement in splendid isolation. Invariably, there will be a whole variety of things going on around us which may detract us from our ability to concentrate and to extract the full message being sent by the advertiser. The decoding process may, therefore, be incomplete or confused. In any case it will be influenced by the recipient's preconceptions of the sender. If he or she regards the company as being reliable and trustworthy, then it is likely that the message will be interpreted in that light. However, if the individual has previously had some form of negative experience with another product or service from the same company, then it is less likely that the message will be interpreted in a positive manner.

The Times newspaper recently ran a series of advertisements for the newspaper itself with a theme highlighting *The Times* coverage of important issues with the heading 'WHAT'S IMPORTANT' above *The Times* logo. The visuals used depicted a series of photographs of the same object with words describing various interpretations of how these objects might be perceived without further explanation. This provided a good example of the complexities of decoding. One of the ads showed six photographs of a banana on a plate. Under each photograph were different words describing how the photograph might be interpreted. The words were banana, vitamins, slapstick comedy, sexual innuendo, trade wars and racist weapon. Taking things at face value does not always allow the correct meaning to be understood.

The response which the receiver makes will vary according to the nature of the message and these extraneous factors. Depending on the objectives for the campaign, some advertisements simply convey information, others contain some form of invitation to purchase. The response of the receiver to the specific message will be of great importance to the sender, who will need to build in some form of feedback mechanism in order to better understand the nature of the response and, if appropriate, be in a position to change the message if that response is negative. This is, of course, the dialogue that we identified earlier as an important aspect of marketing communications.

One final comment on the communication process – the effectiveness of communication is determined partly by the elements we have highlighted here. However, there are a number of other elements that need to be considered when developing marketing communications, and these concern the environment in which the communications are expected to work and the behaviour (e.g. mood) of the people involved in either sending or receiving communications.

Case study

What consumers do when the ads are on

Research by the London Business School has looked at the behaviour of TV viewers during commercial breaks. This involved placing miniature cameras and microphones in a small sample of homes which showed what happened when advertisements were being shown. In relation to the communications process, it demonstrated the response to advertisements including decoding and the influence of noise. Results showed a number of activities taking place other than watching the TV screen. These included 'social interaction', viewers talking to each other about other issues, 'reading' of newspapers and magazines, 'tasking' – household jobs, etc., 'flicking' between channels. Actual viewing extended to interaction with advertising being shown, conversations about brands being shown and singing of jingles.

This research was based on a small sample but it does illustrate the point that not all communications messages are received as the sender would ideally want them to be.

What do you do when the ads come on?

Source: Financial Times Creative Business, 4 February 2003.

Personal influences (Syllabus 1.1)

The communication process is influenced by a wide range of other factors. One of the skills of the communications manager is to manage these other elements in such a way that they enhance the effectiveness of the communications and improve the efficiency of the communications spend.

One of these factors is the influence other people can have. Messages received from individuals rather than the media have the potential to deliver a stronger message than those delivered through media alone. One of the ways in which this can be effected is through the use of opinion formers. These are people who are either experts or who are actively involved in the subject area. Messages received from these people are more likely to be believable as they contain higher levels of credibility. For example, specialist journalists relay information and are perceived to be objective in their analysis and the comment they pass on.

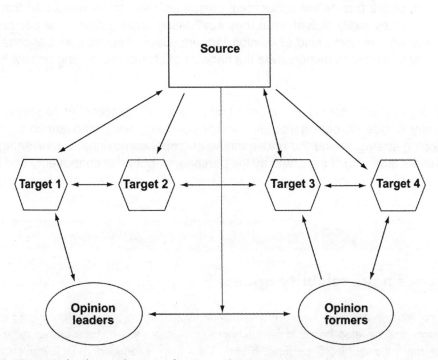

Figure 1.3 Opinion leaders and opinion formers in the communication process
Source: Fill (2002)

Opinion leaders, on the other hand, are usually members of our own peer group. Their expertise is based upon their own interest as a hobby or pastime in the subject areas. It is certainly not their career or part of their job. Therefore, word-of-mouth communications from these individuals carries even higher levels of credibility than those borne by opinion formers (Figure 1.3).

Opinion leaders play a significant role in our everyday decision-making. They can include the media, subject specialist consumer interest magazines such as *Which?*, published by the Consumers Association, who bring influence to bear on the decision-making of anything from computers to motor vehicles, washing machines and so on. They will provide opinions, weightings and ultimately a significant influence upon the decision-makers, particularly those who need confidence and reinforcement of their behaviour and of their decisions.

Opinion leaders can take many forms, for example, pressure groups. They may force us to consider very carefully the basis of our decision-making. They will ensure that we consider not only what the product has to offer, but perhaps some of the principles of the organization that is providing it to us, and perhaps the basis of their supply chain.

With both invasive and investigative media, customers and consumers are coming to realize that there is no such thing as a 'pure' or 'value-free' offer, which makes them concentrate very seriously on the broader aspects of their decision-making process.

Behind every brand, product and service offering, lie the people who are making decisions and choices in a more informed way, and according to priorities, motives and perhaps personal goals.

Increasingly, customers are getting to know more about the product and perhaps the ethos of the organization. In some instances, customers will even want to establish a relationship between themselves and their suppliers based upon trust. Customers are becoming more 'sophisticated' both in their purchase decision-making and the ways in which they respond to communications.

Where high-profile brands are concerned, customers want to be reassured that promises will be met. Can they really deliver what they say? Many organizations use personalities in their communications as some kind of opinion formers. David Beckham and Michael Schumacher are used by Vodafone to demonstrate the benefits of picture messaging on new types of mobile phone.

Zafer Erdogan (1999) considers the pros and cons of using celebrities to endorse brands. The former may include increasing attention, image polishing, new brand launch support, as part of repositioning strategies and the underpinning of global campaigns. Disadvantages suggested are the overshadowing of the brand by the personality, potential controversy and image change or loss of public recognition. Also in some cases, such endorsement may be expensive.

Case study

Luxury goods have celebrity appeal

Luxury goods of many types have for many years been supported by heavyweight media advertising in order to promote and develop brand image. Chanel have taken this a stage further recently in a new campaign for the flagship No. 5 perfume brand. They have produced a TV commercial based on cinematic values which lasts nearly three minutes. It stars Nicole Kidman and directed by film director Baz Luhrmann who also directed Kidman in the movie Moulin Rouge. The agency J. Walter Thompson say the approach is based on adding an emotional story to the visual aspects of the ad, consumers buying luxury brands are paying premium prices to feel special and need the feel of personal connection that can be gained via the celebrity element.

Source: Friedman (2004).

Thomas (2001) suggests some ground rules for celebrity endorsements to work:

o Articulation between the brand promise (What am I?) and the personality involved (Who am I?)
o Agreement among the brand team on the communications objectives to be achieved
o Focus on the characteristics the celebrity should possess to provide synergy with the brand
o Clearly establish what the celebrity is going to communicate.

Because of the strong brand character of the endorser, a potential mismatch could be counterproductive to the brand being promoted.

 ## Activity 1.2

Identify some examples of where celebrities have been used to endorse well-known brands. Do you think the criteria outlined above have been achieved?

Opinion leaders are playing a more and more significant role in responding to customers' thirst for knowledge. They are individuals who are predisposed to receiving information and then using it to influence others.

Opinion leadership manifests itself through a number of channels, in advertising, public relations, editorials, journals, pressure groups, to name but a few.

For marketers therefore, the role of opinion leaders should never be underestimated and they should never be excluded from a communications agenda. The emergence of new technologies and media means that 'news', good and bad, spreads very quickly. This includes information about organizations and their products and services. Opinion leaders' and formers' thoughts can be across the world in seconds.

It is important as an organization, therefore, not just to have customers and consumers, but also to have friends and supporters, who may, to your advantage, be opinion leaders, who will exert positive influence upon your organization. This will be vitally important as you, along with your competitors, are in a desperate race for competitive edge.

It is also important that you have an understanding of the role of opinion formers. Effectively, they are people who exert personal influence because of their authority, status, education or perhaps association with the product or service offering. They are likely to provide information and to advertise, and in some instances may take on roles as 'expert witnesses', that is they use their experience and expertise to justify particular situations in relation to various products. A good example of this could relate to the roles played by specialist journalists in fields such as motoring and travel. Many people thinking about purchasing cars and travel will closely monitor press and broadcast media to help them in their purchase decision-making. Clearly, they act as expert witnesses and therefore become expert 'opinion formers'.

The influence of opinion formers is quite significant and can act as a vehicle to reinforcing the credibility of products and services, or indeed the validity of such products can actually be questioned and found to be deficient in some areas.

In order that organizations can 'win friends and influence people' they will often seek support through lobbying in addition to various other activities to win the opinion formers' support. Public relations has a major part to play in providing information to media sources for them to use in producing favourable editorial material.

It is not surprising, therefore, that some campaigns seek to generate word-of-mouth recommendation as this form of personal influence has a far greater impact than advertising, sales promotion or direct marketing is ever likely to achieve.

In the world of new media, this idea of personal influence is used through viral marketing. This involves the transmission of e-mail messages from friend to friend and is referred to as word-of-mouth (WoM) communications. Picture messaging is now enhancing this communications method.

Word-of-mouth communications (Syllabus 1.1)

Word-of-Mouth communications are an important part of the communication process. Campaigns such as those for the launch of Häagen Daz super premium ice cream and energy drinks such as Red Bull have been launched with the specific aid of WoM communications. It is said that 70 per cent of Dyson floor cleaners are sold through the power of WoM communications. Using the influence of opinion leaders and opinion formers, WoM communications provide high levels of credibility and are relatively free of media and production costs.

A key question concerns why do people talk about products and services and if we know that then it may be possible to stimulate WoM as part of a marketing communications campaign.

Dichter (1966) suggested that there are four main reasons why people engage in WoM.

1. *Product interest* – People like to talk about products that they find pleasurable and those that give them unfavourable experiences. The latter is particularly significant when products fail to reach expectations and cognitive dissonance sets in.
2. *Message interest* – People like to talk about messages (ads, news items and stunts) because they are outstanding, interesting or which stimulate controversy or curiosity. Benetton, Black Magic and Tango ads are classic examples.
3. *Self interest* – People like to talk about ads because the watch they have bought (or been given), or the car they are driving is believed to bestow status and prestige on them.
4. *Other interest* – The final form of interest concerns the feelings people have towards others and their need to communicate information about particular products and brands in order that other people may enjoy or avoid the hazards of ownership.

How does marketing communications work?

The short answer to this question is that we do not really know! Although a great many theories have been put forward to explain the mechanical operation of marketing communications, many of them have either been too simplistic or have simply not stood up to empirical examination.

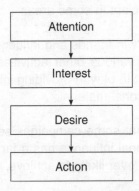

Figure 1.4 The AIDA model

Originally proposed in the 1920s to explain the process of personal selling, the AIDA model was rapidly adopted to explain the process of communications in advertising (Figure 1.4). The basic principle was that, in order to have effect, the first task of any campaign was to gain the *attention* of the viewer or reader. The second stage is the stimulation of an *interest* in the proposition. In most cases, it would be reasonable to assume that if the first requirement – attention – had been met, the second would follow on almost automatically.

The third stage is to create a *desire* for the product or service being promoted. Often, this will take the form of a 'problem–solution' execution in which the advertiser seeks to position the product as the answer to a problem which has previously been identified.

 Activity 1.3

Identify at least three examples of current advertising from which you can identify the AIDA process being utilized.

The fourth and final stage of the AIDA model is the stimulation of some form of response on the part of the audience – the *action* stage. Many advertisements have a specific call to action, and are linked with promotional offers designed to induce a purchase of the product or some other desired end result.

From the outset, it was recognized that a fundamental aim of communication was to cut through the surrounding clutter and arrest the attention of the potential purchaser. Moreover, it suggested that the process of communications required the audience to pass through a series of sequential steps, and that each step was a logical consequence of what had gone before. The principle of sequential activity or learning is used commonly in many marketing models, and is often referred to as *hierarchy of effects*. It is clear that the attention phase is key to the process, since whatever follows will be of little value if the attention of the audience has not been achieved.

However, this model and other 'hierarchy of effects' models are now discredited as valid interpretations of how advertising (marketing communications) works. Many other models have been developed to explain consumer interaction with advertising and the way advertising messages are processed. For example, the 'heightened appreciation model' is a valuable tool for explaining some of the mechanics of the advertising message and, importantly, assists in determining advertising strategy. What the model suggests is that, by identifying a desirable attribute of a product (through the use of consumer research) and linking it directly with the brand, the consumer is made more aware of that attribute and is able to associate it with the brand. The direct result of this activity is to create a more positive awareness of the product or service, which results in more frequent usage and the building of a better image.

A good example of how manufacturers focus on a specific attribute and can arouse heightened appreciation of that attribute can be seen in the soap powder market. For many years, the primary benefit of all products within the category has been their ability to get clothes whiter. As a result of changes in the formulation of the product, the focus has shifted towards colour fastness or freshness or ease of use. Advertising in this category now stresses one of these benefits, with the result that the consumer now compares competing products against the dimension that is important to them rather than the degree of whiteness which is delivered by the product.

 ## Activity 1.4

> The model described above stresses heightened appreciation. Find examples of marketing communications campaigns which attempt to heighten the consumer's awareness of a specific attribute of a product or service.

Contemporary thoughts about how marketing communications (very often just advertising) work tend to be less specific and less inclined to suggest that buyers move sequentially. The learn–feel–do sequence suggested by the hierarchy of effects models is now generally considered to be out-of-date and inaccurate.

Today, ideas such as Hall's four frameworks, Jones's Strong and Weak theories of advertising (and Ehrenberg's ATR model) and general descriptions such as Prue's Alphabetical model are more widely accepted as suitable interpretations.

What emerges from this is that co-ordinated marketing communications (CMC) work through an interaction between the brand and the communications that surround it. As we will see later in this coursebook, brand-related communications can be orientated to the rational factual aspects of a product or may be orientated to image and emotional brand associations. Brands can remind people about category needs and also about the advertising and the associations that surround a brand.

Advertising can work by persuading people to buy a brand (Strong theory) or they might work by reminding people of a need they may have (Weak theory). Advertising and marketing communications work in different ways in different situations (contexts) and it is not right to say that it works by any one single method.

Information processing (Syllabus 1.2)

There are a number of topics associated with information processing. However, you are required to know about perception and attitudes, and how they influence and are influenced by marketing communications.

Perception

Consumers are continuously bombarded with vast quantities of information. Whether the information is orchestrated by the marketer or the media, in general, is less relevant than the fact that there is simply too much information for the average consumer to process effectively. The inevitable consequence is that much of the material is simply screened out and discarded. The result is that the consumer may make purchasing decisions based on limited knowledge, or even a misunderstanding of the real facts. The individual is far less concerned with the average advertising message, which makes the task of ensuring appropriate communications with the target audience an even more daunting prospect.

As consumers, our awareness of specific advertising messages is treated in a similar way. Some form of trigger mechanism is usually required to encourage us to pay attention to the variety of marketing communications messages. Usually, this is an internal recognition of an unfulfilled need, which heightens the levels of awareness of pertinent advertising and other information. The principle can be commonly observed. If, for example, you have recently purchased a new hi-fi system, your awareness of the brand will be enhanced and you will immediately become aware of messages received about all competing brands for a period of time after purchase.

The process of decoding a message, whether it be from an advertiser or simply in the form of an article which interests us, will be substantially influenced by a number of perceptual factors. All of us, whether we think about it consciously or not, are influenced by a number of factors in our perception of a situation. And, as we will see later, perception itself is a key factor in the field of marketing communications.

Often, the consumer will possess only limited information on which to base a purchase decision. Some of that information, gleaned from other sources, will be incomplete.

Value judgements will be based on that limited understanding since, for the individual involved, their perceptions are reality. It is irrelevant that what they understand about the nature of a product or service is lacking or even wrong. In the field of marketing communications, we must deal with those perceptual values and either play to them or seek to change them if that be the appropriate course of action.

Essentially, perception is about how we manage the various stimuli that we encounter. From a marketing communications perspective we are dealing with advertisements, promotions, members of the salesforce, direct mailers and so on, all of which represent stimuli. The perception of stimuli involves three components – attention-getting, organizing and interpretation.

Gaining the attention of the target audience is an essential prerequisite of other levels of the process. If the attention of the potential consumer is not secured by the marketing communications message, then it is impossible to communicate salient aspects of that message. In some respects, attention is determined by the consumer's attitudes towards the product category and the brand within it. If there is little interest in the product category, then gaining attention will be a difficult task. By the same token, however, if the consumer has become interested in the particular category (heightened awareness) for some reason, then significantly more attention will be devoted to the advertisement and its contents. This may come about, for example, because the consumer has decided to purchase a new car. Following that emotional decision, advertisements for cars, particularly those in the area of interest and relevance, will be more readily perceived. Typography, colour, shape, presentation, sex, music, tone of voice, brand name and voice-overs are all variables used to get attention.

 ## Activity 1.5

Identify different types of marketing communications that you have received recently, advertisements, direct mail, telephone calls and determine the devices used to get your attention.

Whilst advertising is important to gain awareness for a brand, sales promotions such as sampling can be an important part of the process. Sampling aims to generate behavioural responses, whereas advertising develops mental pictures of a brand. Therefore sampling has proved to be a popular method of stimulating brand awareness and understanding, particularly in the food and drinks industry. Recently, Fox's Biscuits launched its new Echo brand using sampling teams who distributed challenge cards. The brand's message is based on getting people to talk, so the card invites people to hug a passer-by or talk to a stranger or do a little dance and they are then rewarded with a free sample. Brand experience accelerates the normal development process of brand knowledge and perception. It is becoming common practice for new products to be launched using the so-called 'teaser' campaigns. This starts by providing limited amounts of information about the product and service, and then building up gradually until actual launch.

The organization of the stimuli, once perceived, is necessary in order for us to understand what it is that has attracted our attention. Various devices are available but of these contour and grouping are often used techniques. So, our attention is drawn to a bottle with a dark liquid, it means Coca-Cola because we understand the shape of the bottle. This is an extreme example but it illustrates the principle well. Just mentioning the words Coca-Cola will create images in consumers' minds, very often the contour-shaped bottle. In fact so strong is the bottle in branding terms, that it became the UK's first registered trademark in packaging.

New or misunderstood products can be shown with products and brands that are well known and understood so that we learn that the weaker product is similar to the recognized brand. So, healthy foods are pictured next to a gymnasium, top sporting stars or people working out.

Finally, the organized stimuli need to be understood or *interpreted*. The Coca-Cola stimuli means something about American life and quenching thirst. This aspect of perception is influenced by our background, family values, the society in which we live and the culture to which we belong. All exert a significant impact on our own decision-making process. A product which is wholly acceptable in one society might be taboo in another because of social, religious or moral values. Even the colour of the packaging may mean something different in different markets. The advertiser must be conscious of these factors when developing a communications campaign.

Perception is at the heart of positioning. This part of the context analysis provides information that feeds the objectives, positioning, message content and media vehicle scheduling.

Attitudes

As we have seen elsewhere, the consumer holds a series of *attitudes*, some of which may relate to the brand and the purchasing decision. Although most of these attitudes will be formed by external factors – age, sex, class, the influence of relatives, friends and peer groups, cultural factors and so on – some are the direct result of the impact of an advertising message. In some instances, the *advertising* will serve to reinforce existing beliefs; in others, it will modify existing attitudes. If the consumer already believes that a well-balanced diet is essential to good health, then a product which promotes itself with this proposition is likely to be well received. The advertising will reinforce held beliefs and attitudes, and strengthen the perception of the brand. In some instances, the advertising message may modify attitudes, perhaps by presenting a potential solution to a problem which the consumer previously felt could not be resolved.

Attitudes are an expression of an individual's feelings towards a person or object, and reflect whether they are favourably or otherwise disposed towards that person or object. Attitudes are not directly observable, but can be inferred either from behavioural patterns or by some form of interrogation, typically using market research methods. Attitudes consist of three main components: cognitive, affective and conative. These are more easily remembered and understood as learn, feel and do (Figure 1.5).

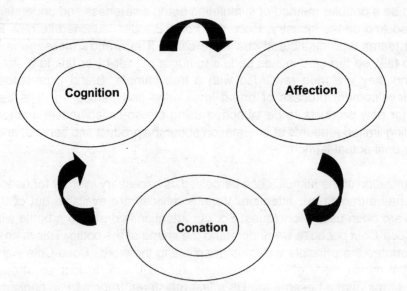

Figure 1.5 The three-component attitude model
Source: Fill (2002)

What this means is that when we buy something we learn something first, then feel something (about the product) and then do something (reject it, buy it or ask for more information).

These feelings (the affective component) are often attached to significant attributes (tangible or intangible). So, when looking at attitudes towards, say, tinned soup, the feelings (like or dislike) may be a reflection of the taste (tangible attribute) or the brand name and the associations that they bring to the individual (intangible). Marketing communications can play a very important role in modifying the attitudes people have. By changing negative attitudes into positive attitudes, a person's predisposition to buy that brand at the next opportunity increases.

Marketing communications can change attitudes by the following methods:

Change the physical product or service element – At a fundamental level, attitudes might be so engrained that it is necessary to change the product or service and then claim in the marketing communications that it is 'new', or 'revised' or 'reformulated'.

Change misunderstanding – By product demonstration, it is possible to change misunderstanding about the function of a product.

Build credibility – Through use of an informative strategy based on product demonstration and hands-on experience (e.g. through sampling) it is possible to build credibility – a brand to be relied on.

Change performance beliefs – By changing perceptions held about the attributes, it is possible to change the attitudes about the object. So, if product performance is in doubt, provide evidence to correct the misperception.

Change attribute priorities – A strategy to emphasize a different attribute can change attitudes. By stressing the importance of service attributes, airlines might have an advantage over their rivals who stress punctuality.

Introduce a new attribute – This action might create a temporary advantage if it is valued by the target audience.

Change perception of competitor products – By changing the way competitor products are perceived, it is possible to differentiate your own brand.

Change or introduce new brand associations – By using celebrities or spokespersons with whom the target audience can identify, it might be possible to change the way a product is perceived on an emotional basis rather than relying on attributes and a more rational argument.

Use corporate branding – By using the stature of the parent company, it is possible to develop a level of credibility and brand values that other brands cannot copy.

Change the number of attributes used – Today, two or even three attributes are often combined with strong emotional associations in order to provide a point of differentiation and a set of benefit-orientated brand values.

A fuller account of this important aspect of marketing communications can be found in the essential textbook for this unit (Fill, 2002).

 Activity 1.6

> Select a market sector with which you are familiar (travel, convenience foods, alcoholic or soft drinks, financial services, etc.), determine the leading brands and find examples of their communications. How have they used attributes to communicate? Are any of them trying to change the attitudes held of the target audience?

Attitudes towards products and services are an important dimension, since they will affect the individual's propensity to purchase. Products for which favourable attitudes are held are far more likely to be purchased than are those which create negative attitudes.

It is important to recognize that attitudes are not easy to change. Most consumers adopt fairly consistent behavioural patterns which can only be changed over time. If the consumer is of the view, for example, that all drink is evil, then no amount of advertising for alcoholic beverages is likely to alter that attitude.

Activity 1.7

Identify examples of communications which:

Seek to change existing beliefs and seek to reinforce beliefs.

However, we have to remember that the consumer will not necessarily take in all of the advertising message, or may modify the content of the message to suit their existing views. Advertising promoting healthcare insurance will be irrelevant if the consumer believes that they are too young, for example, to be likely to fall seriously ill.

In turn, these attitudes will influence the *purchasing* decision. In some instances, held beliefs will arouse interest in a product category or a brand. Exposure to a specific advertising message may induce the consumer to go and buy the product. It is important to recognize that this is a two-way process. If the consumer is dissatisfied with the purchase, or feels that it does not live up to the promises of the advertising, then a process of dissonance will take place. Their attitudes towards the brand will be modified to reflect this lack of satisfaction and the advertising message will be viewed in a different light.

Attitudes, in general, reflect changing patterns over time. The activities of pressure groups, peer groups and others will make some purchases more desirable, while others are less so. One only has to look at the growth in the awareness of environmental issues to see how brands have had to respond. Product ingredients which were once widely accepted can now no longer be included if the brand is to enjoy wide acceptance. Fashion exerts a similar influence. Once popular brands are now scorned by consumers as being unfashionable, while others have grown from limited acceptance to broad popularity as fashion dictates their purchase.

The purchase decision-making process (Syllabus 1.3)

Depending on the nature of the product or service that we are intending to buy, we tend to follow a series of distinct 'steps' which form the decision-making process. Commonly, we recognize five stages in the decision-making process, although it must be noted that not every purchase decision involves each of the stages, nor can we say that the consumer always begins the process at the beginning and ends at the end! A model of the purchase decision-making process is shown at Figure 1.6.

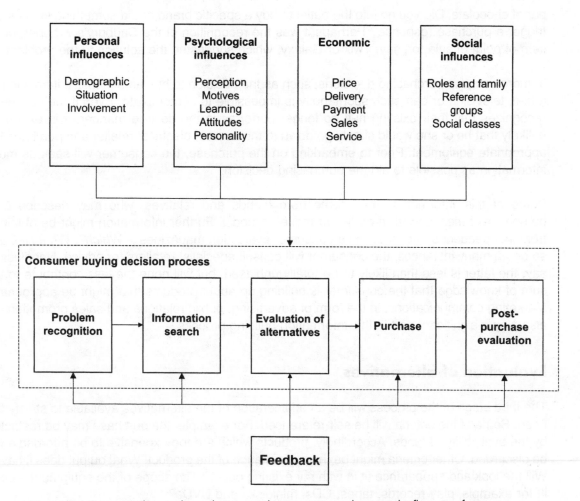

Figure 1.6 Stages in the purchase decision-making process and potential influencing factors

Problem recognition

The starting point in the purchasing process is the identification of a problem or unfulfilled need on the part of the consumer. In some instances, these will be the basic human needs relating to, say, hunger or thirst. In other instances, the stimulus to problem recognition may be derived from some external source – the comment of a friend or relative, seeing a television commercial or press advertisement and so on. In all cases, the consumer recognizes that there is a difference between the actual state and the desired state, and that in order to resolve the imbalance, a purchase may need to be made.

The search for information

In many purchase decisions, there is little time between the identification of the problem and the purchase of the product to fulfil the need. Impulse purchase decisions typically illustrate this type of decision-making. The consumer may, for example, pass a confectionery outlet and feel slight pangs of hunger. He or she will enter the outlet and select a product, say a bar of chocolate, to satisfy that hunger. We will see, shortly, that this is indicative of what is known as *routine problem-solving*. Indeed, many purchase decisions, particularly of fast-moving consumer goods (fmcg), are of this nature. In essence, the consumer has previously stored sufficient information about the product category in order to make an appropriate brand selection without any need for additional information. Think about the last occasion on which you purchased a bar of chocolate. Did you go into the outlet to buy a specific brand or did something in the store trigger a purchase response? Perhaps it was the recognition of the Cadbury's wrapper, or an item of point of sale for, say, Twix or Galaxy, which suggested the solution to the problem.

In more complex purchasing decisions, such as the decision to buy an expensive item such as a hi-fi, television or car, such spontaneity is impossible to contemplate. Even if the consumer recognizes that their existing hi-fi no longer performs in the desired manner, it is extremely unlikely that he or she would simply go down to the nearest electrical retailer and purchase the appropriate equipment. Prior to embarking on the purchase, the consumer will seek as much information as possible to aid the purchasing decision.

Some of this 'information' may come from friends and relatives, who may describe their personal experiences with a particular make or model. Further information might be obtained from independent sources, such as consumer evaluation magazines – *Which*?, *What Hi-fi* and so on. In many instances, the consumer will consult specialist retailers for advice. Needless to say, the latter is less than likely to be totally unbiased, but will none the less contribute to the sum of knowledge that the consumer is building up about products that might be appropriate. Marketing communications, in the form of advertising, public relations and sales promotion will also play a significant part in this information-building process.

Evaluation of alternatives

The third stage of the process will be a consideration of the alternatives available to satisfy the need. Some of the criteria will be self-referenced. For example, the purchase may be restricted by the availability of funds. Accordingly, products which are too expensive to be affordable will be discarded. Other criteria might be the performance of the product. What output does it have? Will the look and appearance fit in with my existing decor? The scope of the equipment – does it, for example, play records, tapes, CDs, minidisks and DVDs?

Here again, marketing communications make an important contribution to the evaluation process. As we will see later, some advertising is specifically designed to identify appropriate criteria on behalf of the consumer. Indeed, much advertising for expensive consumer durables is of this nature in which comparisons are made between the advertiser's product and those of his competitors in order to assist the consumer in the purchase selection.

Only when the consumer has gathered sufficient information and evaluated the various alternatives against the established criteria, will the consumer pass to the next stage – the decision to purchase.

 ## Activity 1.8

What are the factors which, in your opinion, influence the evaluation of alternatives?

Relate this question to a recent purchase of an infrequently purchased item which you have made.

Purchase decision

Even having passed through the previous stages, it would be naive to assume that the process invariably ends with a decision to purchase. Personal or other considerations may dictate that the consumer either defers the decision or abandons it completely.

If, as was suggested earlier, the consumer has insufficient money to purchase the 'best' equipment at that time, they may feel that cheaper items lack some of the desired features. Accordingly, the decision might be made to delay the purchase until such time as the desired product is affordable.

Alternatively, the consumer might feel that none of the available alternatives really satisfies the need. Perhaps the improvement sought represents too great an investment and it would be better to remain with the existing equipment, at least for the time being. However, it is equally reasonable to assume that many consumers reaching this stage of the decision-making process end it by making a purchase selection.

Post-purchase evaluation

Once the consumer has returned home with the selected item, a stage known as 'post-purchase evaluation' begins. We have already seen that the consumer has built up an idealized image of the desired purchase during the earlier stages of the process, resulting from a variety of internal and external influences. Inevitably, they will make comparisons of the performance of the product with those criteria.

Where the consumer is satisfied that the product meets the level of expectations, then we have consumer satisfaction. Obviously, this may well impinge on the purchase decisions of other consumers, since the purchaser will, in this instance, comment favourably on the performance and other attributes of his or her purchase to others seeking advice and input.

However, where the consumer feels that the product does not live up to expectations, he or she is said to experience 'dissonance' or 'post-purchase dissatisfaction'. The latter may be brought about, for example, by an advertising message which overclaims for the product. Or, there may be an imbalance between the true needs and the product delivery. In either case, this post-purchase dissatisfaction is an important element to understand. Consumers who have this response will comment unfavourably on the product, perhaps undermining the impact of marketing communications campaigns. They may write letters of complaint to the manufacturer or, in extreme cases, begin their own programme of publicity by writing to newspapers, specialist publications and so on. Certainly, it is extremely unlikely that they would purchase the same brand again on another purchase occasion.

Television programmes such as *Watchdog* may serve to accelerate this dissonance. By exposing deficiencies in product performance, some viewers may be motivated to re-evaluate their own recent purchasing decisions. Yet others may conclude that their intended purchase is inappropriate, given the new information. Major brands such as Hoover and Hotpoint have been the subject of investigation by the programme, with a resultant negative impact on their sales.

Activity 1.9

Why is a consideration of post-purchase satisfaction so important in the context of marketing communications?

The nature of purchasing

We have already seen that purchase decisions will be made more or less spontaneously, depending on the nature of the purchase. We can distinguish between three types of decision according to the nature of the 'problem-solving' in which the consumer is involved:

1. Routine problem-solving
2. Limited problem-solving
3. Extensive problem-solving.

Routine problem-solving
As we have already seen, many purchases, especially those involved with low-priced fmcg, are of this type. In many cases, because the consumer has prior experience of the product category and the variety of brands that are available, little information-seeking is involved in the process. Moreover, where the price of the item is comparatively low, little risk is involved in the purchase decision. Hence the decision will tend to be taken quite quickly, in a routine and automatic way.

 Activity 1.10

Some consumers purchase products spontaneously. What role do marketing communications play in this context?

Limited problem-solving
Sometimes, when a consumer is considering the purchase of a new or unfamiliar brand, even when it is within a familiar product category, there may be a limited amount of information-seeking, and the consumer will tend to spend slightly more time before making a purchase decision. This is also associated with slightly more expensive purchases, where the cost involves a slightly more detailed consideration or where there is a degree of risk in the purchase. The selection, for example, of over-the-counter medicines is likely to involve some careful consideration of the ingredients, the identity of the manufacturer and so on, before the decision to purchase is made.

Extensive problem-solving
The consumer will become involved in a more detailed search for information and the evalua-tion of alternatives in those instances where the product category is unfamiliar or where a purchase is made on a very infrequent basis.

Obviously, purchases which involve a high capital outlay on the part of the consumer (durable items, cars and houses) or a high degree of personal commitment (life insurance, membership of clubs and societies) will be of the extended problem-solving variety.

Organizational purchasing

This area will be studied in more detail later in the coursebook, but it is important to recognize that in purchase decision-making, there are significant and more complex issues arising when considering organizational purchases. First, the amounts concerned are usually much larger and can run into millions of pounds. Secondly, it is often the case that more than one person is involved in the decision-making process. For example, if a large company is setting up or replacing a computer system there are technical issues finance requirements and probably the requirements of a range of different user groups to be considered. The communications needs of all these interested parties will need to be met, often via a mix of communications tools. Timescales are usually longer often involving complex negotiations. Influencing factors are also more wide ranging and complicated. These and other issues will be studied later in Units 4 and 5.

 Activity 1.11

Identify four examples of:

- ○ A routine purchase
- ○ A purchase involving limited problem-solving
- ○ An extended problem-solving purchase.

Case study

Decisions

The stages of the purchase decision-making process play a key role in determining the kinds of marketing communications that are used by marketers in 'moving' customers through the process. An extensive purchase decision, such as a new car, requires many different types of communication in order for the customer to make an informed decision.

At the problem or need recognition stage, TV advertising will be used to create awareness of the latest models and initiate interest. This also provides the first level on information searching. Press advertising will be used to provide more detail on specifications and allow alternatives to be evaluated. The evaluation stage will also involve seeking information from personal influencers, opinion formers and leaders via editorial in specialist magazines and word of mouth.

The evaluation will be furthered by visits to dealers where personal selling becomes important. Customers can also view and test drive different models. Negotiation will lead to concluding sales. The post-purchase stage has become increasingly significant for car producers as they seek to maintain relationships with purchasers. Communications will include direct mail, telemarketing and PR activity. This provides reassurance that the right decision has been made and continues until the next purchase cycle commences.

Perceived risk

Our propensity to involve ourselves in the purchase decision-making process is partly a reflection of the level and type of perceived risk that we each see in these decisions. The extent of the risk involved may be proportionate to the type of purchase involved – routine, limited or extensive. Further, the influence of different types of risk may be apparent at different stages of purchase decision-making process. Mitchell (1999) suggests 'perceived risk is more powerful at explaining consumers' behaviour since consumers are more often motivated to avoid mistakes than to maximize utility in purchasing'. Recognition and understanding of the potential risks from consumers' perspectives, therefore, provides the opportunity to use marketing communications messages to eliminate concerns associated with type of risk involved. These risks may be a function of the following six elements:

1. *Performance risk* – Will the product wash my clothes clean?
2. *Financial risk* – Is this good value? Will I get the goods? (e.g. Internet shopping fears)
3. *Social risk* – What will my friends think?
4. *Ego risk* – How will I feel about myself?
5. *Physical risk* – Will the product harm me or others?
6. *Time risk* – How long have I to make this decision, buy this product?

These risks will be present in all decisions, but to varying degrees according to product/category experience, confidence, wealth, education and so on. The risks will vary across product sectors for each individual. How some of these perceived risk issues might be overcome in using marketing communications is considered below in examining the types of appeal that are used in advertising and other forms of communication.

 ## Activity 1.12

Find some examples of recent advertisements or direct mail. Which 'risks' are being addressed?

Communication appeals (Syllabus 2.8)

Many forms of communication, particularly those aimed directly at consumers, contain some type of appeal. These appeals can be categorized into two basic forms – those based around emotional criteria, and those of a more logical or rational nature. Bovee *et al.* (1995) describe the differences in these approaches in terms of appealing to the head and the heart. Logical appeals focus on quality or performance factors (thinking), whilst emotional appeals are based more around feelings. They suggest the following types of appeal as being prevalent in different forms of communication:

- o Price/value
- o Quality
- o Star appeals and testimonials
- o Ego
- o Fear or anger
- o Sensory
- o Sex, love and social acceptance
- o Novelty.

The creation of different types of appeal has much to do with the positioning of the subject – brand, service and organization. It will, of course, be a key element in the creative communications process discussed further in Unit 2. De Pelsmacker *et al.* (2001) also discuss appeals in terms of emotion. Based on reviews of earlier studies, they consider rational or logical appeals as 'informative'. Emotional appeals are classified under humour, eroticism, warmth and fear. The latter grouping considers issues of perceived risk which were discussed earlier.

Butterfield (1999) highlights the need to consider functional and emotional appeals 'in combination'. This helps in differentiating competitive brands, as unique selling propositions are increasingly difficult to sustain over anything other than short timescales. He goes on to propose that emotional appeals alone 'result in emptiness which, however glossily presented, stays superficial and will be found wanting in time'.

Case study

Mixed emotions

Like many not-for-profit organizations, the childrens' charity Barnado's uses a combination of functional and emotional appeals in its communications. In late 2003, they ran a press campaign highlighting issues surrounding child poverty. The advertisements presented information relating to the problems against a background of photographs of children in distressing circumstances. The advertisements were successful in stimulating further media interest in the campaign as a result of the disturbing nature of the photographs. Similar examples were discussed in an article in *Marketing Business* July/August 2003 which discussed the effectiveness of shock appeal in communications. An earlier campaign by Barnado's won an award in *Campaign* magazine's annual press awards. This focused the charity's Abuse through prostitution campaign.

Other examples of functional or emotional appeals that are common in communications of different kinds include:

- o Aspiration – luxury goods
- o Features – technical equipment
- o Cost – discount, extended credit
- o Nationality – German engineering – Vorsprung durch technik
- o Experience – of staff, customer service
- o Tradition – established manufacturing techniques
- o Benefits – meeting needs, core product
- o Security – reassuarance, financial services.

 ## Activity 1.13

Find examples of communications from which you can determine which types of appeal are being used. Look particularly for examples which 'combine' functional and emotional appeals. Compare direct competitors – What differences are apparent?

Likeability in communications (Syllabus 2.8)

The relationship between different types of appeal used in marketing communications and their effectiveness is considered in the concept of likeability. Research over the last decade or so has been examining the relationship between communications, most specifically advertisements that are seen to be 'liked' by consumers, and which are more likely to be enjoyed, remembered and effective in generating sales. Biel (1990) suggests where consumers expressed liking a commercial, there was an increase in brand preference. The term 'liked' should not be mistaken. It does not refer to a superficial take out of an ad but refers to some deep seated, personally meaningful feelings that an ad can create in individuals. The appeals in such communications may be relevant to a person's current lifestage or situation, and therefore change over time. Even serious functionally orientated communications for financial services can drive feelings of likeability if, for example, a person is currently considering revising a will, seeking financial advice or is about to invest in an ISA or other financial product. Humour is one of the key creative devices that is used to engender likeability. Smiling or laughing at a commercial could suggest that we might like what is being said in the message. Whilst there is probably some truth in this proposition, care also needs to be taken in the use of humour. This relates to potential decay effects. The initial response to something funny is stronger than after exposure to the same message over and over again. Frequency and exposure need to be carefully considered, therefore.

Activity 1.14

Put the coursebook down and go and watch TV for an hour or so! Write down a scale of one to five with one being like a lot and five being dislike very much, a measure of how much you like or dislike each advert you see. What kinds of factors are you taking into account?

Ethics, corporate and social responsibility (Syllabus 1.5)

The high-profile cases of financial irregularities at Enron and Worldcom have brought these issues to the fore in a general business and marketing context. Failure to recognize the significance of these issues may have a potentially serious impact on brand reputation and their consideration figures prominently in the field of marketing communications. It has to be recognized that the use of marketing communications is often described as an immoral business activity, responsible for exerting a pernicious influence on society in general. By the promotion of products and services which are beyond the reach of many consumers, marketing communications is often held responsible for many of the underlying ills of society.

Cause-related marketing has been developed as a response to the perceived need to provide increased credibility and authority for some brands in the form of sponsorship. This approach enables brands to work together so that both share the benefits of working with the other brand. So, Tesco have been involved with their Computers for Schools campaign, Microsoft provided financial and marketing support for the NSPCC 'Full Stop' campaign and many other companies such as Walkers, British Gas and Avon, attempt to meet some of their social responsibilities through similar schemes.

Undeniably, marketing communications stimulates the desire of individuals to aspire to a superior lifestyle and, with it, to have access to a wider range of goods and services.

However, whether this is a reflection of the values of marketing communications, or of society as a whole, is a more difficult question to resolve.

Activity 1.15

Defend the position of advertising against the argument that it creates unnecessary needs and wants.

It is a fundamental dimension of human nature to 'seek to improve one's lot'. What was an acceptable lifestyle 20 or 30 years ago would be significantly below the level of today's desires. Products which were then considered aspirational, are now considered to be the very staples of existence. Inevitably, it is a facet of an open society that individuals have the right to choose the products and services which they wish to have access to. The alternative is a more rigid society in which choice is restricted – based on the value judgements of others.

On a more fundamental level, criticisms of advertising often relate to the issues of selective emphasis and exaggeration. Since advertisers choose to highlight only those areas in which their product performs well, or better than their competitors, rather than providing a comprehensive analysis – warts and all! – such advertising may be criticized as failing to communicate the true nature of the products or services it promotes. By the same token, some advertisers use exaggerated claims to promote the appeal of their products.

Ultimately, there are a series of responses common to all societies which will limit these excesses. It may be a cliché, but if the product or service fails to deliver against the expectations of consumers – largely created by marketing communications – the product will fail. We have already seen that the area of post-purchase satisfaction (or dissatisfaction) is an important dimension of marketing communications. Manufacturers who seek to use marketing communications to promote inferior products, or whose claims for performance exceed their ability to deliver, will rapidly appreciate the impact of the dissonance which such activity creates.

However, it must remain true that there are a number of areas in which the consumer must be protected against the excesses which might otherwise be against their interests. To this end, the governments of most countries have created a variety of legal and other regulatory frameworks which ensure that marketing communications perform in a manner which is acceptable to the public at large. These, in turn, are augmented by self-regulatory procedures which have resulted in the creation of codes of conduct to which practitioners are required to subscribe.

There has been a progressive realization that those practising marketing have an ethical responsibility towards society. This area has proved to be contentious, since it is difficult to define the nature of ethical behaviour. The fundamental role of marketing is to satisfy the needs of consumers. However, there may be times when although seeming to satisfy those needs, they are in fact being misdirected. A recent *Watchdog* TV programme demonstrated that many products labelled as 'light', implying a low-fat content, in fact, were higher in fat than regular versions of the same brands.

In the same vein, an increasing number of products claim to be 'environmentally friendly'. However, when their packaging fails to meet standards of biodegradability, can they really substantiate this claim? Often products serve to satisfy the needs of one group of consumers, but at the expense of others. Environmental pressure groups have demonstrated that products containing chlorofluorocarbon (CFC) gases may work efficiently, but in so doing they deplete the ozone layer. Here again, there is an ethical conflict.

These examples serve to illustrate that, while it may be accepted that a company must first serve the needs of its customers, there are increasing concerns that companies should also recognize their responsibilities to society as a whole.

In recent years, a wide variety of issues have been raised to further the debate.

Advertising to children

In many countries it is permissible to advertise products directly to children. Elsewhere, as in Sweden such activity is banned. However, opponents of the ban point to the restricted availability of children's products – toys and confectionery – and the relatively higher costs of those products.

Case study

Tesco promotion provides lasting rewards

The Computers for Schools promotion launched by the retailer Tesco in 1992, has provided benefits not only for the schools involved but also for Tesco themselves in driving trade. The programme is based on a voucher collection scheme which can be redeemed against equipment contained in a catalogue.

The scheme is communicated to stores via bulletins, manager briefing packs and a staff incentive scheme maximises the potential. This involves staff visiting schools to assist in training and presentations. Tesco utilize TV advertising, online information, point of sale, receipt messages, Tesco Bank statements and Tesco Clubcard mailing to maintain the high-profile nature of the promotion.

By 2002, equipment valued at over £77 million had been distributed to over 24 000 schools. More research has shown that a significant majority, 94 per cent of respondents, believe the scheme was good for local communities. The Tesco programme is often seen as a benchmark for cause-related promotional schemes.

Adapted from: An article in *The Marketer*, January 2005, a special edition on ethics and corporate and social responsibility.

The depiction of women in advertising

Concern has been expressed over the way that women are shown in advertising campaigns. Many believe that these serve to reinforce stereotypical roles. Care must be taken to depict all people in an appropriate and socially acceptable way.

Product labelling

There is increasing pressure on companies to declare the full contents of their products on labelling, particularly of those ingredients which might result in harm to some consumers or where their consumption might conflict with their beliefs.

Confusion pricing

It is argued that many companies deliberately use different bases of pricing to preclude the consumer from making direct price comparisons.

The issue of the ethical responsibility of companies is a complex one. As noted earlier, companies which pursue policies which are in conflict with contemporary beliefs will often find that consumers respond by rejecting their products or services. However, the issue remains as to whose ethics should be followed.

In some countries, providing a financial incentive to an intermediary to secure a contract is regarded as an accepted part of the selling process. In the West, such activity would be regarded as bribery!

Similarly, some commentators regard the provision of inferior products to developing countries as being immoral. However, supporters of these policies would argue that even inferior products represent a significant improvement on what is currently available!

It is important to appreciate the ethical and moral concerns which relate to both marketing and marketing communications practices.

The historical development of marketing and, with it, marketing communications, has entered a new phase. As described by Kotler (2000), we are entering a new phase in which marketers must balance their own needs with those of society in general.

> *The social marketing concept holds that the organization's task is to determine the needs, wants and interests of the target markets and to then deliver the desired satisfactions more effectively and efficiently than competitors in a way that maintains or improves the consumer's and the society's well being.*

The underlying changes in consumer attitudes will result in the exertion of a number of pressures on marketing organizations. The ultimate power of the consumer remains the freedom of choice. If manufacturers fail to recognize and respond to these changes, then they must accept that they will be forced to accept the consequences of their actions, or lack of them. If manufacturers act in ways that consumers find detrimental or harmful to their well-being, they will reject their products. By the same token, if they are seen to be taking positive steps to improve the general environment in which the consumer exists, the same consumer will reward them by buying their products.

These concerns should not be overstated. An annual survey conducted by the Advertising Association repeatedly reports that the level of those expressing concern or disapproval with advertising is falling progressively. Only 7 per cent of the population express such mistrust. For most, the field of marketing communications makes a positive contribution to the society in general. It communicates information about products and services efficiently and cheaply, and provides consumers with confidence in the goods and services that they purchase. It stimulates competition to produce new products and to improve old ones, and helps to ensure that consumers have a choice. It helps to fuel economic prosperity, with the subsequent contribution to employment, by the opening up of new growth areas, and it expands media choice, by funding diverse and independent media which, substantially, rely on the income derived from advertising.

Undertaking marketing activities in a way that is socially acceptable, ethically driven and is proactively incorporated into the organization's vision, mission, ethos, culture and day-to-day business dealings, is becoming increasingly significant.

Summary

In this opening unit, some of the key issues facing marketing communications have been identified and we have started to explore the key theories and concepts that underpin the subject. In order to maximize the effectiveness of communications, it is important to have some knowledge of how they work. Definitions of marketing communications have been examined which highlight the spread and depth of this aspect of the marketing mix. The purchase decision-making processes of consumers have been explained and how these are influenced by individuals and groups. The use of emotional and functional appeals in communications have been considered. The risks involved in product and service purchase have been considered. Issues surrounding ethics, corporate and social responsibility and the relationship in marketing communications have been highlighted.

Further study

References have been made to the Strong and Weak theories of communications. These are explored in more detail in the essential text for this module Fill (2002). Before moving on, you should read the relevant chapters on these and other issues raised. The essential text will also provide further examples to illustrate the application of different concepts. Where other sources and references have been included, you should attempt to follow these up in order to gain a wider perspective and more detail on the issues concerned. There are few texts which deal specifically with the role of celebrity endorsement. A recent publication, Pringle (2004), is a welcome addition to the academic and practitioner perspectives in this area.

Typical exam questions

In this section, references are given to specific examination and assignment questions from the June/July 2004 assessments. The questions are set out in Appendix 5. Detailed feedback on these questions from the CIM Senior Examiner and specimen answers can be obtained from the CIM website. Also included are some general examples of question types, briefings on which are included in Appendix 3.

June 2004 Examination Questions 1a and 1b. July 2004 Assignment Question 1, part 1 and Question 5, part 1.

Question 1.1

Explain the characteristics of informational- and emotional-based messages and provide examples based on the L'Oréal mini-case.

(5 Marks)

This question refers to the L'Oréal mini-case presented in the Appendix 4.

Question 1.2

Examine the ways in which marketing communications can be used to change consumers' perceived risk towards a leading car manufacturer.

(10 Marks)

Question 1.3

Explain how promotional messages might be adjusted according to the different stages of the purchase decision cycle.

(10 Marks)

Question 1.4

Evaluate the extent to which relationships with consumers should be based on the development of suitable attitudes and strong source credibility.

(10 Marks)

Hints and tips

Now you have embarked on a course of study in marketing communications, you should start to take a more critical perspective of the marketing communications you 'receive'. Ask yourself questions about what the communication is designed to achieve. Make mental and written notes to help you develop your understanding about communications.

References

Anonymous (2005) *The Marketer*, Issue 9, p. 26.

Biel, A. (1990) 'Love the Ad. Buy the product?' *Admap*, September, pp. 35–40.

Bovee, C.L., Thill, J.V., Dovel, G.P. and Wood, M.B. (1995) *Advertising Excellence*, New York: McGraw-Hill.

Butterfield, L. (1999) *Advertising Excellence*, 2nd edition, Oxford: Butterworth-Heinemann.

De Pelsmacker, P., Geuens, M. and Van den Bergh, J. (2001) *Marketing Communications*, Harlow: FT Prentice Hall.

Erdogan, Z. (1999) 'Celebrity endorsement: A literature review', *Journal of Marketing Management*, **15**(4), 291–394.

Fill, C. (2005) *Marketing Communications: Engagement, Strategies and Tactics*, 4th edition, Harlow: Pearson Education.

Friedman, V. (2004) *Financial Times*, 11 November, p. 13.

Kotler, P. (2000) *Marketing Management: the Millennium Edition*, Englewood Cliffs, NY: Prentice Hall.

Mitchell, V.-W. (1999) 'Consumer perceived risk: Conceptualisations and models', *European Journal of Marketing*, **33**(1,2), 163–195.

Pringle, H. (2004) *Celebrity Sells*, Chichester: Wiley.

Shannon, C. and Weaver, W. (1962) *The Mathematical Theory of Communication*, Urbana, IL: University of Illinois Press.

Thomas, R.J. (2001) *'Brandspeak'*, Accessed 17 February 2004, www.brandchannel.com.

unit 2 marketing communications mixes

Learning objectives

There are many different terms used to describe the various methods used by organizations to communicate with customers and other stakeholder groups. Indeed there are alternatives to the word 'communications' in this context, promotions is often used interchangeably to describe the same thing. Advertising, sponsorship, selling, direct mail, point of sale, exhibitions are different elements of what can be called the 'marketing communications mix'. Some firms will use a range of different methods, others might focus on one specific element. These tend to be terms that are used by marketers to distinguish between different types of activity. In consumer terms, many do not use different terms but perhaps classify everything they receive as publicity, advertising, promotion or selling. As marketers attempt to achieve a co-ordinated approach to communications, this may actually be helpful in achieving effectiveness.

After completion of this unit you will be able to:

o Understand the broad objectives for marketing communications

o Explain the roles that different elements of the communications mix play

o Understand the importance of co-ordinating the communications mix for maximum effectiveness

o Explain the different terminologies used by practitioners to describe communications activities

o Evaluate the role that marketing communications plays in the launching of new products and supporting brands at different stages of their development.

Syllabus references include: 2.1, 2.3, 2.4, 2.8 (see also Unit 1) 2.12.

Key definition (Syllabus 2.3)

Above- and below-the-line communications – Traditionally, most forms of advertising have become known in the communications industry as 'above-the-line' communications. This term identifies advertising through a variety of media in broadcast and print forms. Most other forms of marketing communications have, not unsurprisingly perhaps, been defined as being 'below-the-line'. These include sales promotion, PR, point of sale, personal selling. The 'line' being referred to is based on accounting terminology. Because advertising agencies have most commonly received payments by way of commissions paid by the media companies with whom they place their advertising, rather than direct payments from their clients, these payments were treated differently in profit and loss accounting.

Although these terms are still commonly used, their meaning has become increasingly blurred on two major counts. First, many clients are now establishing mechanisms for paying their agencies on results achieved and not on commission payments. Second, it is becoming difficult to actually determine what is advertising in its traditional form, compared to other forms of communication. The term 'through-the-line' referring to direct marketing has emerged in an attempt to accurately define these marketing communications activities. As organizations seek a co-ordinated or integrated approach to their communications, differentiation between above- and below-the-line becomes less important.

These are industry terms which might be considered helpful in defining responsibilities and roles in creating communications. They are less important from a consumer perspective where communications are seen in terms of specific methods used to communicate – advertising, publicity, promotions, sales, sponsorship, exhibitions and so on.

Communications mix elements (Syllabus 2.1)

Organizations use an increasing variety of marketing communications tools and media in order to convey particular messages and encourage us to favour their brand or products. As consumers, we are exposed to a vast amount of information on a daily basis – everything from news reports on television, radio and in the press, to weather forecasts, traffic information, store signs, product packaging, in-store point-of-sale material and so on. Advertising is just one of the elements with which the consumer must deal every day. A recent report published by CIM highlights the changing role of marketing in modern society. It describes the modern consumer as being 'under siege – being exposed to over 1500 communications messages every day'. The report suggests one of the most significant causes of this 'overload' is media proliferation. Cable and satellite broadcasting, the Internet and mobile technologies are having a significant impact on both how and how often marketing communications are being delivered.

Activity 2.1

Access and read this CIM report 'You talkin' to me?' – www.shapetheagenda.com. How might some of the issues raised impact on organizations with which you are familiar – your own company?

The major elements of the marketing communications mix are:

1. Advertising
2. Sales promotion
3. Public relations
4. Personal selling
5. Direct marketing.

Now, these five basic elements are supplemented by other forms of marketing communications. For example, you may have been thinking about sponsorship and telemarketing, or exhibitions and the Internet.

Well, these are either subsets of the five basic tools or they are media. So, sponsorship may be considered by some to be a part of public relations, telemarketing is a part of direct marketing, exhibitions are part of personal selling and the Internet is technically not a tool of marketing communications, it is a communications medium.

A communications medium is a part of the range of media available to carry promotional (often advertising) messages. Communications mix elements and media are separate. Media will be considered in more detail later in the coursebook but because of the close relationship between the communications mix and the media used to transmit them, it is worth noting here the main forms of media.

- o *Broadcast* – Television, radio
- o *Print* – Newspapers, magazines
- o *Outdoor and transport* – Billboards, taxis
- o *New media* – Internet, mobile phones, text messaging
- o *In-store* – Point of purchase, packaging
- o *Others* – Cinema, product placement, ambient.

Activity 2.2

Identify a practical example of each of the marketing communications mix elements.

Define the task that each has been designed to fulfil and decide whether it is likely to achieve its primary goals.

The communications mix is the use of any or all of the above-described elements in a unified and cohesive manner designed to achieve specifically defined and measurable promotions objectives. It is important to understand at this stage that these are the tools used in all forms of marketing communications, whether they be for packaged consumer goods, consumer durables, industrial products or services. In terms of marketing communications planning, the nature of the product or service which is to be promoted makes little difference – the same communications tools will be employed. Each element of the marketing communications mix will, however, have a specific task to achieve and it is the deployment of the tools to achieve the objectives which will be an important part of the overall understanding of the subject.

The elements of the marketing communications mix all have different properties and different potentials to achieve different tasks. Therefore, managers must mix the tools in such a way that they achieve the actual tasks at hand, within the resources available.

Activity 2.3

Identify a product (this may be something from a supermarket or chemist) and a service (such as banking or dry cleaning).

Do some research and make a list of the elements of marketing communications which are used by the company to support the brand.

Obviously, each element of the marketing communications mix can be used on its own. In fact, though, this is rarely the case. Most companies use some combination of the marketing communications tools in order to achieve their objectives. Most advertising campaigns will be supported with sales promotions activities, or public relations or both. A direct mail campaign may follow media activity designed to stimulate interest in the product. Most companies use point-of-purchase material to remind the consumer of their advertising message at the point where purchase decisions are made. A recent yet long-running car campaign included, among other things, a major television, print and poster advertising, public relations activity resulting in major articles in the national press both about the car and the advertising, dealer support activity, exhibitions, sponsorship and direct mail.

What is important, and vitally so, is that each element of the communications mix should co-ordinate with the other elements in the mix in order to achieve the communication of a single and unified message. Clearly, the impact of the message will be enhanced if it is reinforced by other parts of the mix, and the campaign objectives will be achieved in a more cost-effective manner.

Activity 2.4

Find examples of each of the elements of the marketing communications mix used by two directly competing organizations. Are there any differences between how the elements are being used by the two organizations?

Marketing communications is an essential part of the Marketing Mix – sometimes described as the 'Four Ps' – with the communications aspect represented by P for promotion. It is important to understand that each of the elements interacts with each of the others. Thus, the nature of the product – and its appeal to the customer – will be influenced by the price which is charged. Similarly, the availability of the product at specific retail outlets and through different dealerships may influence a customer's perception of the quality of the product. And marketing communications can affect and be affected by all the other components of the marketing mix.

Marketing communications is just a part of the marketing mix and its role is to communicate information of various kinds about the company, and its products and services to target audiences. However, it is not as simple as this might imply; its role may vary according to circumstances and the particular task at hand.

So, marketing communications may be required to provide information, to persuade a potential customer to buy a product or it may be used to remind a lapsed customer of the need to purchase brand *X* at the next opportunity. Indeed, there is a fourth role – a strategic role associated with the positioning of a brand so that a customer might understand quickly what the brand is offering and what the value might be to them. This is all part of the differentiation role that marketing communications has to play.

The role of marketing communications is to either:

1. *Differentiate* – a product/brand (to make it different to a competitor's brand or seem different through effective positioning)
2. *Remind* – and reassure a target audience with regard to benefits (to encourage (re)purchase)
3. *Inform* – a target audience by providing new information (e.g. of a new brand or flavour)
4. *Persuade* – an audience to take a particular set of actions (e.g. buy a brand).

These four roles might be more easily remembered as the *DRIP* roles of marketing communications (Fill, 2002). They are important factors when considering the objectives for marketing communications and in determining the roles of individual elements of the communications mix. At various times, marketing communications may be utilized in order to achieve more than one of the DRIP-related objectives, maybe all at the same time! Examples of campaigns in which all of these factors were incorporated were seen when the new UK directory inquiry services were launched. All of the competitors had to try and differentiate from the others, inform customers of the changes that were taking place – the replacement of the existing systems, persuade them to use their service and to continue to remind given the fragmentation of the market. TV advertisements formed the basis of these campaigns, supported by press, radio and billboards. The emphasis and role of different elements of the communications mix need to be considered against the DRIP factors when designing and implementing supporting tactics and selecting appropriate media.

There will be further references to the DRIP concept in other units when considering different types of communications and applications.

 Activity 2.5

Find examples of marketing communications being used to achieve different DRIP objectives.

Co-ordinated marketing communications (Syllabus 2.2)

Choosing the ultimate communications mix is a complex task that requires skill, creatively matching the profile of the customer and the target group with a promotional mix that will essentially attract them to the product. Of course the complexity of the exercise will differ based upon the market, certainly from a Business-to-Business (B2B) perspective; it is highly complex given the number of people involved in the decision-making process.

It has been suggested on a number of occasions that the key to success in implementing the ultimate communications mix is understanding customers and their characteristics, something that is a consistent theme to implementation of communications and promotional objectives.

The development of a co-ordinated approach to marketing communications is growing in impetus and importance in marketing today, as more and more organizations realize the importance of taking a more structured, ordered and co-ordinated approach to their marketing communications activities.

In the simplest form, it involves the co-ordination and cohesion of all elements of the marketing communications mix. A campaign that is co-ordinated needs to be planned, and is uniform in terms of its design, and communicates the same message. By combining more than one element of promotion, the message that is communicated is more powerful.

For example, Walkers Crisps have been involved in implementing a co-ordinated campaign. This has been both on TV and poster advertising. In addition to that, they are developing a consistent approach to advertising, using key personalities to identify with their products. As a result of this, Walkers' market grew by 21 per cent, while the crisp market generally rose only by 11 per cent.

Another prime example was Häagen-Dazs. They demonstrated an effective use of CMC when they entered the UK market. They positioned their products as luxury, fashionable food for adults and used a number of key personalities to promote the product for them. They gave themselves a quality positioning and used quality press in which to advertise. The net effect is that they are a main player in the ice cream market in the UK today.

Brook (2004) discusses the ways in which even major 'advertisers', such as Procter & Gamble, are looking at utilizing a range of co-ordinated but different forms of communication to promote brands with a budget of £600 million to spend on advertising, in-store promotions, direct mail, public relations and market research. £200 million of this is spent on advertising. Eighty per cent of the media budget is spent on TV but increasing sums are being spent in other areas. This is in part as a result of industry research which shows that there has been a reduction from 70 per cent to a little over 40 per cent in what consumers recall from TV ads. Interactive TV is playing a part as is the development of WoM communication via PR, sponsorship, text messaging and sending products to opinion leaders and opinion formers such as makeup artists and celebrities.

As customers, we require a variety of different communications and promotional activities to fulfil our need to know about products and services, and then to purchase them. You must consider the need to co-ordinate all of your marketing and communications/promotional activities.

Communications plans can be successfully developed only if the key factors within the marketing plan are clearly defined, identified and developed. Communications objectives need to be consistent with the firm's marketing and ultimately business objectives.

Co-ordinated marketing communications are mostly likely to occur when organizations attempt to enter into a dialogue with their various internal and external audiences. The communications elements used in the dialogue and the message sent should be consistent with the organization's objectives and strategies. Co-ordination and consistency are important when considering the role of marketing communications in maintaining long-term customer relationships.

The 4Cs Framework

It is essential that whilst considering each element of the promotional mix in isolation, to understand its role in the promotional operations process, ways should also be found for maximizing the mix potential by co-ordinating and aligning it with other promotional tools in order to optimize the marketing communications effort. Given the potential impact of the communications overload described in the CIM report discussed earlier, the question of co-ordination is a significant one. Increasingly it is probably becoming more appropriate to consider communications 'holistically', rather than in its constituent elements such as advertising, PR and so on.

Table 2.1 provides a brief summary of the key characteristics of each of the major communications tools. This categorizes the four principal elements: communications impact, credibility, costs and control – the 4Cs – used to determine the role and benefits of using each tool in CMC plans. Each tool is considered in more detail later in the unit. It is important to recognize these characteristics in this format as in many situations more than one tool is used in any given campaign. Ultimate decisions on which co-ordinated combinations of the communications mix need to consider the relationship between all of the elements and their respective characteristics. The framework developed here focuses on the major elements of the communications mix, for many organizations, other communications will be used as well which will make decisions on co-ordination even more complex. Consideration of the impact of the 4C elements should be given when evaluating the use of other communications tools.

Table 2.1 The 4Cs Framework – summary of the key characteristics of the tools of marketing communications

	Advertising	Sales promotion	Public relations	Personal selling	Direct marketing
Communications					
Ability to deliver a personal message	Low	Low	Low	High	High
Ability to reach a large audience	High	Medium	Medium	Low	Medium
Level of interaction	Low	Low	Low	High	High
Credibility					
Given by target audience	Low	Medium	High	Medium	Medium
Costs					
Absolute costs	High	Medium	Low	High	Medium
Cost per contact	Low	Medium	Low	High	High
Wastage	High	Medium	High	Low	Low
Size of investment	High	Medium	Low	High	Medium
Control					
Ability to target particular audiences	Medium	High	Low	Medium	High
Management's ability to adjust the deployment of the tool as circumstances change	Medium	High	Low	Medium	High

Adapted from: Fill (2005)

You will read and, no doubt, hear about the term 'Integrated Marketing Communications' (IMC). This term is often misused and refers to a variety of marketing and related activities. Different agencies, researchers and clients all attribute different meanings to IMC. There is no empirical evidence available to support the term and due to the inconsistency in the way the term is used, it is not used in this module. The term has been used to refer to the strategic use of marketing communications and, as the real focus of this module is operational the term 'Co-ordinated Marketing Communications' (CMC) has been adopted. CMC refers to a harmonized, planned and synchronous use of promotional and media mixes. Issues relating to IMC are explored during Professional postgraduate diploma in marketing.

Butterfield (1999) identifies several more Cs in considering successful 'total' brand communications – clarity, coherence, consistency, control, commitment, contact and customer-driven. He suggests that these factors might be considered 'obvious', but they are often ignored as companies fail to understand the nature of branding as being a holistic, longer-term process and not, as exemplified in many cases, as a series of short term, TV advertising driven executions.

Advertising

Advertising is one of the most influential forms of communications within the promotional mix, and the one that perhaps has the most impact upon our everyday lives. It does not matter where we go during a day, it is likely that we are bombarded either by newspaper, magazine, radio, billboard, TV, cinema or banner advertising on a regular basis.

 Definition

> **Advertising** – Is a paid form of non-formal communication that is transmitted through mass media such as television, radio, newspapers, magazines, direct mail, public transport vehicles, outdoor displays and the Internet.

Advertising benefits

Each element of the communications mix can deliver specific benefits, those for advertising include:

1. The ability to reach large numbers across different geographic markets when required
2. More effective targeting and media allow large audiences to be reached with specific messages
3. Depending on media used, costs of reaching individuals can be lowered compared to other forms of communications
4. Can be used to provide information for consumers at different purchasing stages
5. Effective in awareness creation at early stages of new product launch
6. Wide range of media vehicles available to carry advertising.

It is likely that advertising will serve a number of purposes in terms of communicating with both individual and organizational customers. It is used to meet a number of specific marketing and promotional objectives as you have already seen, but its main emphasis is to inform, persuade and remind customers to purchase products and services.

One of the significant roles for advertising particularly in respect of its ability to reach large numbers of consumers, often very quickly, is that of awareness generation. This can apply to new product launches where there is a need to create initial awareness and positioning, and also to established brands where messages regarding repositioning might be the main objective. Advertising is the main communications tool used by organizations in different market sectors and is the tool on which most budget is spent. This is due in no small part because it is the tool used by the large consumer goods firms in supporting brands on a global basis. Whilst there are major benefits in using advertising as listed above, the disadvantages relate to the costs involved in both production and media purchase. Additionally, although advances are being made in this area, measuring effectiveness is still a difficult issue for advertisers and their agencies. As identified in Unit 1, the volume of advertising (and communications in general) that exists, makes it difficult for consumers to retain messages and decode in the way in which they are intended to be. Refer back to Table 2.1 which summarizes the respective strengths and weaknesses associated with advertising.

Ideally advertising is used to promote products and services, but it is also a source that creates long-term images and perspectives of the organization. It is likely that there have been a number of adverts that stick in your mind, that have impacted upon you in a direct way, created an image and perception in your mind.

Take, for example, 'Orange Tango' – being 'Tangoed' became a way of life for young people for a long time as a result of the orange-coloured man running around and slapping an unsuspecting person in the face. It is probably one of the most successful advertisements in achieving 'recall'.

Advertising objectives

You will see later in this unit where advertising objectives actually come into play, and how they break down into different categories. Advertising objectives should be SMART in the same way that marketing objectives are SMART and they should relate directly to achieving the marketing objectives overall. It is therefore likely that advertising objectives will reflect some of the following components:

- ○ Promoting product, organizations and services
- ○ Stimulating demand for products
- ○ Competitive advertising – offensive/defensive advertising
- ○ Increasing sales (growth)
- ○ Educating the market – brand and product awareness
- ○ Increasing the use of products and services (market development)
- ○ Reminding and reinforcing (market penetration)
- ○ Reducing fluctuations in sales performance.

For example, a typical advertising objective could be to increase sales by 10 per cent from £500K to £550K by the end of the financial year. A further example might be to increase brand awareness from the existing 70 to 100 per cent within the same timescale. These are obviously the two very different types of objectives. Indeed, it could be argued that the former is not a specific communications-based objective at all in that increasing sales levels also depends on other elements of the marketing mix; communications can play a limited role if there are problems with the basic product or the price is not right. Attributing the significance of communications to sales response has proved notoriously difficult to measure as a result of the difficulties in 'isolating' its effects from other marketing elements.

There is thus a fine line between using advertising to increase sales and advertising to create awareness, and each of these will require a different approach in order to achieve the long-term goals of the organization.

Case study

Putting your shirt on advertising

A new campaign by Ben Sherman, the shirt manufacturer, will be based on posters and magazine advertising. The campaign will cost some £3 million. Nothing unusual so far. Where the campaign differs from many others of its kind is in how the star of the adverts will be paid. The Manchester United and England soccer player, Rio Ferdinand, is being paid a guaranteed £100 000 plus a share of profits based on sales volume. This structure is a move away from the normal fee-based approach paid to personalities.

Although unusual in the UK marketing, it is not uncommon in the USA. Michael Jordan is in part rewarded by Nike for his endorsements with shares in the company.

Source: *Metro*, 3 February 2003.

It is quite clear that one of the key tools of the promotional mix to support the sale of products is advertising. This is particularly so for consumer-based products, where advertising serves to create an awareness of the product, its characteristics, its image and buying habits.

A good example to demonstrate how consumer-based products interact with advertising is chocolate. A low involvement, low unit-price bar of chocolate would not, of course, warrant an investment in personal selling to the millions of consumers who purchase it on a day-to-day basis. In this situation, it is much more likely that the emphasis would be through some form of advertising, or even sponsorship through advertising. Sponsorship-based advertising is becoming increasingly common, with organizations such as Cadbury sponsoring the UK soap opera *Coronation Street*, for example.

It is critical that you understand the impact of advertising and the role it plays on the product, and the link between the advertising campaign and the different stages of the product life cycle. However, it is also important that first you understand the appropriate media and their characteristics, and how, therefore, they can be used.

 ## Activity 2.6

Why is it important to define advertising objectives?

Advertising and the marketing mix

Advertising is used to support many elements of the marketing mix, but in most instances the product and brand are the key focus to advertising activities.

Advertising for both distribution and retailing is very much related to the 'push' and 'pull' strategies that are discussed later. In essence, an organization at this stage may be developing a strategy related to increasing the number of outlets it has, for example a marketing objective may have been set to increase the number of retail outlets by 15 per cent within a 12-month period.

Advertising will be focused on encouraging retailers to stock their products. In this situation, advertising will be very closely linked to a high level of promotional activity to support the product and give an incentive for distribution outlets to stock their products.

A push strategy would often include a range of personal selling, trade (sales) promotions, advertising and direct marketing activities, in addition to public relations.

For a retail outlet, a pull strategy would be developed. The key to developing this is to create an awareness of the brand and its associated product, and encourage consumers to purchase from them. The strategic approaches to marketing communications will be discussed further in Unit 6.

Advertising on this occasion will take several forms, such as TV, radio, press advertising and possibly a big poster campaign. Clearly, the level of advertising will be based on the budget available through both the manufacturer and the retailer.

Quite often, in retailing situations, some promotional support will be available from the manufacturer, such as various brochures, point-of-sale display materials and merchandising support. Again this is very relevant with the sale of electrical goods. Electrical retailers such as Comet, Dixons and Currys will commonly use advertising to promote specific brands supported by incentives from the manufacturers.

As a marketing communications planner, you will need to undertake the following activities in this area:

1. Liaise with channel members to ensure that stock is available
2. Be aware of the needs of the channel and how and when they need communications support
3. Provide consistency for all communications
4. Ensure that all members of the channel support and are empowered by the message the advertisement seeks to deliver.

Case study

India advertises for tourists

In world travel terms, India accounts for less than 1 per cent of global tourist traffic, around 3 million tourists. More Indians travel abroad than they receive visitors. In order to try and counter this, the Indian Government launched a major advertising campaign, 'Incredible India', depicting striking images of the country. Launched in December 2002, major objectives were to improve brand image by positioning India as a premium tourist destination. Media selection included international print and electronic media such as the *Financial Times*, Conde Nast Traveller and CNN. The advertising budget was £1.7 million in 2002/03 and some £5 million in 2004/05. The success of the campaign led to an increase in tourist visits by 17 per cent in the year to February 2003 and by over 30 per cent for the following year. Foreign exchange earnings have increased by 40 per cent.

In addition to the advertising, the Indian Government is investing significantly in infrastructure projects and service provision. Such marketing changes and objectives are consistent with the communications objectives to raise the country's profile and positioning.

Adapted from: An article by Ray Marcelo in the *Financial Times*, 4 November 2004.

 ## Activity 2.7

Why is it important to co-ordinate advertising with other elements of the promotional mix?

Advertising campaign planning

Planning for an advertising campaign is a complex process, often very involved, drawn out and resource intensive.

As regards the campaign itself, it is likely that it will involve a pre-determined theme but communicated through a series of different messages in different media, carefully chosen for maximum impact on the target audience. The campaign will need to be managed carefully and synergy of advertisements will need to be planned. Campaigns will run over various lengths of time, from the quick burst or seasonal burst to the DRIP–DRIP approach that goes on over a long period of time, in some instances for many years.

Regardless of the time period of the campaign, it needs careful planning and the client and agency need to be able to work together and move from stage to stage assessing each situation as it arises and making a range of important decisions.

Figure 2.1 clearly explains the stages in an advertising campaign.

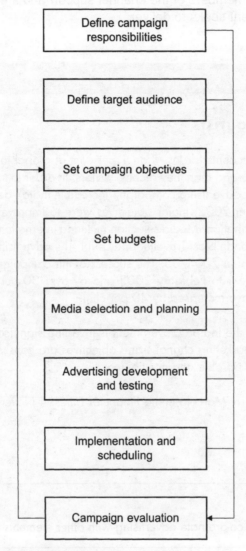

Figure 2.1 The campaign planning process

Setting campaign objectives is a very strategic role and will involve a series of meetings to ensure that the campaign objectives link clearly to the marketing and corporate objectives from which they actually evolve. It is sensible to point out at this stage, however, that the other strategic component of the campaign is the budget. This will most likely have been set within the budgeting round and it is therefore likely that the budget appropriation has been defined in advance of the campaign commencement.

Sales promotions

Sales promotions traditionally are complementary to advertising. They are used to reinforce and encourage customers to try the product and then purchase it. Sales promotion provides a range of short-term tactical measures to induce sales of particular products or services now rather than at some point in the future. In that sense they are sales accelerators. Its aim is to provide extra value to the product or service, creating the extra impetus to purchase products that we might not normally buy.

 Definition

> **Sales promotions** – A range of tactical marketing techniques designed within a strategic marketing framework to add value to a product or service in order to achieve specific sales and marketing objectives.

Sales promotion should be part of a planned approach and very much an integral part of the marketing communications planning framework. It should be planned and executed in parallel with associated advertising and possible public relations campaigns.

Marketers will, therefore, rely upon sales promotions to enhance the performance of other components of the promotional mix. Again this reinforces the nature of a CMCs approach to promotional activity.

The main aims and associated objectives of sales promotions are usually:

- To increase brand and product awareness – attracting new customers
- To increase trial and adoption of new and existing products
- To attract customers to switch over brands and products from competing organizations
- To level out fluctuations in supply and demand
- To increase brand usage
- To increase customer loyalty
- To disseminate information
- To encourage trading up to the next size or the next range – particularly pertinent to the car market.

Sales promotion benefits

Sales promotions are rarely used as a solus form of communication, but are now a widely accepted form of promotion, seen almost as part of the product or service 'package'. Consumers may actively seek out where they can get the best sales promotion offer when making purchases, whether that might be whilst shopping in a supermarket or evaluating alternatives in more limited or extensive decision-making situations. Benefits for consumers come in adding value to their purchases. Manufacturers and retailers, therefore, find it beneficial to use a wide variety of techniques to attract and retain customers. As indicated in Table 2.1, sales promotions can be a highly targeted and flexible form of communications. Sales promotions are most often considered to be short-term devices intended to prompt brand or supplier switching. In evaluation terms, effectiveness can quite readily be measured as response is often an integral part of the communication, coupon redemption or competition entries, for example.

Sales promotions techniques

There are a range of sales promotion techniques that can be used to achieve each of the above aims and objectives. Typical techniques in both sectors will include:

- Money-off vouchers/coupons
- Buy one get one free
- Customer loyalty bonus schemes
- Twin packs
- Bulk buying
- Discounts
- Try before you buy
- Cash rebates
- Trial-sized products
- Prize draws
- Competition codes
- Point-of-sale displays.

Case study

Guinness use Rugby World Cup to promote drinks sales in pubs whilst watching sport

Consumers tend to default to lager when watching sport in pubs. In an attempt to counter this behaviour, Guinness ran a major pub-based sales promotion during the course of the 1993 Rugby World Cup held in Australia, Targeting 18–24 males who were not committed Guinness drinkers but who tried it periodically, 12 000 pubs in the UK received promotional kits which included supplies of Up & Down Under hats, POS and external LIVE RUGBY HERE banners, posters, cut-out pints, show cards, table talkers, wipe clean fixture posters. The unique hats were available when buying four pints of Guinness. Pubs were incentivised to return tokens to Guinness with rugby shirts and tee shirts, 650 000 hats were distrubuted, volume of Guinness sales increased by 2 per cent year on year in strong rugby areas including Scotland and the North East, against a market decline of 5 per cent. Brand awareness increased from 23 to 46 per cent during the promotion.

Adapted from: Institute of Sales Promotion, 2004, *Awards Winners section*, ISP website – www.isp.org.uk.

 ## Activity 2.8

Draw up a list of products or services that you have purchased or seen recently that have included each of the sales promotions identified above.

Trade promotions

Earlier on, we looked at the nature of the 'push and pull' promotional strategies, whereby manufacturers are looking to encourage their wholesalers and retailers to take their products and effectively 'take them to market'.

As a result of this process, trade promotions are often based around ensuring that product penetration is achieved. However, in order to achieve product penetration, the incentive levels often have to be quite high, as product penetration is likely to be contrary to the typical 'volume stock traffic' aims of the wholesalers.

It is likely that manufacturers will encourage organizations to *increase their stock levels* in order to gain some level of commitment to increase sales potential in the marketplace, but also perhaps with the view of gaining some kind of supply chain relationship, with priority given to one particular supplier.

Alternatively, there is intensive competition for *increased shelf space* within retail outlets. The greater the incentive provided by the manufacturer, the more potential there is for greater shelf space in the retail outlet. 'White Goods' products are often at the heart of this scheme, with particular brands securing more floor space or shelf space than some of the lesser brands. There is the potential in this situation for a joint promotional activity between the manufacturer and perhaps the retailer to give incentives for a greater number of sales, from which both organizations will clearly benefit.

Good trade promotions, that is a good 'push strategy', highly incentivized, backed up by appropriate merchandising and appropriate advertising may be advantageous. Alternatively, policies such as sale or return are also a good incentive and ultimately reduce the financial risk involved.

Seasonal fluctuations – are often problematic to both manufacturers and suppliers, and therefore it might be that through a range of sales promotion activities, incentives to buy the products outside the typical season could be achieved. The likely nature of these would be to involve the manufacturer in both the push and the pull strategy context, in line with both consumer and trade promotions.

Competitor response – sees sales promotion being used very much as a tactical weapon to dilute the impact of competitor activities. Therefore, during the launch of a new competitor product, it might be that the focus of trade activity relates to creating high barriers to entry for the trade in order to sustain your market share in the wholesale community.

Specific methods might include:

- o Allowances and discounts
- o Volume allowances
- o Discount over-riders – based upon retrospective performance, for example, on a quarterly or annual basis
- o Free merchandise
- o Selling and marketing assistance – co-operative advertising, merchandising allowances, market information and product training
- o Sales contests
- o Bonus payments.

Case study

Nikon sales promotion for Coolpix launch

Nikon were launching their new range of compact digital cameras, Coolpix, into a crowded and saturated market. A sales promotion campaign, Coolpix Adventures, was aimed at both the trade and consumers in order to create differentiation from the other brands in the market. Incentives for counter staff encouraged pro-active demonstration and recommendation. The consumer aspects were to drive traffic to participating dealers. Purchase data collection would provide a basis for future relationship development and retention offers.

The specific target audience were TGI digital camera users/buyers of which 58 per cent were men in the age range 35–44, 81 per cent of whom were married and in households with incomes over £35 000. A leaflet was delivered to over half a million homes containing a photo memory card for the Coolpix and invitation to their local dealer where the card could be activated. The card idea provided the opportunity for consumers to interact with the Nikon brand. This visit would also determine success in other parts of the campaign with 'adventure' themed prizes.

Store staff were sufficiently motivated for sales to exceed targets in each month of the promotional campaign.

Adapted from: Institute of Sales Promotion, 2004, *Awards Winners section*, ISP website – www.isp.org.uk.

Retailer to consumer sales promotions

The key aims and objectives of this process will be to increase sales through a range of promotional techniques, as follows:

- o *Increase in-store trade and customer traffic* – The use of coupons and money-off vouchers.
- o *Increase frequency of purchase* – Discounted promotions for next purchase.
- o *Increase in-store loyalty* – Through the use of storecards and rewards systems.
- o *Increase own brand sales* – Encourage customers to purchase own brand products through a range of sale promotion incentives such as trial packs, in-store demonstrations, and so on.
- o *Achieve consistent demand* – Reduce fluctuations, provide sales promotions in particular time bands to encourage a more consistent approach to shopping.

Manufacturer to consumer sales promotions

This relates very much to the 'pull' strategy, whereby the manufacturers take responsibility for creating awareness and demand in order to pull products up through the supply chain to the customers.

Typical sales promotion activities might include:

- o *Encouraging trial* – Samples, gifts, trial drives of vehicles – allows customers to decide for themselves
- o *Disseminating information* – Information packs on a door-to-door basis, perhaps closely linked with a direct marketing campaign (again utilizing the IMC approach)

    o *Trading up* – Encouraging customers to trade-up from their existing models – a typical activity of car manufacturers and white goods manufacturers.

The list of promotional activities is endless, but the important issue from a promotional operations' point of view is to ensure that demand for the products is continuously stimulated and is consistent with the marketing plan.

We will look at the impact of sales promotions on a B2B basis later in the coursebook.

As with advertising, a planned approach must be undertaken and programmes tightly managed. Therefore, the typical planning process will include:

    o Identification of the target market.
    o Sales promotion objectives versus budget appropriation.
    o Identification of the cost of communication for the sales promotion campaign and the actual cost of the campaign, that is the 'fulfilment cost' – the cost of actually hosting the campaign in terms of postage, free gifts and so on – effectively, the cost of the promotion to the organization. Obviously, this should be looked at in association with the ultimate benefits in the longer term.
    o Implementation – the same applies here as to the advertising programme, but clearly the promotion will probably run in parallel with the advertising programme; therefore issues relating to timescales, drip and burst style promotions and so on will apply.

Activity 2.9

What are the most likely sales promotion alternatives open to a manufacturer when trying to attract consumer attention?

Public relations

The role of public relations is to look after the nature and basis of the external relationships between the organization and all stakeholder groups. It is aimed at creating a sustainable corporate brand and an overall company image within the marketplace.

Definition

Public relations – The planned and sustained effort to establish and maintain goodwill and mutual understanding between an organization and its publics. (Institute of Public Relations)

Publics, in the main, consist of:

    o Customer groups
    o Local and central government
    o The general public
    o Financial institutions – investors/shareholders/borrowers

- o The media – TV, press, radio (locally and nationally)
- o Opinion leaders/formers
- o Internal marketplace – employees, trades unions, employee relations bodies, trade associations
- o Potential employees.

It is of primary importance that the organization specifies precisely the use of public relations in respect of both the promotional and marketing mix, and PR objectives must be expressed in SMART terms. Failure to target the PR campaign precisely will potentially mean that the campaign could be wrongly directed and, at the worst, be a complete failure.

PR benefits

Public relations is perhaps one of the most misunderstood communications tools in the sense that it is considered to generate 'free' messages. An editorial feature in a magazine or newspaper which says good things about a product, service, organization or individuals associated with them, might be considered 'free' when compared to purchasing equivalent amounts of advertising space. However, the costs of employing PR staff and agencies who act on their behalf and the additional expenditure in organizing events, press conferences and so on, need to be added to the 'free' bill. As a lot of PR activity is based on personal level communications and relationships, perceived credibility of communications generated via PR activities is considered to be higher than those of other communications tools. See Table 2.1.

Just as direct mail suffers from connotations and references to 'junk', PR also has to deal with the media image of 'spin'. This infers that messages can be twisted or spun to create different perspectives on issues other than those representing the actual position. High-profile areas such as politics and financial services are sectors which suffer from allegations of spin. When firms announce unfavourable financial results, some attempts are usually made to present these in as positive light as possible in order to retain confidence amongst stakeholder groups such as investors and employees.

Aims and objectives of public relations

Typically PR aims and objectives will closely link to the following:

- o To create and maintain the corporate and indeed the brand image
- o To enhance the position and standing of the organization in the eyes of the public
- o To communicate the organization's ethos and philosophy, and corporate values
- o To disseminate information to the public
- o To undertake damage limitation activities to overcome poor publicity for the organization
- o To raise the company's profile and forge stronger, lasting, customer and supply chain relationships.

Public relations, as with all other elements of the marketing mix, requires a planned approach and plays an important role at a strategic level. It is also subject to strategic level objectives. For example, the launch of a new model by Mercedes-Benz will be subject to a significant PR campaign running in parallel with significant advertising and direct marketing, perhaps on a local level by the local dealerships. Therefore, PR becomes a high-level communications objective and it is critical that it is subject to the same intensity in respect of targeting specific groups of the public.

Marketing information to underpin public relations activities

As explained in the previous section, marketing is more likely to provide an underpinning role in relation to public relations and will on many occasions be the think tank behind a lot of the planning and development of PR strategies.

However, marketing also supports the PR process by providing a range of relevant information, both in respect of primary and secondary data. Therefore, the following activities are undertaken:

- ○ Consumer and trade press scanning
- ○ Competitive comparisons
- ○ Production of publicity materials
- ○ Promotional videos
- ○ Management and publicity of special events
- ○ Development of corporate logos/symbols and identity
- ○ Internal marketing tools
- ○ Preparation of literature to support corporate activity.

Public relations and attitude change

The whole basis of public relations is to continually reinforce a positive attitude towards the organization in the minds of the public, therefore for PR to be successful it has to change a range of negative attitudes into positive attitudes (Figure 2.2).

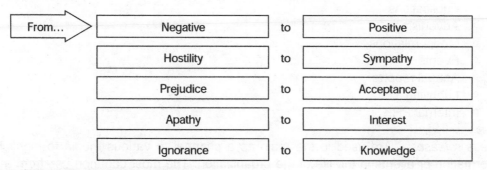

Figure 2.2 Attitudinal change
Source: Worsam, 2000

In order to undertake this level of attitudinal change, you will require a clear and specific understanding of the nature and breakdown of the market in which you operate, both from a customer perspective and also from a media perspective.

Case study

Domino's Pizza chose PR to change perceptions

Domino's wanted to radically change the way the brand was perceived and be seen as pioneers in every part of the delivery process. The main focus was to generate media impact in men's magazines and national press to benefit local stores and franchises. Agency Cohn & Wolfe created the Domino's Pizza 'Test Base' which pulled together existing innovations from within the business and introduced future technology that could improve delivery efficiency. Test Base initiatives were rolled out through the selected media over 6-month period. These included Hoverboard trials, use of GPS tracking and security processes. Journalists were invited to a world preview to see what happened in the Test Base. Press relations included a video news release, photography of Domino's delivery experts, press packs with quotes from the BSM Road Safety Consultant highlighting commitment to safety and regional press targeted to coincide with April Fools Day.

The campaign created 44 million opportunities to see with 12 000 cm^2 of positive print coverage with significant exposure of the Domino's logo and other brand graphics. The Commitment to Innovation theme appeared in all articles.

Adapted from: Case study *IPR Excellence Awards* 2004. See www.ipr.org.uk.

Public relations techniques

It has already been identified that PR has two roles, one which is a long-term developmental role, and the other that reflects the need to have contingency activities in place. From a marketing operations' perspective, you need to understand when to use which particular public relations technique to optimize the level of 'positive publicity' the organization can deliver.

Typical techniques include:

o Press releases
o Press conferences
o Publications
o Advertising
o Media relations
o Events
o Annual reports
o Lobbying
o Internal PR.

Press releases – Are used in the main as a channel to various media to highlight specific information or events in the life of the organization. The most common use from a marketing perspective will perhaps relate to either product launches or new initiatives. Most press releases are now sent electronically.

Press conferences – Are particularly pertinent at a corporate level, whereby press conferences are usually the channel for announcing a major story or indeed having to respond to a crisis that is in the public domain and the media spotlight. Videoconferencing allows simultaneous and recordable broadcast opportunities to those audiences unable to attend the conference at a specific venue.

Publications – Are in general the work of the marketing department, and they will provide a range of information, through a range of different media, that can be sent to current and potential clients. This approach would be helpful when organizations are looking at a marketing development programme, and therefore raising corporate awareness is vital.

Media relations – Both at corporate and marketing level, it is helpful to have good media relationships with both the general press and also the specialist press. Having close media contacts and good relations may gain both favour and greater access to the potential media spotlight when required. Quite often, inviting the media to undertake a particular role in the public relations exercise may gain favour with them.

Events – Covers a whole range of both corporate and marketing activities, and highlights yet again close links with other elements of the promotional and marketing mix, with areas such as sponsorship or events linked very closely to a product launch. It is likely that a wide range of publics will be invited to such events in order that the organization's corporate image is enhanced.

Annual reports – Are an extremely important publication. They are usually widely distributed, but are especially important for providing shareholders and the financial media with organizational performance levels for the previous year. They provide an opportunity to present the organization in a positive light, reflecting upon past achievements and defining its future direction.

Lobbying – Is a very specialist area, which is designed to develop and influence a number of high-level relationships in order to influence organizations such as local, national and, where appropriate, international governments. Lobbying, therefore, is seeking to influence people in authority in order to secure their support to achieve a desired action. All who have an interest, for and against, any piece of legislation will set out to lobby support. Public relations, of course, has a major and highly specialized part to play in this process.

When considering lobbying, remember that it is likely to be a long-term process, which will involve highly targeted contacts with individuals and groups.

You are, of course, selling an idea, persuading others to take a certain course of action. Therefore, a decision-making process is operating and there is a decision-making unit (DMU) to be identified.

Lobbying is not exclusive to the legislature. Its principles, adapted as needed, are used wherever there is a need to persuade a person in authority to take a certain line of action. There are of course usually pro- and anti-lobbyists. It is likely that lobbying of this nature will be handled at a corporate level, the materials and information for the lobbying exercise will be provided by the marketing function.

It is important to note here the role that electronic forms of communications are playing in the field of public relations. Press releases no longer have to be printed and mailed. E-mail provides an effective method of distribution, as does text and picture messaging. Videoconferencing can be used to organize and/or support press conferencing or employee briefings.

Internal PR

The importance of developing a structured and meaningful communications process in order to win over the confidence of the workforce, and gain support for strategy implementation and the associated change is growing in significance. Internal PR plays a vital role in respect of this communication and while they are part and parcel of the overall publics, the workforce requires a more tailored and organizational approach.

The likely emphasis of internal PR will be based around keeping people informed, avoiding cloak and dagger-style internal politics. Should a successful PR campaign be implemented internally, then motivation and attitude levels might appear to be more positive within the organization.

Particular techniques included in this area will relate to journals, newsletters and internal briefings.

It is likely that on some occasions internal PR will be based around 'crisis' style PR, perhaps announcing redundancies, changes in management structure, disaster and so on.

When selecting the appropriate public relations technique, it is essential to ensure that you undertake an assessment of three criteria:

1. *Suitability* – It is vital to ensure that the techniques chosen are targeted and, therefore, appropriate to the target market, in respect of tone, content and style; that the appropriate medium is chosen, which again meets the profile requirements of the customer base; of primary importance will be the necessity to establish the level of influence and impact the actual technique will achieve.
2. *Feasibility* – As with any other promotional activity, PR will be restricted by a budget – therefore any activity or programme of activities will need to come within the required budget. Particular considerations will relate to resourcing the programme both physically, financially and from a human resource perspective. Ultimately, it is important to establish whether the programme is considered achievable or realistic.
3. *Acceptability* – Are the activities chosen acceptable to the organization as a whole, are they appropriate and in keeping with the corporate identity? An assessment of alternative sources of PR should also be undertaken to ascertain which is the most acceptable approach to achieving the desired level of publicity.

Case study

Employees as brand ambassadors

In late 2001, SEEBOARD Energy launched a new customer vision – *Passionate about finding new ways to save you energy and give better value for money.* SEEBOARD wished to match internal employee behaviour with this new vision. They recognized that this would require a culture change but wanted to avoid a specific 'change' programme and looked to present a series of stages that moved employees from where they were to where they wanted to be.

The specific objectives were to:

o Communicate the details of the new customer vision
o Explain the vital role staff played in its achievement
o Reward staff who exhibited the right kind of 'behaviours' which had laid the foundation for the new vision
o Advocate involvement
o Contribute towards increasing satisfaction and morale
o Evaluate effectiveness.

The activities involved employees being cast as extras in the new TV advertising campaign, workshops for team leaders who would then cascade information in briefing sessions, Employee Awards scheme, Christmas gifts, staff magazine content, videos and an All Staff Communications event. The Company's intranet site was also used, and field sales employees received text messages.

Evaluation showed that 99 per cent understood the new customer vision, 94 per cent thought the new TV commercials were very good, 98 per cent understood the key achievements in 2001, 98 per cent understand the contribution they can make to the new vision and strategy, and 99 per cent believe that this is the right direction for SEEBOARD.

Adapted from: IPR Excellence Awards (2002), IPR website – www.ipr.org.uk.

Crisis management

One of the key functions of any PR role will be to handle 'crisis' situations. These can range from management fallouts to serious incidents, accidents and disasters that might need reporting on.

At some stage in the life cycle of an organization, it is almost inevitable that they will be hit by some form of crisis that will invoke a whole range of contingency plans, or even the immediate development of an emergency PR plan. For example, Air France suffered a devastating blow when one of its Concorde airliners crashed on take-off from Paris during 2000. This invoked a range of public relations exercises, informing the public of the basis of the incident and providing regular updates, as the situation unfolded.

As a marketer you should be alert to potential situations that might emerge as a result of the use of your products or services, in order that you are prepared to deal with the unknown or perhaps unexpected event. It is therefore your role to ensure that, on behalf of your organization, you:

- ○ Are aware of what could happen
- ○ Know how to manage PR should this particular situation emerge
- ○ Develop a number of contingency plans based on the possible situations in readiness for the event.

Since September 11, of course, crisis management has become a significant issue for all firms.

Activity 2.10

In what ways do public relations complement other elements of the promotional mix?

Direct and interactive marketing communications

Definition

Direct marketing – An interactive system of marketing which uses one or more advertising media to effect a measurable response at any location. (Institute of Direct Marketing)

This is one of the most rapidly evolving and changing areas of marketing communications and promotional activities. Key driving forces of change relate to:

- ○ Changing dynamics in demographics and lifestyles
- ○ Increasing competition
- ○ Customer power
- ○ Fragmentation of the media
- ○ Increasing costs of media
- ○ Emerging distribution channels
- ○ Changes in market information (EPOS, smart cards, etc.)
- ○ New technologies.

One of the key drivers of growth is the massive movement in technologies, including the rise of databases, improving analytical systems, developments in phone technologies and the information superhighway.

Added to these, it would appear that in today's marketing environment, organizations know more and more about their customers. Their profiling and research techniques are far more sophisticated, making direct marketing an excellent tool for very specifically targeted communication campaigns.

These drivers are the common denominator in almost all change strategies; therefore direct marketing is not an exception to the rule.

The use of direct marketing by an organization effectively demonstrates that the organization has taken a decision to avoid dependence on marketing channel intermediaries and has also decided to deal with customers in a highly targeted way. This, of course, has implications for the level of marketing and management information that a company may need to obtain and retain in the future.

Direct marketing has in the past been viewed as a very tactical approach to meeting marketing objectives, and like sales promotions and PR has been used as part of both an ongoing programme of marketing communications and promotional activities. However, in cases of emergency, that is in crisis or indeed in competitive response, direct marketing has proved to be a useful tool.

As a marketing tool, direct marketing evolved from the mail-order business and now it is seen as another compatible element of the promotional mix that supports and underpins the marketing communications activity and can often be found conveying the good news of sales promotions.

However, over the years direct marketing has come under fire as 'junk mail' and has also been found to be the source of 'confusion marketing'. In addition to this, direct marketing has been subject to considerable change due to the Data Protection Act, and therefore the introduction of issues such as permission-based marketing have had a tremendous impact upon the future shape of direct marketing.

While this is quite a broad definition, it does however, identify some of the key component characteristics of direct marketing. For example, it provides the basis of the relationship, which is defined as interactive, being a two-way relationship between the organization and the customer. At the customer's location this could be via phone, fax, e-mail, the Internet, post, to name but a few. However, whatever the nature of the communications and wherever and whoever they go to, it is essential that as with every other form of the promotional mix, there is an underpinning and SMART set of quantifiable objectives.

Objectives of direct marketing

Direct marketing performs a number of tasks, depending upon which element of the promotional mix it might work in parallel with and support.

The aims and objectives of direct marketing might include:

o Increasing direct mail-order levels from new and existing customers
o Dissemination of information and provision of information to aid customer enquiries and support the adoption process
o Generation of sales leads to increase the number of sales leads and ultimately to influence a rise in sales income

    o   Generation of trial leads to increase the number of customers willing to trial the product, to influence the process of adoption and to influence a rise in sales income.

The aims and objectives of direct marketing can be achieved in a number of ways, and can often play a pivotal role in enhancing the selling process, by way of providing sales leads, that might directly result in a sale.

Furthermore, direct marketing objectives can be achieved through techniques such as direct mail, direct response advertising, telemarketing and the Internet, all of which are aimed at increasing sales leads and sales turnover.

Database marketing

For an organization to really optimize its effectiveness in relation to building and developing long-term customer relationships, it is essential that they secure as much relevant information as possible about their customers and retain it in a database system. This in turn provides an opportunity to create closely defined profiles in order that a tightly defined targeting exercise can take place.

> *Database marketing is the application of digital information collected about current and/ or potential customers and their buying behaviour to improve marketing performance by formulating a strategy and building personalized relationships with customers.* Source: Chaffey *et al.* (2000)

As information technology plays such a tremendous role in day-to-day business operations, it is increasingly likely that databases will be built to collect information from customers accessing websites. Databases are essentially known as the 'brains' behind the website, which enables a high level of customer profiling and personalization to take place.

Typical consumer information for database building might include:

    o   Name
    o   Address
    o   Occupation
    o   Geo-demographic profile
    o   Psychographic profile
    o   Previous contacts
    o   Previous responses
    o   Frequency of purchase
    o   Purchases made
    o   Value of purchases
    o   Type of purchases
    o   Media responsiveness
    o   Promotional responsiveness.

Source: Dibb *et al.* (2001).

However, many underpinning database systems have failed as yet to achieve the level of sophistication required in developing appropriate data-mining opportunities. In addition to this, unless the site is a transaction-based website, that is where customers actually carry out a transaction online, it can be difficult to glean sufficient information about the customers to develop the typical profile basis you might prefer.

A further consideration in database marketing currently is that where databases are highly sophisticated, organizations do not understand how to use the information and put it through the data-mining process.

One of the key benefits of a good database, whether it be based on information gleaned from websites or through other sources, is that it forms the basis of the relationship and how it might be maintained in the future. While databases aid relationship management, database marketing does not constitute relationship marketing, in fact it only provides the means by which the relationship might be maintained.

Direct marketing techniques

Direct marketing provides significant scope for communicating directly with customers and can cut across just about any promotional activity, as part of the CMC activity, and is not used exclusively for the consumer B2C market. It is also used very much in the B2B market and has always been a central component of marketing strategies in the consumer market for years.

Direct mail

Direct mail has probably been the most used form of direct marketing over the years, but probably the one subject to the most abuse. It has also commonly been termed by the media (and consumers) as 'junk mail'. This term refers to incorrectly targeted mail. What is the point of mailing details of gardening products to people who live in high rise blocks of flats! This can quite rightly be termed 'junk' by both receivers and senders who have wasted money on the mailing contents and postage. The advent of sophisticated database systems, and geo-demographic and lifestyle profiling systems has reduced much of the vast wastage of this kind. Consumers still complain about the amounts of direct mail they receive but at least in most cases the information is relevant to them as individuals.

Direct mail is widely used in both consumer and business markets to target their customer groups directly. The financial services sector is a major user of direct mail. Even with the Data Protection Act, it is likely that some households receive as much as one piece of direct mail per day, in relation to mortgages, pensions, insurance, offers of credit cards, to name but a few.

Some UK direct mail facts:

o 5438 million items were mailed in 2003, of which 78 per cent was consumer mailings
o Direct mail volume has increased 139 per cent over the last 13 years
o Estimates suggest consumer direct mail generates over £27 billion worth of business each year
o 60 per cent of direct mail is opened
o 52 per cent of consumers like to receive special offers through the post.

Source: Direct Mail Information Service, www.dmis.co.uk.

These statistics both illustrate the size of the direct mail industry and suggest higher levels of consumer acceptance than that which might generally be perceived when considering the effectiveness of direct mail communications.

There are many advantages associated with using direct mail, such as targeting. Targeted campaigns can include working on a basis of either geographic segmentation or geo-demographic segmentation. This level of segmentation combined with the level of knowledge that exists in relation to market segments means that targeting can become a very exact science.

Other advantages include being able to personalize messages, improve response rates and provide flexibility in terms of the range of activities available.

Case study

Whisky and socks

The whisky brand Macallan used a highly effective direct mail campaign to help protect market share and form a longer-term relationship programme. The campaign was run at Christmas time when whisky sales are at their peak and also when promotional activity is at its highest.

The mail pack was headed 'If you don't ask for Macallan this Christmas, you'll get the same pair of boring socks'. This was mailed to their existing database and a list of known purchasers bought from a lifestyle survey. Around 14 000 pieces were mailed which also included a questionnaire to help establish the relationship programme and a £1 off voucher.

Response rates far exceeded expectations, 58 per cent from the existing database and 39 per cent from cold prospects. This was Macallan's first venture into the use of direct mail but it is now a regular part of their communications activities.

Adapted from: Case study on Royal Mail website – www.royalmail.com.

However, when developing a direct mailing campaign, it is vital to ensure that the information being used is accurate, that customer groups are profiled and then targeted specifically, and that the content matches the needs, wants and expectations of the group. This process will be assisted through the database marketing process, and ultimately the information collected will provide a greater insight into the customers and their buying behaviour. At the end of the day, the mailing will only be as good as the marketing research information that underpins it. When purchasing a list externally, it is essential that you ensure the list provides you with relevant and up-to-date information, and is inside the data protection limits, defined in the Data Protection Act.

There are a number of organizations now that specialize in the development of appropriate automated mailing lists:

- o Dun and Bradstreet
- o Wyvern Direct Response – based around occupational groups such as accountancy, medical practitioners and hospital contacts
- o Wise and Lovey – website address – http://www.mailing-labels.com.

It is expected that more and more online automated mailing lists will become available to keep abreast of the changes in technology and the direct marketing sector.

It is essential that if you are purchasing a list, very clear criteria have been developed in relation to:

- o Relevance of the list in relation to the target market
- o The source and ownership of the list
- o The level of detail in the list
- o Frequency of updates

- ○ Whether the list is of enquirers, purchasers or respondents
- ○ Frequency of purchase
- ○ Level of accuracy.

Direct response advertising

This is another form of direct marketing, and appears in the standard broadcast and standard print media.

Principally, it is different from other forms of advertising, as it actually demands a response, by giving a website address, telephone number or a coupon for a personal visit. This is becoming a popular approach in direct marketing and is growing continually as advertisers try to gain greater value from their advertising experience.

The targeting for direct response advertising is probably a little less scientific than direct mail, and relies much more on an assessment of the average reader or viewer profile than a prepared mailing list. However, the information collected can be used as a database for other forms of direct marketing in the future.

More and more organizations are involving themselves in direct response advertising in order to optimize their expenditure in advertising.

Case study

Smart money on direct marketing for investments company

M&G Investments were able to increase response rates by 32.5 per cent and increase direct sales by 15.3 per cent through the effective implementation of callsic direct marketing principles.

The starting point was the use of qualitative and quantitative market research to identify what consumers were really looking for from an investment company. The core market was 'mass affluents' with assets of £30 000 to £200 000 and/or incomes of £30 000 to £100 000. The research allowed a narrowing of this segment to a target market known as the 'affluent silvers' – over 45s who took investment seriously and prepared to invest large sums who preferred informative advertising.

The promotion started with copy-rich newspaper advertisements used for a brand response campaign. The ads were positioned in the colour pages in main news sections. Crosstrack 48-sheet posters were displayed in main railway and underground stations. Specific product advertising were run in the financial sections of newspapers, financial papers and IFA trade press.

An ISA direct mailshot was sent to prospects which suggested recipients to have a cup of tea and take time to digest the information. Follow up mailings prompted a more urgent call to action via a cup of instant coffee. Coded coupons and response phone numbers were used to track response. All leads were followed up via outbound telemarketing. Conversions were added to databases for retention, cross and up selling.

Media spending compared to the previous year was over 30 per cent less yet response rates rose by 32.5 per cent overall. Cost per enquiry fell by 53.9 per cent and total cost per acquisition was reduced by 35 per cent.

Adapted from: Case study IDM Business Performance Awards 2003 – www.theidm.com.

Telemarketing

We have touched upon the issue of personalization, and how through the use of database marketing we can glean enough information to personalize organizational approaches to customers. However, the difference between telemarketing and other methods of direct marketing is that it is truly a personal approach, whereby there is a direct personal contact, which provides the basis for an interactive relationship between the organization and the customer.

While the personal approach is preferred and is seen as a way of getting closer to the customer, customers can find this approach rather intrusive and are somewhat resistant to embracing deeper and more meaningful relationships with organizations they might purchase from.

Telemarketing, like other components of direct marketing, should be a planned, highly targeted and controlled activity that will both create and exploit a direct relationship between customer and seller using the telephone.

Telemarketing provides the organization with significant scope as telephone rental and ownership is very high, with over 80 per cent of households possessing them across the European Union. The telephone is a particularly powerful communications tool, which gives you direct access to new and existing customers, in a flexible environment, that is, wherever they are.

Telemarketing also provides the scope to be used for customer service initiatives and customer satisfaction surveys, as well as the basis for developing the existing customer relationship overall.

The scope of telemarketing

- o To generate sales leads
- o To screen leads prior to following-up
- o To arrange appointments for sales representatives
- o To direct sales
- o To encourage cross/upward selling
- o To provide dealer support
- o To manage and service accounts
- o To undertake market research
- o To undertake test marketing.

Source: Brassington and Pettitt (2000).

As regards promotional and marketing operations, it is clear that telemarketing plays a pivotal role in:

- o Increasing sales levels
- o Supporting customers
- o Increasing levels of customer service
- o Providing technical support
- o Information gathering
- o Credit control.

One of the key disadvantages of telemarketing is the cost. It is a costly exercise, where few economies of scale can be charged. However, many financial services organizations are given very tough limits in terms of varying sorts of telemarketing in order that economies are achieved, but unfortunately this can be to the detriment of the long-term relationship with the customer.

A key factor of telemarketing as a direct marketing tool is that volume is rather limited in comparison with other direct marketing techniques. While a typical telemarketing representative might make between 30 and 60 calls per day, an equivalent piece of direct mail could actually achieve a significantly greater proportion of contacts.

Telemarketing, while having many qualities, is probably one of the least effective direct marketing mechanisms. It is certainly one of the least cost-effective, personally intrusive and does not achieve the necessary volume of hits on a day-to-day basis.

Use of the telephone plays a significant role in managing customer relationships and whilst there are negative aspects to telemarketing, significant investments are made by organizations in telephone technology to allow them to provide services to customers, handling sales enquiries and providing ongoing customer services. This area has led to the rapid growth of the 'call centre' either operated by companies themselves or most commonly outsourced to specialist agencies who manage the telephone enquiry systems on behalf of a number of different clients. This is in fact one of the fastest growth areas for new business in the UK. It is of course a significantly high cost area and it is for this reason that some major users have moved their call centre operations to places like India where personnel costs are much lower. BT has recently announced that it is opening two call centres in India creating over 2000 jobs. Other firms that have either already done so or are considering similar moves include, British Airways, HSBC and Powergen (*Financial Times*, 10 March 2003).

 Activity 2.11

How can direct marketing communications complement advertising and sales promotions?

Sponsorship

 Definition

Sponsorship – Is a two-way mutually beneficial partnership between an organization being sponsored and the sponsor. Sponsorship works on the premise that the association largely affects image and that the sponsor may exchange money and/or goods or services in kind return for the association that the sponsorship provides. Those being sponsored may include groups or teams, events, charities, individuals, buildings and TV programmes.

Sponsorship can play a significant role in co-ordinating not just marketing communications but the whole of the marketing mix. When Carling undertook a major sponsorship of the UK's football Premiership, in addition to the extensive media coverage generated, they also launched a Premier brand of lager and all of their delivery vehicles carried logos and wording related to football and the sponsorship. In communications terms, the sponsorship facilitated PR and sales opportunities through corporate hospitality at matches and related events. This was in addition to the millions of football supporters who would wear their teams' shirts at games and for leisure which carried the Carling logo on the Premiership badge.

Sponsorship objectives

Typical sponsorship objectives may include:

○ Increasing brand awareness
○ Building and enhancing corporate image
○ Raising awareness of brands related to products restricted in advertising through various legislation, such as alcohol and cigarettes.

There are two perspectives to consider in a sponsorship, the perspective of the organization being sponsored and that of the sponsor. Both parties will need to consider if the alliance created as a sponsorship arrangement is one that is required by the existing image of the organization and will enhance overall organizational credibility. They will also need to consider how relevant the association would be between the two organizations and how both parties will benefit. The sponsor will need to consider what exposure will be gained as a result of the sponsorship and how similar or dissimilar the target audiences are to their own.

Types of sponsorship

The main types of sponsorship include the following:

○ *Programme sponsorship* – For example, *Coronation Street* by Cadbury's or HSBC sponsorship of drama and films – typically this is used at the start of a TV programme, during the interval and at the end. The cinema and major films often form the basis of sponsorship alliances. There has been a significant increase in TV programme sponsorship and the opportunity is providing broadcasters with a valuable new revenue stream as budgets reduce for more traditional forms of TV advertising.
○ *Arts/sports sponsorship* – For example, the Barclaycard Premiership. Barclaycard sponsor the football Premier League in England. Events' sponsorship is expensive but can be of very high profile and potentially the most cost-effective way of getting increased brand awareness.
○ *Sponsorship of other events* – Exhibitions, festivals and awards ceremonies. These are again high profile, and are sometimes very useful forms of sponsorship for smaller businesses that wish to raise their profile locally.
○ *Sponsorship of individuals or teams* – Mercedes-Benz sponsor the British tennis player Tim Henman, and Nike sponsor the golfer Tiger Woods.

Case study

Heineken sales up through TV sponsorship

Heineken is attempting to freshen up it's appeal among younger drinkers with a sponsorship of an anarchic Dutch TV programme. This is a significant change of approach for the brewing company which has traditionally relied on a relatively conservative communications strategy. The late night programme, 6 pack, consists of a number of pranks and off beat reports. The sponsorship consists of the provision of beer for the show. The programmes success is measured by viewing figures of 100 000 against initial forecasts of 40 000. Text messaging and online chat after the programme has finished, extend the communications activity.

Based on an article in *Financial Times*, 26 June 2003 by Ian Bickerton.

Role of sponsorship

Sponsorship can provide a more cost-effective means of reaching your target audience but the design, content and message are much more controlled. From a corporate and PR perspective, sponsorship raises the profile of the organization and its corporate values, and in some instances can really bring the brand name and corporate image to centre stage.

Advertisers are being drawn in by the opportunity to convey their brand values by clever association with programming, that is, in keeping with their product and the desired company image.

Many organizations succeed in ensuring as part of the sponsorship deal that their name is an integral part of the overall event, for example the 'Worthington Cup'.

However, while sponsorship may appear to be a good idea, it is essential that, like all other elements of the promotional mix, it clearly fits a need and will enhance the possibilities of directly achieving pre-determined marketing objectives.

In many ways in fact sponsorship is a term used to describe the co-ordination of elements of the promotional mix. It involves part advertising, part PR, part sales promotion, part personal selling.

Sponsorship offers vast opportunities for the organization in terms of the value-added perspective of merchandising, public relations activities, improved stakeholder relationships, and highlighted ethical and social values. The benefits are quite considerable.

However, a number of key factors should be considered prior to taking the decision to proceed with sponsorship arrangements:

o   What relevance does the particular sponsorship arrangement have in terms of the match between the two organizations and the potential target audience? For example, it is clear that for Worthington and Benson and Hedges, sponsoring sports events will bring in additional sales of both drinks and cigarettes, both during and after the event, as sports effectively, is linked to the consumers of both products.
o   *The period of impact* – How long before and after the event will the sponsorship profile last? Is the event a one-off or a sequence of events?
o   *The uniqueness of the sponsorship agreement* – From a competitive perspective it will be essential that the agreement you hold with the sponsored organization allows you to differentiate your brand, market and competitive positioning in a unique way. In some situations this level of expectation is not achievable, but if the potential fit of the organization and the sponsorship deal is good, then high-profile sponsorship might be achieved.
o   *The level of spin-off promotions is also essential* – For example, the importance of a co-ordinated approach between other elements of the promotional mix will be essential to maximize and optimize cost-effectiveness of particular high-profile events. Here advertising, merchandising and promotional incentives may be a particular match for the promotional mix.

Therefore, for successful implementation of a sponsorship strategy, it is necessary to clearly define the position of sponsorship, and ensure that it is fully representative of corporate and marketing communications goals, and effectively co-ordinates sponsorship with other elements of the promotional and marketing mix.

Case study

Sponsoring to win

It is suggested that consumers are not as cynical about sponsorship as they may be about advertising. This may in part be due to perceived community benefits and it is not as direct or as pervasive as forms of direct advertising. This has advantages for organizations who use it but it requires careful planning if it is to be effective. In the UK, sports sponsorship is estimated to be worth more than £1 billion and globally the figure is between \$20–24 billion. There are however some doubts as to whether major users of sponsorship are getting full value for their investments as the programmes are not fully planned and all opportunities being exploited. Nike is reported to be sponsoring tennis star Serena Williams some \$55–60 million over 8 years but as this timescale will most likely see the individual end her career, can Nike really achieve long-term benefits? Potential problems associated with sponsorship include:

1. Weak targeting – sport attracts large audiences but what proportion of these are core customers?
2. Inappropriate matching of sponsor and event
3. Not integrating sponsorship into the whole marketing and marketing communications strategy
4. Sponsorships based on short-term activity
5. Sponsoring individuals disproportionately to their long-term value.

Adapted from: An article in *The Marketer*, October 2004 – Special Edition on Sponsorship.

Product placement

Of growing importance is the use of product placement in TV programmes and films. Seeing brands being used by well-known personalities in such situations may have an impact on influencing consumer opinion. This might also be considered as a relatively discrete form of advertising. Sherwin and Malvern (2004) identify a number of examples of recent product placements in successful movies. *Die Another Day* had Bond driving Aston Martin and Jaguar brands. *Lost in Translation* had Bill Murray (ironically) making ads for Suntory whiskey. Murray's wardrobe was supplied under an agreement with Helmut Lang. Specialist product placement agencies are receiving upto \$20 000 to find product sponsors.

Tomkins (2003) suggests that advertisers will spend an increasing proportion of their budgets on ways that will attempt to overcome consumer resistance to traditional forms of communication. This might include linkages to different forms of the entertainment industry. An American website – www.americanbrandstrand.com – supplies a listing of the number of brand references in the US Billboard Hot 100 pop charts. Many of these 'plugs' are unpaid for in advance but may lead to future endorsements or other sponsorships. The example of the hit 'Pass the Courvoisier' by Busta Rhymes is quoted. After this, US sales of the cognac brand rose 14 per cent. Allied Domecq, the brand owner did not pay for the reference but would have appreciated the impact on sales which may not have resulted from conventional advertising.

Personal selling

In the context of promotional operations, it is important that you have a clear overview of how the personal selling process can be both compatible with other elements of the marketing mix and also enhance the effectiveness of the marketing mix (Figure 2.3).

 Definition

Personal selling – An interpersonal communication tool which involves face-to-face activities undertaken by individuals, often representing an organization, in order to inform, persuade or remind an individual or group to take appropriate action, as required by the sponsor's representative.

When preparing a marketing communications plan, the role of the sales department will usually include some form of personal selling objectives. Particular emphasis will include an analysis of the specific responsibilities associated with personal selling, the role of personal selling overall, and how it will influence and enhance other elements of the marketing mix.

It is a known fact that personal selling is the most expensive element of the marketing communications mix:

o It is resource intensive
o It is time ineffective
o It contributes little to economies of scale
o It incurs high contact costs and customer maintenance costs.

Some organizations have made changes to their selling structures in order to alleviate some of the cost burden. Personal sales calls to relatively low value, and volume customers have been replaced by direct mail, telemarketing and e-mail. In such cases this often provides for more active and regular contact, leading to increases in sales and strengthening of relationships.

However, it is probably one of the most effective methods of influencing decision-makers to the stage of adoption. At a strategic level, the balance of personal selling versus other more cost-effective methods of the marketing mix must be considered in order that the target market receives the most relevant approach to meet its information-based needs.

Sales force activity will be subject to a number of associated sales objectives that it will directly relate back to the marketing objectives, and will be pre-determined in order that the organization can optimize and maximize the potential impact of the personal selling team in association with other promotional activities.

Sales force objectives

Sales force objectives will not all relate directly to increasing income. They may also relate to cost saving, customer-relationship management and developing new leads.

Therefore, typical sales objectives could be:

o To increase sales turnover by 20 per cent within a 12-month period.
o To reduce the number of clients with minimum viable order levels at the end of a 12-month period.

o To reduce the cost of sales by 10 per cent within a 6-month period.

o To increase the number of distribution outlets by 15 per cent in a 12-month period.

Often, personal selling goals are misunderstood and are assumed to be about an increase in sales, where actually personal selling goals will be about increases in overall revenue and profitability. Profitability might be improved by an increase in minimum order levels in order to achieve economies of scale.

The task of personal selling

There are four key order-related activities of personal selling:

1. *Order takers* – Are effectively personnel who take orders from customers at the place of supply, for example holiday bookings, train tickets and retail outlets.
2. *Order getters* – Are sales personnel who effectively visit organizations/customers in order to try to gain orders and future business from them.
3. *Order collectors* – Are personnel whose role is to gather orders, this is very much a telemarketing role.
4. *Order supporters* – These are back-office personnel who underpin the personal selling process by providing information, customer service and support.

While this is one perspective, the role and task of personal selling is far more extensive than this, and includes activities such as:

o *Prospecting* – Gathering information in order to gain sales leads and prospective clients.

o *Communicating* – Being the provider of information about the organization, its products, services and after-sales care.

o *Selling* – The actual role of convincing a potential customer to adopt the product; overcoming resistance and handling objections relating to, for example, the company, the product, the service, the pricing strategy, the individual, competitive comparisons, need- or want-related issues.

o *Market research/information gathering* – Environmental scanning, competitor intelligence and customer intelligence.

o *Servicing of accounts* – Maintaining and providing ongoing customer service, including technical support, financial contractual arrangements and logistical arrangements.

o *Allocating* – Ensuring that the allocation of products to customers is undertaken at all times, in particular in times of production shortages.

o *Customer-relationship building* – Building and sustaining long-term customer relationships.

Personal selling is a vital role within the organization, but it underpins a range of other promotional activities that it can only achieve through the appropriate level of sales and marketing support and with the appropriate tools of the trade.

It is essential from a marketing and promotional operations perspective that the sales team is kept briefed of any changes to the product portfolio, services mix or any essential information that might either enhance or inhibit sales team performance. As a marketer you therefore have a responsibility to support the sales team in a range of ways in order that they can open and close a sale effectively and efficiently.

o Provision of market information to support the selling process – customer and competitor intelligence.

o Provision of potential leads from the market scanning process.

o Client history – database information about purchasing behaviour, purchasing trends, frequency and value of orders.

- ○ Financial reports – Dun and Bradstreet reports, annual reports and so on.
- ○ Provision of a range of appropriate promotional materials that include company history, product portfolio, services mix, financial package, support packages and so on.
- ○ Sales aids – product samples, service packages and demonstration equipment.
- ○ Provision of promotional plans in order that sales staff can co-ordinate their call plans in line with particular promotional initiatives.
- ○ The provision of promotional incentives, merchandising and so on.

Opening and closing a sale

As advertisements raise awareness and desire a response, as sales promotions provide an incentive to purchase, personal selling provides the opportunity to actually close the sale.

The role of the sales person will be to effectively take the buyer through from the opening of the sale to the closing of the sale and the signing of the purchase order and contract.

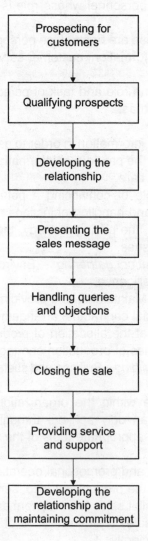

Figure 2.3 The personal selling process

Creativity in communications (Syllabus 2.8)

Generally speaking, all communications contain a balance of informational and emotional content. This area was discussed in Unit 1. Informational or rational appeals contain product-related information and seek to persuade through the benefits and advantages of the product itself. Emotional appeals attempt to provide customers with images that help develop brand associations and favourable feelings. In some cases, these need not contain any directly product-related information at all. However, the vast majority of messages contain informational and emotional content. For example, many TV advertisements for toilet cleaners or disinfectants include men in white coats telling us that our toilets, baths, sinks and so on are full of germs. This use of 'experts' is a technique used not only to gain our attention but also to provide credibility for the message. Refer back to Unit 1 where the use of celebrity endorsement was introduced. By raising the seriousness of the issue it might induce an element of fear into some people, which is essentially an emotional appeal. So, 'Domestos – kills all known germs dead' combines both an informational and emotional element in the ad's message. Consider the concept of perceived risk in cases of this kind. Which risks are being reduced through an ad of this nature? Ronseal claim that their brand of paint and wood stains does 'exactly what it says on the tin' and dries in 30 minutes. This is an informational approach using product-related attributes as the core message appeal. Look back at Unit 1 and consider other types of perceived risk.

A similar approach is taken with disposable nappies/diapers, where the rational element explains how 'Sam will get a sore bottom', from wet diapers; and the emotional appeal is conveyed through images of smiling happy children and their mothers.

Fear is quite a common factor of creative appeals, where advertisers appeal to the emotions of their customers. Financial services organizations often use the fear appeal, when marketing pensions or serious injury claim products. The brand icon used and developed by Scottish Widows depicts a (young) widow dressed in a black cape symbolizing bereavement and isolation.

Other emotion-based slogans are included in the table below:

Company	Slogan
Durex	Feeling is everything
Nokia	Connecting people
Peugeot	The drive of your life
Swatch	Time is what you make it
Toyota	The car in front is a Toyota
Vauxhall	Raising the standard

Source: Brassington and Pettitt (2000)

The creative process

Communications, particularly advertising can be highly creative, and will therefore include a number of creative brainstorming sessions, both internally before the brief is issued and externally in preparation for the pitch. Within an agency there will be a range of activities being undertaken, preparing to meet the brief, both creatively and strategically, with an advertising campaign that is SMART. They will be asking themselves a range of questions, for example:

- ○ What is the role of advertising in this campaign?
- ○ What is it expected to achieve?

- ○ Who is the target audience?
- ○ What is the single most important thing we should convey?
- ○ What is the brand called?
- ○ Why do people want to buy it?
- ○ Why should people buy it?
- ○ What is the proposition?

From answering these questions the creative process gets underway. The creative team will want to know, in particular, what it is about the brand that justifies the proposition. What are its key characteristics? What if anything is physically unusual about the product or even the service? Do people have a special relationship with the brand? Or is there anything special about the people who use it?

Bartle Bogle Hegarty

Creative Brief

CLIENT _____

BRAND _____

THE PRODUCT IS:

THE BRAND IS:

1. THE ROLE OF ADVERTISING:-
   A. WHAT DO WE WANT PEOPLE TO DO AS A RESULT OF SEEING THIS ADVERTISING?

   B. HOW DO WE BELIEVE THE ADVERTISING WILL WORK TO ACHIEVE THIS?

2. WHO ARE WE TALKING TO?

3. **WHAT IS THE SINGLE MOST IMPORTANT THING THIS ADVERTISING SHOULD CONVEY?**

4. WHY SHOULD PEOPLE BELIEVE THIS?

5. WHAT PRACTICAL CONSIDERATIONS ARE THERE?

DATE	
JOB NO.	
1ST REVIEW	
FINAL SIGN OFF	
CREATIVE DIRECTOR	
TEAM LEADER	
BUDGET ESTIMATE £	
MEDIA	

Figure 2.4 A creative brief form

Figure 2.4 represents an example of a briefing form used by the advertising agency Bartle, Bogle and Hegarty (BBH). This might at first glance appear somewhat simplistic. However, it is intended to encapsulate the key information required by creatives in order for them to focus on developing the right kind of messages associated with the brand. Overloading with detail at this stage of the process is likely to be counterproductive.

How might this process work? Those involved in the creative process, copywriters and art directors will attempt to combine their skills, working closely together in an attempt to produce effective communications ideas. Typically the elements that they might work with include words, pictures, imagery, sound, music, people or characters, space and colour. In the course of producing communications campaigns, ideas and different creative executions will go through a series of iterations before a mutually acceptable (to client and agency) solution is arrived at. This could involve intense testing and research of various concepts. A TV advertisement lasting only 30 or 60 seconds will usually have taken many months in design and production.

In addition to the creativity involved in actually producing the communication, it is also important to recognize that creativity plays a role in other aspects of communication planning and associated activities. Creative approaches to planning itself, objective setting, evaluation techniques, budgeting, co-ordination, media selection may all play a part in generating successful communications.

Marketing communications and brand development (Syllabus 2.12)

Recalling that one of the prime roles of Marketing Communications are to differentiate (and position) a product or service, it is important to understand that this is paramount when considering how to launch new products and develop a brand and keep it alive in the minds of the target audience.

Marketing communications can develop and establish key brand values in one of two main ways. These may be considered as the advertising route or the name route. With the advertising route, advertising is used to develop brand-related associations for consumers such that they make connections between a brand and its advertising. These associations may be linked to tangible attributes such as taste, colour or price, for example. Alternatively, they may be linked to intangible elements such as prestige, status and ego-related aspects of ownership. Therefore, branding may be entirely emotional or image-based. Alternatively, brands may be based entirely on rational information, for example Ronseal's 'It does exactly what it says on the tin'. In many cases, a blend of emotive and rational messages may well be required to achieve the objectives and goals of the campaign.

If the naming route is to be adopted then the brand name will be linked to the functionality of the brand itself. The packaging and associated communication devices (often in-store/ merchandising) will provide further points of brand association reinforcement. All aspects of the promotional mix, if used appropriately, can be used to develop, maintain and extend a brand. Mass-media advertising used to be the tried and trusted way of brand development. Times have changed and now CMC can be used to develop and reinforce brand messages. Co-ordinated marketing communications can be used to establish brand values which consumers then use to understand those brands that are important or significant to them.

Branding, therefore, can augment products in such a way that buyers can understand that it is different to other brands, recognize it quickly and make purchase decisions that exclude competitive products in the consideration set. Premium pricing is permissible, as perceived risk is reduced, and high quality is conveyed through associated trust and experience. Loyalty develops, facilitating opportunities for cross-product promotions and brand extensions. Integrated marketing communications become more feasible as buyers perceive thematic ideas and messages which, in turn, reinforce positioning and values associated with the brand.

Launching new products (Syllabus 2.12)

In both B2C and B2B marketing, the main objectives for communications are to create awareness. This might take the form of heavyweight TV campaigns for consumer products or specially designed launch 'events' for business products. Of course in both circumstances, there would be appropriate support from other communications tools. Opinion formers and opinion leaders would be targeted for attention in order to influence initial purchases utilizing PR activities. Trade activity would focus on achieving distribution. Sales promotions, both consumer and trade, would be used to promote trial.

Case study

Adidas PR focus for new ball launch

1 December 2001 saw the worldwide launch of the new Fevernova football, the official matchball of the World Cup in Japan and Korea in 2002. This date was selected because it was also the date of the competition draw. The 'normal' communications method would probably include pull-based advertising. The launch was taking place over the competitive and commercially significant pre-Christmas period. In the UK, the decision to use PR, involved releasing information to the UK media the day before the launch with the intention of seeking coverage on the Monday which would be a relatively 'quieter' day after extensive coverage of the draw itself on the Sunday. PR was selected because of its ability to selectively target key individuals within the media who could influence the editorial content.

Personalized 'media kits' were prepared for 45 key journalists which included the ball in a box wrapped with a red ribbon and the St. George's cross motif to highlight the link between Adidas and the England team. Digitally manipulated photographs of England players David Beckham and Steven Gerrard, shown heading the balls side by side, were provided for picture stories. Media kits were presented personally, and an exclusive was arranged with *The Sun* newspaper with additional materials. This provided for front page coverage on the Monday.

This was a highly cost-effective campaign compared to the alternative of advertising. The communications were given added credibility through the use of Beckham and Gerrard, and linkages to the actual World Cup draw. Effectiveness was achieved with the ball selling out in the UK by Christmas, with first month sales 11 times greater than any previous ball launch.

Source: IPR Excellence Award, 2002 – www.ipr.org.uk.

Maintaining market share (Syllabus 2.12)

As products develop and build market share, the role for marketing communications change. In the growth phases of the product life cycle, there is a continued need to increase awareness. Levels of expenditure may increase as share and volumes grow. Advertising and PR may still dominate the mix as repeat purchase is encouraged. Messages would change, and sales promotions would still play a part in attempting to gain loyalty and deter competitive activities. Direct and interactive tools can be used to target specific groups again to build loyalty and provide information for database development.

As maturity approaches, differentiation becomes significant. This might include communications to support product development and reposition, where necessary, depending on the level of competitive activity. Further efforts at relationship and loyalty building would be necessary. These issues will be dealt with in detail in Unit 4.

Case study

Advertising relaunch for Magnum

Unilever's concern over flagging sales of the Magnum ice cream brand, first launched in 1986, has prompted a £25 million advertising campaign in the UK to support an effective relaunch. The ice cream sector as a whole has been suffering weak sales with the two major players, Unilever and Nestlé buying up local brands around the world.

The campaign included extensive TV and cinema advertising with the theme of 'Seven Deadly Sins'. This theme was successfully used in the relaunch in Australia where sales were 400 per cent above targets. The ads are targeted at women with an empowering theme and message that indulgence is acceptable.

Source: The Times, 6 March 2003.

Case study

Repositioning 'heritage' brands

There are a number of brands that may lay claim to some kind of 'heritage' status both in terms of how long they have been on the market and to some extent the way in which they have been promoted. The latter point is also connected to the nature of the product and how it has traditionally been positioned.

One such brand is Horlicks, the 130-year-old malt-based bedtime drink owned by GlaxoSmithKline. The target market has been in the older age ranges and principally female. Updating the packaging has had a limited effect on the look and feel of the brand, aimed at attracting a younger audience whilst keeping the existing market happy. The softly-softly approach was further enhanced with TV ads with a tag-line 'Horlicks could help anyone get a restful night's sleep'.

More recently, the product itself was given a creamier taste and further packaging changes resulted in an eye-catching carton. PR activity has now resulted in the drink being adopted as an after-dinner digestive in hip London venues such as the Groucho Club. Such an approach represents a reinterpretation of the brand's values. Other examples where brands have taken a more contemporary view of the brand and how it is communicated include Tetley Tea who have run ads with personalities such as Kim Cattrall from *Sex and the City*.

Adapted from: An article by Alicia Clegg in the Financial Times, 28 October 2004.

Summary

This unit has been particularly extensive as it seeks to provide an overview of the key components of the promotional mix.

One of the critical success factors of implementing the promotional operations plan will be the degree of synergy and co-ordination that exists between each of the promotional mix elements.

It is clear that the mix elements are indeed complementary to each other. Some of them are more effective and efficient in terms of targeting volumes, while other elements have a key strength in developing customer relationships in the long term.

Ultimately, the key success factor for any promotional mix will be its ability to meet the marketing objectives and bridge the successful implementation of the marketing strategy. Promotional planning in complete isolation of the marketing plan could be untargeted and a complete waste of valuable resources.

It is necessary to clearly identify the direct objectives, relate them back at all times to the marketing plan, undertake a co-ordinated approach of promotional mix tools to optimize the effectiveness of a combined campaign and, of course, evaluate the implementation for measurement of success.

Further study

The essential textbooks for the module provide more depth and breadth of most of the issues covered here. Applications using the various elements of the communications mix are considered throughout the coursebook. The website of the branding and identity consultancy, Interbrand, contains a wealth of research and information on branding and related topics – www.brandchannel.com.

Typical exam questions

In this section, references are given to specific examination and assignment questions from the June/July 2004 assessments. The questions are set out in Appendix 5. Detailed feedback on these questions from the CIM Senior Examiner and specimen answers can be obtained from the CIM website. Also included are some general examples of question types, briefings on which are included in Appendix 3.

June 2004 Examination Questions 1d, 2a and b, 3a and b, 4a and b. July 2004 Assignment Question 1, parts 1 and 2 and Question 4.

Question 2.1

Using appropriate criteria, compare and contrast the effectiveness of the following two promotional tools: sales promotions and personal selling.

(10 Marks)

Question 2.2

Recommend the key processes and procedures necessary to develop and implement an effective direct marketing campaign.

(10 Marks)

Hints and tips

Check the websites of the major communications bodies such as the IPA, IDM, IPR and so on. These provide details about the specific areas covered as well as containing case studies of effective implementation. Some of these will be used to illustrate issues throughout the coursebook.

Keep practical examples of different kinds of communications that you receive making notes about what you think the objectives were, what creative devices are being used and, what is the expected response?

References

Brassington, F. and Pettitt, S. (2000) *Principles of Marketing*, Harlow: Pearson Education.

Brook, S. (2004) *Media Guardian*, 25 October, p. 10.

Butterfield, L. (1999) *Advertising Excellence*, Oxford: Butterworth-Heinemann.

Chaffey, D., Mayer, R., Johnston, K. and Ellis-Chadwick, F. (2002) *Internet Marketing*, 2nd edition, Harlow: FT Prentice Hall.

Clegg, A. (2004) *Financial Times*, 28 October, p. 12.

Dibb, S., Simkin, L., Pride, W.M. and Ferrell, O.C. (2001) *Marketing Concepts and Strategies*, 3rd European edition, Boston, MA: Houghton Mifflin.

Fill, C. (2005) *Marketing Communications: Engagement, Strategies and Tactics*, 4th edition, Harlow: Pearson Education.

Marcelo, R. (2004) *Financial Times*, 4 November, p. 13.

The Marketer Sponsorship Works October 2004, pp. 6–7.

Metro, 3 February 2003.

The Times, 6 March 2003.

Tomkins, R. (2003) 'The hidden message: Life's a pitch, then you die', *Financial Times*, Friday, 24 October.

Worsam, M. (2000) *Marketing Operations*, Oxford: Butterworth-Heinemann.

www.cim.co.uk/www.shapetheagenda.com
www.dmis.co.uk
www.ipr.org.uk
www.isp.org.uk
www.marketing-labels.com
www.royalmail.com
www.theidm.com

unit 3
the marketing communications industry

Learning objectives

For many years, the marketing communications industry and the communications mix have been dominated by advertising. Large agencies such as J. Walter Thomson, Saatchi and Saatchi, Bartle, Bogle and Hegarty (BBH) have grown to service the needs of international clients most often competing in consumer markets. More recently this picture has been changing. The large agencies still exist, although in many cases they have become part of larger marketing services groups such as WPP and Omnicom. Also, the focus on advertising has been shifting towards a need for providing a range of co-ordinated services based on wider application of the communications mix and media neutrality – not dominated by TV.

After completion of this section, you will be able to:

o Explain the role of the communications agency in helping organizations to develop and implement communications strategies and tactics

o Understand the structures of agencies and how they manage relationships with clients from a domestic and international perspective

o Understand the role of marketing communications in an international and global context

o Describe the regulatory and voluntary arrangements that exist to monitor and control communications activities in order to safeguard customer interests.

This unit covers Syllabus references 2.15, 4.4–4.7.

Key definitions

Agency – The term 'agency' in marketing communications terms represents an external supplier which an organization contracts to provide services that assist in the creation and implementation of effective communications.

Communications agencies (Syllabus 4.5)

Agency structures

Traditionally, agencies (predominantly advertising) have been structured around two main areas of activity – creative development in copywriting and art direction, and media planning and buying. Account managers or directors have responsibility for client liaison which includes research and strategic development. This kind of structure typifies the so-called 'full service agency', which attempts to meet all client needs from a single source. Gradually, there has been a shift from this type of approach. This has been partly driven by clients looking for a wider range of communications activities beyond advertising and the growth of specialist service consultancies in areas such as media buying. Those issues considered in other units concerning co-ordination have led to changes in agency structures and range of activities.

The response by some agencies has been to acquire service expertise via purchase of specialist companies as a whole, or recruiting individuals to head new divisions. Some have created 'networks' of specialists who can be brought together to collaborate on specific projects. A plethora of new agencies have emerged which specialize in different areas such as creative, media, production, strategic planning, direct response, sales promotion, sponsorship or other communications mix variants. There has, of course, also been a rapid growth in the number of agencies with capabilities in advising on using new technologies and media for marketing communications.

The structures required to meet the needs of clients operating internationally and globally are discussed later in this section.

Case study

Not just another agency

As already discussed, many agencies are changing their focus from being advertising led to a more holistic communications approach. The new head at Saatchi & Saatchi, names synonymous with advertising, suggests that they 'have done the phase of being an advertising agency'. Kevin Dundas, Chief Executive, says the new focus will be on ideas and planning. Account management has now become brand management and other old distinctions between roles and functions are being broken down as relationships between consumers and brands are developed. This change has extended to a move of payment by results with over half of the agencies clients.

Source: Financial Times Creative Business, 13 January 2004.

A similar perspective is being taken by a new agency created under the leadership of Andy Law, formerly of the St Luke's advertising agency. Boy Meets Girl S&J sets its stall out to be 'a non-advertising led creative services agency', promising clients '360 degree creativity with communications management led by brand directors rather than account staff'. Law recognizes the limitations of advertising and proposes the use of any form of (integrated) communications in articulating creative ideas.

Source: Financial Times Creative Business, 13 January 2004.

Activity 3.1

If you can, identify the structures of any agency used by your own organization. If you cannot do this, try and find the websites of some agencies and see how they are structured.

Full service agencies

This is what might be considered the 'classic' large agency. Full service agencies provide a complete range of services:

- ○ Creative
- ○ Strategic planning
- ○ Production
- ○ Media planning and buying
- ○ Market research.

Examples of full service agencies include well-known firms such as Bartle, Bogle and Hegarty (BBH), Abbott Mead Vickers and Leo Burnett. There are a number of advantages to a full service provision. For many organizations, it means that there is an additional resource with which to work, to share ideas and responsibilities. Working with a full service agency will see a huge pool of skills under one roof that can be drawn on as needed; new, different perspectives on the communication problem may be gained, which ultimately will contribute towards the corporate and the marketing objectives of the organization being achieved.

For an organization preferring a CMC approach, using a full service agency means that all of the elements of the promotional mix can be managed under one roof and the marketing communications operation then becomes easier to manage and control. Moreover, from a security angle there is less chance of sensitive information leaking out into the competitive domain.

One key disadvantage to a full service agency, on the other hand, is 'having all your eggs in one basket'. This can be a dangerous way to operate, and within the volatile world of communications this must be considered. For example, if an organization is channelling all of its marketing communications through one agency, should the relationship break down and the contract be breached in any way, the organization could have every element of the promotional mix left high and dry, with no agency to manage the process for them.

Therefore, in a full service agency it is critical to have a relationship built around quality, trust and understanding. This is imperative for the successful implementation of the marketing communications strategy.

The type of customers who use full service agencies in the main will be organizations who have significant budgets, but possibly little internal resource to support the co-ordination of communications campaigns. Large multinational organizations often use full service agencies, which will co-ordinate their global activities in order to provide a consistent approach.

Limited service agencies

Limited service agencies tend to specialize in particular elements of the marketing communications process. For example, an advertising agency may specialize the level of artwork and creative skill, and therefore focus on the design and development of advertisements. They will then rely on significant information being provided by their client to enable them to meet the brief. Another agency may specialize in media buying and therefore be able to achieve a high level of competitive advantage to enable a more effective use of the advertising budget.

The key advantage to using limited service agencies is that an organization can shop around to get the best skills to suit a range of marketing communication needs.

'A la carte' agency

Many organizations now want greater flexibility and choice in the way in which communications are managed. To do this they need to have a broad range of options, which do not necessarily come from a full service approach; rather they want to select a range of services from a range of different specialist agencies. While this gives choice and the desired flexibility, it takes a lot of time, effort and commitment to manage the potential number of relationships involved.

For example, Lloyds TSB gave their Internet bank advertisements to Saatchi but they also appointed a company called Inter-focus to work on their strategy for the launch and handle the direct marketing and customer-relationship management for the project.

Another good example is Wrigley's. They took the decision to expand their web activity across Europe. To do this, they decided to manage the project via a joint committee of marketers from Wrigley's operations in the UK, Sweden and Germany. The company's local operations spent time talking to a handful of new media houses. The key here is that Wrigley's works with a number of agencies and in this case they have chosen to work with a different agency specifically to deal with their web activity.

An 'à la carte' agency would be able to help resolve this problem by co-ordinating the range of specialist agencies. For example, an organization preparing for a launch of a new product may require market research, sales promotions and perhaps on this occasion their launch will take place at an exhibition. The à la carte agency would act on behalf of the organization, take away the brief, define their role and then outsource the remainder of the work, across a broad range of other specialist agencies. The à la carte agency then co-ordinates the project activities.

Over the years, there has been some erosion of the status of full service agencies, with a resultant decline in the numbers and the emergence of companies specializing in media planning and buying, sometimes known as 'media buying shops' or 'media independents'. Zenith Media and CIA are two examples of major media specialists. Effectively, this means that an agency is buying in services to support a project that has been outsourced to them.

Agency selection criteria

Choosing an appropriate communications agency is a very time-consuming process; it is not simply a matter of choosing the agency which is capable of producing the best campaign, but choosing an agency which is creative, which has something your own organization does not possess.

When selecting an agency it is important to establish criteria on which the decision will be made, based around the aims and objectives of the communications.

Therefore, the following questions should be addressed:

○ Does the agency fully understand the requirements of a brief?
○ Do they know and understand how to use market research?
○ Is their strategic thinking sound?
○ Is their thinking imaginative and creative?
○ Are they professional and business-like?
○ Can they work with senior people?
○ Are their capabilities high in all key areas – management, strategy, creative media?
○ Do they work well as a team?
○ Is their creative work of a high quality?
○ Is their work confined to TV or does it go across all media?
○ Does this include below-the-line activities, new media?
○ Can they offer an integrated communications approach?
○ How do they propose to evaluate the campaign?
○ Can they work internationally?
○ What is their attitude towards costs? Will they work effectively to reduce costs?
○ How will they relate to our media-buying agency?
○ Will they fit with our working practices?
○ How important to them will our account be?

Source: White (1999).

 Activity 3.2

> What are the advantages of using a full service-advertising agency over a limited service agency?

Managing the agency relationship

Managing an agency relationship can be complex. Once an agency relationship has been established, the marketing team and the agency team will need to establish operational teams, systems, contracts and reporting lines.

At the same time that this is all going on, the agency team will be wanting to learn everything they can about the organization, its business, products and services portfolio. They want to be conversant with the supply chain and want to review all available market research in order that they have a full understanding of the organization and its purpose.

The most important element to establish within an agency relationship is a communication line and a day-to-day communication contact.

Key contact points which provide relationship development include:

○ Structuring initial and ongoing contract negotiation
○ Scheduled meetings and other contacts via e-mail and fax
○ Creative presentations.

In Units 4 and 5, various aspects of relationships are discussed. Many facets of relationship building and development apply very well in client and agency relationships. The successful relationship will be built on foundations of trust and commitment. Agencies are often selected on the basis of personal compatibility between individuals in the respective teams. Often when marketing communications staffs leave a particular organization, they will attempt to 'transfer' their agency with them to the new company they join. The client agency interface is usually maintained by account managers who will take the client brief and then brief relevant parties in the agency, creatives, media, planners and so on.

It is interesting to note here the differences between the different elements within the agency. Major character and personality differences can emerge. Creative individuals will be very different characters than those involved in client management and research. Indeed, there may be antagonism between the account planners who present research which queries the outputs of creatives. The latter group do not always like to have their 'creative' judgement queried by 'mere' research! Managing internal relationships within agencies is not without its difficulties.

The agency brief

The success or failure of the implementation of a communications campaign can depend on the quality of the brief given to the agency, but they are not easy to write. These are some elements that might be contained in an agency brief:

o *Current situation* – The history of the brand, previous campaign successes (or failures) and the reasons for mounting the new campaign.
o *Promotional objectives* – Having set your marketing objectives (often expressed in terms of sales volume), you then have to address the promotional objectives. These will vary according to your overall plans, but could include:

  – To encourage product trial
  – To raise awareness levels
  – To encourage direct sales
  – To increase distribution outlets.

o *Target markets* – A good definition of the target market will include not only socio-economic details (e.g. age, class, sex), but also psychographic information on users. This will have a bearing on the nature and tone of the promotional activity, its overall focus and content.
o *Product/service* – In providing your agency with a detailed brief, this section is very important. It should include any original research results or focus group research to establish what the perceived benefits are, so that these can be promoted strongly, both visually and in words.
o *Budget* – The budget should be carefully planned with consideration given to your total budget as often it includes funds not only for the cost of the media, but also for the production of promotional material.
o *Competitors* – You should know your competitors and their products as well as you know your own. Make it your business to find out and include the results of your findings in your brief.
o *Timescales* – This should include the start date of the campaign and the period over which it is to run. Media scheduling will play a vitally important role at this stage, with the need to establish the consistency of the campaign in terms of the 'drip–drip' approach or indeed the necessity for a 'burst'-style campaign.

The creative team will be responsible for the direction of the artwork, ensuring that visualization and copywriting match the needs of the organization and would be meaningful and attention grabbing to the target audience. They will be directed by the Account Manager within the agency who will also brief the media and planning functions.

From the agency perspective, every opportunity must be taken to send a message that is succinct, effective, dynamic, exciting, meaningful and able to incite 'action'. Technology today allows for a highly creative range of opportunities to convey the message in a positive way. The use of multimedia campaigns is likely to be a very attractive option and more effective than a single medium.

Agency pitching

When clients seek the assistance of communications agencies, the process of briefing will be followed by what has become known as the agency pitch. More often than not, more than one potential agency is briefed on the client's needs and they are asked to pitch or bid for the account. This will involve the agency in conducting research into the marketing and communications situation, and presenting creative and media plans to the client in a pitch meeting. Clients, who have been using the services of one or other agency, will also from time to time look to switch agencies either to meet new needs or to seek refreshment of current approaches. This may or may not include the incumbent agency.

Agency pitches involve the agency in considerable amounts of activity and expense. It is viewed as a necessary element of their business development processes. However, because of the length of time and direct costs involved, it also carries risks as there is no guaranteed return at the end of the process if the account is not awarded. The pitching process has over the years been viewed sceptically by agencies who sometimes see it as a no or at best a low-cost exercise by clients simply seeking fresh ideas. Few clients offer any financial incentive for agencies to participate in pitches, other than the value of the account if successful. The case study on agency selection describes recent attempts by those agency groups involved in pitching to arrive at some agreed principles for pitching and selection.

Case study

Guide to agency selection

Given some of the relative uncertainties involved in the agency selection process, particularly those concerning pitching, several communications bodies have recently published a set of guidelines aimed at establishing a fair and equitable framework for all parties to work to. Known as 'The Guide', this has been developed by the DMA, IPA, ISBA, MCCA and the PRCA as a set of joint industry guidelines on agency search, selection and relationship management.

This includes considerations to be made prior to undertaking the review and the principles to be applied to the appointment.

The guidelines call for:

1. Clear preparation of all background information.
2. Identification of the response required and preparation of written brief.
3. Consideration of the time required for response.
4. Invite up to three agencies to pitch, four if incumbent agency involved.
5. Give background market data, interpretation and clarification.
6. Demonstrate commitment with financial contribution.
7. Understand roles of those involved and set up objective evaluation system.
8. Insist on necessary commercial disciplines before an appointment is made.

9. Decide and inform quickly and fairly.
10. Develop guidelines on implementation and relationship management.

'The Guide' extends to 103 pages and it will be interesting to see how closely it is followed.

Source: IPA website – www.ipa.co.uk.

 ## Activity 3.3

Go to the IPA website www.ipa.co.uk and download a copy of the Guide discussed in the case study.

Agency remuneration

Agencies have traditionally been paid for their work on the basis of receiving commissions from media owners when they buy space or time. There has been a view held by many clients that agencies make media recommendations based on how much commission the agency receives rather than how much is actually required for the communications to be effective. This has been a long-running agency/client debate. The debate has taken a new turning more recently with clients becoming more demanding of their agencies in the measurement of communications' effectiveness. This has to some extent reflected the shift from focusing on advertising as the main element of communications towards a more co-ordinated approach. Incorporation of response mechanisms into advertisements, direct mail and telemarketing, and electronic delivery, have made the measurement process more quantifiable.

Case study

Holsten pays on results

The Incorporated Society of British Advertisers (ISBA) estimates that around 50 per cent of major advertisers now include some element of payment by results in their contracts with agencies. The TBWA agency which handles the Holsten beer account, has agreed a deal that links their remuneration solely with product sales. For each hectolitre (176 pints) sold, TBWA receives 40 pence. Both the agency and the client are more than happy with this arrangement. Holsten's marketing chief, Andy Edge, says that this means that both parties share the rewards and the risks. Under media-related commissions, if the campaign underperformed there was no comeback on the agency who were 'paid' regardless of how well the ads did. It was the agency's idea to introduce the scheme, which is called 'Risk and Reward'. The concept will effectively reward the agency for ideas that bring commercial success. Just as they would benefit if campaigns were not successful, agencies do not benefit if results go beyond expectations. This type of remuneration deal puts more onus on the agency to perform but this is considered acceptable to those agencies who are confident of their abilities to producing high standard work that is effective. Other TBWA clients who operate on a similar basis include Air Miles and Virgin One.

Source: FT Creative Business, 13 August 2002.

The development of multinational communications agencies (Syllabus 4.6)

In the same way that companies have become international, so too have advertising agencies, public relations and sales promotion consultancies and so on. Two important and parallel trends have occurred.

There has been a progressive 'internationalization' of the service companies to the point where few do not have representation in all of the key markets. As a result of mergers, acquisitions and alignments, the major practitioners in the field of marketing communications have subsidiaries or associates in all the major countries of the world. In addition, global clients are increasingly appointing global agencies to handle and co-ordinate their marketing communications business across all their territories.

Cisco Systems announced in April 2001 that it was in talks about its £120 million worldwide creative account and the possibility of reducing the number of agencies on its roster. This and a large number of similar moves by other major organizations are typical of the process of global realignment. Indeed, the key requirement to inclusion on the shortlist for many such accounts is the extent to which a company has the ability to service the business on a multinational basis.

Often, companies will maintain a roster of agencies to handle their business, particularly where they have multiple brands. In most cases, the same agency will be used across the brand in all markets. Examples of this practice may be seen with Procter & Gamble, Mars and others.

Multinational agencies

The trend has been for the large agencies either to acquire or establish branches in all those markets in which they might reasonably expect to generate international client opportunities. Indeed, some of this process has been client inspired, in the sense that the agency is encouraged to establish an office in a country in which the client is intending to operate. Over the past two decades, led originally by US agencies, but more recently by British and Japanese agencies, groupings have been assembled to respond to clients' needs.

Independent networks

To offset the competitive threat posed by the multinational agencies, networks and confederations have been formed to provide the global coverage demanded by some client companies. CDP Europe, Alliance International and ELAN (European Local Advertising Network) are three examples of such groups. From the agency perspective, these associations meet clients' needs to operate on a global basis, while preserving their own independence. Usually, these groupings are based on 'like-minded' philosophies, with agencies of similar views of the marketing communications process (creative style, media prowess, the role of planning, etc.) coming together.

Local independent agencies

In many countries, newly emergent agencies remain bitterly jealous of their independence and, at least in the short term, are prepared to forgo some international accounts. Indeed, many such agencies remain independent in the longer term as a means of offering their own unique positioning in a crowded market.

Case study

WPP – a global approach to communications

WPP is one of the world's leading communications services groups. Through its companies and associates, it offers a comprehensive and, when appropriate, an integrated range of services. The Group is divided into a number of disciplines covering Advertising and media investment, Information and consultancy, Public relations and public affairs, Branding and Identity, Healthcare and Specialist communications. Well-known agencies such as J. Walter Thompson, Young & Rubicam and Ogilvy & Mather are part of the WPP empire.

In terms of co-ordination, over 300 clients work with three or more WPP companies, 150 clients work with four or more and over 100 clients are served in six or more countries. In 2003, WPP turnover was over £18.6 billion (Gross billings).

The WPP client list is something of a Who's Who of the world's largest and best known brands across many different sectors – Coca-Cola, IBM, American Express, Ford, Disney, Nestlé and Rolex. J. Walter Thompson has a global network covering 90 countries and a mix of multinational, regional and local accounts. There has been a move by some large brand owners to place all of their communications needs with such marketing services agencies as WPP. In November 2004 Samsung, the giant Korean electronics business, announced that WPP would handle their global branding account worth £120 million. This provides some further evidence of a move toward such integrated holding companies. Other WPP clients, Ford and HSBC, also work on a similar basis.

Source: www.wpp.com, accessed 21 January 2005.

Criteria to be considered when selecting an international agency

Before deciding on its agency, any client must consider a set of important criteria in the international context.

To what extent is it planned to implement a single communications strategy in all markets?

For those companies wishing to pursue a global communications strategy, it is sensible to consider only the first and second options, that is a multinational agency or an independent network. The benefits of already established links will ensure the speedy transfer of knowledge and understanding which, in turn, should facilitate the process of implementation in the variety of countries in which the campaign will run.

To what extent will the intended agency be precluded from operating in other market areas?

Some companies adopt a strict policy whereby the incumbent agency is not only precluded from handling directly competitive business, but also from those other areas in which the client company has an interest. This, it has to be said, is becoming an increasingly untenable situation. As multinational companies expand their businesses, both horizontally and vertically, they embrace increasingly diverse market segments.

Acquisitions of companies and brands result in taking an interest in markets far beyond their original businesses. For example, Procter & Gamble have interests in diverse fields including haircare preparations, sanitary protection, cough and cold remedies, soap powders and toothpaste, to name just a few. Apart from their coffee interests, Nestlé operate in the following markets: confectionery, bottled waters, cereals, tinned soups and yoghurts and mousses. Here again, the list is only a partial one.

Clearly, to function profitably, the multinational agencies have to think carefully about client conflicts, both current and the future, before taking on a new account. Though the short-term increase in billings might be attractive, their tenure of a particular client might inhibit their growth potential in the future. In turn, therefore, some agencies with otherwise desirable credentials may be precluded from consideration.

Do the multinational or network agencies possess all the appropriate skills in all markets?

Often, a multinational agency may have relatively weak representation in one or more of the markets considered important to the company. The same is equally true of agency networks, where not all of the participants may have the same reputation and skills.

Are there specific local skills which need to be accessed?

In some instances, a local independent agency may have a far greater in-depth knowledge or understanding of the market, the consumers or the general environment which it may be important to access. Indeed, the independent local agency may have greater prowess, for example, in media planning or creativity. It should not be assumed that simply because an agency is part of a wider international grouping it will possess all the skills required.

Where co-ordination is not a requirement, some companies have taken the decision to locate the creative development with one agency – usually referred to as the 'lead' agency – and to appoint several local agencies to handle the implementation. In other instances, they have chosen to appoint the 'best' agency in each market, to ensure access to the necessary skills in all areas.

How will the company cope with co-ordinating the campaign globally?

Deploying company personnel to the co-ordinating task may be one solution to this requirement. An alternative, particularly where a multinational agency is appointed, is to devolve that responsibility to the agency. Usually, a senior member of the agency structure is appointed to the specific role of ensuring consistency, both of creative work and implementation, throughout all markets. It will be his or her role to ensure cohesion between all aspects of the campaign in all markets, although ultimately it will be the client's responsibility to determine whether the role has been fulfilled adequately.

Activity 3.4

What are the benefits of using a local marketing communications agency to launch a new product rather than the branch office of an international network?

This internal agency role is often of considerable importance to other aspects for the smooth running of the campaign. The task involves overcoming the 'not invented here' syndrome, whereby the local brand responsible for the implementation of the activity may feel detached from it, since it was created elsewhere.

Similarly, the international co-ordinator may have the responsibility for allocating funds between branches to ensure that tasks such as market research are carried out adequately. In many cases, although the work is an important aspect of the understanding of the communications task in the market, the branch office may not generate sufficient income to afford their contribution.

 Activity 3.5

> Coca-Cola was a major sponsor of the 2002 World Cup. To what extent should they, as sponsors of other global events, integrate this activity with the other aspects of their marketing communications programmes?

A final point to consider concerns the degree to which clients seek effective co-ordination of their marketing communications and the necessity to have the best people in each application area, working on their account. Some research suggests that because of their structure, agencies (normally advertising) are unable to provide both co-ordination and expertise. As a result, there has to be a trade-off between the degree of co-ordination and the availability of expertise. A loose consortium of independent agencies allows for high levels of expertise (and poor co-ordination), while centralized multinational agencies are better able to provide for co-ordination but cannot always provide the very best expert in each promotional area.

Marketing communications in international and global contexts (Syllabus 4.4, 4.6)

In addition to considering the use of marketing communications agencies in an international context, it is important to understand the wider issues underpinning the role of marketing communications at an international and global scale.

The trend towards globalization

Recent years have seen an increasing tendency towards the globalization of brands. As domestic markets have reached positions of virtual saturation, manufacturers have turned to new and often distant markets to ensure a continuation of their growth potential. It is argued that global marketing is the final phase in a progressive process of this desire for market extension (Table 3.1).

Table 3.1 Phases of international marketing development

Domestic markets	These comprise the first stage of the process, in which companies design products and services to satisfy the identified needs and wants of domestic consumers
Infrequent foreign marketing	This is often dictated by a short-term need to eliminate production surpluses which cannot be absorbed by the domestic market. However, there is no real desire on the part of the company to exploit these opportunities on a long-term basis, and once the domestic 'problem' of over supply or low demand has been eliminated, overseas sales are curtailed
Regular foreign marketing	The manufacturer devotes some resources to the exploitation of overseas opportunities on an ongoing basis, but the primary focus remains the need to respond to domestic demand. In these instances, the company often uses middlemen, but may create its own selling operations in important markets
International marketing	As companies perceive the major opportunity to derive profits from foreign markets, they progressively commit more resources to the development of this potential and, in the process, become more committed to the tasks of international marketing. In general, they perceive their markets as possessing unique characteristics for which individual marketing and marketing communications strategies must be developed
Global marketing	At this level, companies view the world as a single market. This is accompanied by a tendency towards the standardization of business activities, and the adoption of marketing and marketing communications strategies which reflect those elements of commonality throughout the many markets they serve

Source: Caetora (1993)

A further impetus to the process has come from the expanding rate of globalization. Mergers and acquisitions, together with organic growth, have resulted in many corporate operations opening up in different parts of the world. As operations expand and become more dispersed, there is an inherent danger that each operating unit, by retaining responsibility for its own communications programme, produces materials which are inconsistent with other parts of the operation. The development of a cohesive corporate identity programme has the twin benefits of avoiding inconsistencies and of binding the diverse parts of the operation together. The alternative is the lack of a shared identity, with the risk that the operations move apart and the benefits of globalization are lost.

Inherent in this statement, however, is the recognition of the need for corporate identity programmes to work across national divides, and with different languages and cultures. Not only words, but symbols and colours may also communicate a different impression from the one intended and desired. There is a need to ensure that companies in competing industries identify a means of differentiating themselves from each other. But it must be remembered that image and identity change is no panacea for other ills. A simple audit of the present identity will establish whether images perceived by the target audiences are positive or negative. In the latter instance, work needs to be done to enhance the image. However, if the reality falls short of the image – actual or desired – then it is clear that there is a fundamental problem within the organization which needs to be addressed. The corporate identity can provide the focus for the organization and provide a unique position in the marketplace. In many respects, the corporate identity reflects the personalities and values which are associated with a company.

Activity 3.6

Think of some global companies. What image do you have of their organizations?

Activity 3.7

What are the key factors motivating the shift towards globalization?

Multinational versus global marketing

We can make an important distinction between these two approaches to foreign markets, and these have significant implications for the determination of marketing communications strategies.

The *multinational company* readily perceives the fundamental differences between the various markets it serves. In general, it believes that its success is dependent on the development of individual marketing and marketing communications programmes for each of its territories. As a result, it tends to operate through a number of subsidiaries which, for the most part, act independent of each other. Products are adapted, or developed independently, to meet the needs of the individual markets and the consumers within. By the same token, the other elements of the marketing mix are developed on a local basis. Although there may be some cross-fertilization of ideas through some form of central function, the primary aim is to satisfy the needs of individual country markets, rather than the specific identification of common elements which might allow for the standardization of activities.

The *global organization* strives towards the provision of commonality, both in terms of its products and services, and the propositions which support them. As far as possible, it attempts to standardize its activities on a worldwide basis, although even within this concept there is some recognition of the need for local adaptation to respond to local pressures. The fundamental objective is the identification of groups of buyers within the global market with similar needs, and the development of marketing and marketing communications plans that are as standardized as much as possible within cultural and operational constraints.

Activity 3.8

Find examples of three or four similar magazines from different countries. Examine how the advertising presentation differs in each of them.

Are there any advertisements for the same product in the different magazines?

Are they the same or different?

The impetus for a more detailed examination of the implications of international marketing was provided by a seminal article by Theodore Levitt (1993). The thrust of his argument in 'the globalization of markets' is that a variety of common forces, the most important of which is shared technology, is driving the world towards a 'converging commonality'. The result, he argues, is 'the emergence of global markets for standardized consumer products on a previously unimagined scale'.

It could be argued that it is the convergence of communications which has, and will continue to have, the far greater impact. We know that consumer motivations towards the purchasing of products and services are the result of the influence of a wide range of factors. One central factor which impacts upon many, if not all, of them is the mass media. As the people of the world are exposed to the same messages via television, film and other media, it is inevitable that their attitudes towards the products and services depicted will move towards a common central point.

Irrespective of our geographical location, it is likely that most of us will listen to the same music (the bands that top the charts in one country enjoy similar levels of success in others), the same films (which country has not yet been exposed to the film *Titanic* or *Lord of the Rings*?), the same television programmes (note the spread of *Who Wants to be a Millionaire?* and *Pop Idol*), the same computer programmes and games, and even the same articles in the media. While it is undeniable that cultural differences will continue to prevail, at least for some considerable time, so too are we witnessing the coming together of many attitudes and beliefs, which enhance the potential for products and services that respond to those common and shared values.

The forces of internationalization

There are many factors that can be cited as contributing to this growth of an international rather than a purely domestic outlook. We have already seen that, from an attitudinal perspective, there are growing similarities between countries. With improved communications, the physical distances between markets matter far less. There is, as mentioned by Levitt, the integrating role of technology. The capacity to produce similar or even identical products in dispersed markets is enhanced as the technological base of manufacturers becomes similar. At the same time, we are witnessing the progressive removal of the former barriers to international trade – tariffs. Most regions of the world are joining together in supra-national groupings for their mutual economic benefit. Among others, these include the EU (European Union), NAFTA (North-American Free Trade Agreement), ASEAN (the Association of South East Asian Nations), CARICOM (the Caribbean Community and Common Market) and CACM (the Central American Common Market).

With slowing domestic economic growth in many areas, manufacturers are being forced to seek potential markets away from their home base. Indeed, specific government actions are being taken to increase foreign trade. A similar impetus comes from the recognition that, as products reach the maturity or decline phase of the product life cycle, they will need to identify new markets which are in a different stage of development.

The intensity of domestic competition may also force companies to look elsewhere, where the costs of market entry are lower or their offerings appear to be more innovatory and exciting. Of course, there is the opportunity for manufacturers to secure the benefits of differential pricing. A product sold for a premium price in one market can be sold in another for a lower price and still make a profit contribution, so long as the marginal costs are covered. The changing base of competitive advantage and the emergence of global competitors is forcing other manufacturers to seek joint ventures and coalitions, often with foreign partners. Apart from the benefits of shared technologies, the participants in such deals obtain 'ready-made' set-ups which enable them to access other markets in return for a comparatively low investment.

The forces restraining standardization

As much as there are many forces driving the move towards internationalization, so too there are a number of factors which preclude, or at least slow down, the rate at which manufacturers from one country can introduce their products directly into another. National and cultural characteristics remain a fundamental point of difference. Although, as many have argued, there is a progressive convergence of attitudes and behaviours, many such patterns are sufficiently ingrained to be unchangeable in the mid-term. We will discuss these factors in more detail later in this unit, as they have important implications for the determination of marketing communications strategies.

The different levels of economic growth and national living standards will, similarly, act as restraints in some areas. However attractive a particular offering may be, if the individual is on a low income or unemployed, he or she will not be able to make the desired purchase.

There will be fundamental differences between markets which cannot be altered in the short term. While some will relate to the ingrained behavioural patterns mentioned above, others will be a direct consequence of environmental factors – the comparative penetration of items such as fridges and freezers, the availability of domestic storage space, distribution factors and so on.

There may be a more basic resistance to change which will inhibit the acceptance of products and services which are commonly accepted in other markets. Also, there remain a number of legal and regulatory factors which may preclude the penetration of particular markets where the sale of individual products may be limited or even banned. Finally, there is the political environment which may discourage foreign trade in general, or that from individual companies in particular. At the same time, manufacturers may be wary of making substantial investments in markets with unstable economic or political environments where they do not have sufficient confidence of being able to secure an adequate level of return because of underlying changes.

 Activity 3.9

How does the information required for the development of an international communications campaign differ from that required for domestic planning?

The development of global brands

It is inevitable that the progressive standardization of products results in significant economies of manufacture which, potentially, lead to lower prices and a more competitive positioning for the brand. The high investment in product development will be rapidly amortized if the market for the resulting product is global and enormous, rather than domestic and limited. Such developments, however, will not obviate the need in many instances to adapt the product to meet 'special' local needs, however these are occasioned.

Some manufacturers perceive the world of the future to be one in which global brands dominate. The perceived benefits of a single worldwide brand identification outweigh those of country-specific products with separate brand identities. However, it is important to remember that, even here, it is not essential that the product delivered in each market is identical – only that the branding and the imagery associated with it are the same. Nestlé, for example, have adopted the same packaging and style for their leading brand of instant coffee across most international markets. However, the specific product may well be different in many of those markets to reflect local tastes.

Activity 3.10

Locate examples of some products sold in your country but originated elsewhere. How have they been adapted to suit local needs? Consider product, packaging, advertising and so on.

Even where it is necessary to subjugate the current brand identity in favour of a single consistent worldwide brand mark, major manufacturers have determined that the long-term benefits are likely to outweigh the short-term losses. Despite enjoying considerable consumer acceptance in the UK with their Marathon brand, Mars opted for a standardization of the brand under the name of Snickers across all markets. In 2001, the household cleaner Jif was renamed as CIF to provide consistency across the markets in which the brand was offered.

Activity 3.11

In what ways does the construction of a marketing communications campaign differ in an international context?

Global marketing communications

In the same way that we have seen a progressive move towards the standardization of brands, so too has there been a movement towards the development of standardized marketing communications programmes. For example, Canon announced in February 2002 that they were to try and reduce the emphasis on individual product promotion across Europe, and try to develop loyalty across different product lines with the strapline 'you can'. In an attempt to move from an information-based approach to an emotional-based approach in its communications, the strategy also involved a reduction from the 50 plus different agencies to just two networks, one for its consumer and one for its business accounts. The rapidly accelerating costs of producing separate campaigns for individual markets, the difficulties of co-ordinating separate campaigns in physically close markets, together with the desire for the establishment of a single worldwide identity for its brands, have induced many companies to explore the potential of single campaign development across many, if not all, markets. Inevitably, there are polarized views on the merits of such moves.

At one extreme, as a response to the pressures indicated above, some companies have developed central campaigns which provide the core of all of their marketing communications activity in all markets. For a number of years, Coca-Cola have run essentially similar campaigns in many markets, with all or most of the elements being constantly applied in all of the territories in which they operate. Promotional activities and sponsorships, wherever possible, operate globally. Similarly, identical advertising, save only for the language of the voice-over, has been run by the brand across all territories.

At the other end of the spectrum are a wide range of international brands for which 'local' advertising propositions have continued to be developed and which, in their producers' view, enable them to reflect more readily the needs and desires of the individual markets in which they operate.

Between these two positions are those brands which adopt a common communications strategy, but allow for the local development of specific executions. In these instances, there is a cohesion in the underlying message of the brand in all of its markets, but room for the development of tightly focused and tailored propositions which reflect the subtleties and nuances of the local marketplace. Some manufacturers have developed this approach to the position where they develop 'pattern book' communications campaigns. An overall stance for the brand will be taken centrally, with semi-finished examples of advertising and sales promotion approaches laid down centrally. These, however, provide the 'shell' of activity and the local operations have the flexibility to adjust the specific content to meet their local requirements. It is this latter area which has witnessed the greatest growth over recent years. Indeed, even the ubiquitous Coca-Cola have recognized the need to develop specific messages for individual markets to respond to pressures on the brand's position.

 Activity 3.12

The expanding European Union and the opening up of certain Chinese markets represent a major market opportunity for many manufacturers' products and services. To what extent should they plan to use existing marketing communications campaigns to support the introduction of their products to these markets?

Standardized marketing communications

It has already been seen that the proponents of standardized communications campaigns cite the cost savings to be accrued from the development of a single campaign, together with the comparative ease of co-ordination, as partial justifications for the move towards common global marketing communications activities.

It cannot be denied that the cost savings may be enormous. For example, the average cost of production of a television commercial is of the order of £300 000 to £500 000 and, very often, very much more than that. Moreover, if several creative teams are working in different parts of the globe to resolve the communications needs, the time involved and the associated costs will be considerable. As we have seen, there may be an underlying commonality of requirements, and thus much of that time will be spent covering the same ground as others in the search for the communications message.

Not only does a standardized process eliminate the problems of conflict arising from dissimilar messages being communicated in adjacent territories, but also saves a considerable amount of management time involved in resolving such difficulties. Similarly, management would otherwise need to be involved – within each market – in the briefing and approval of creative work, the development of separate sales promotion campaigns, public relations activity and even packaging changes.

Ultimately, the key benefit results in the creation of a single consistent image for the brand across all markets. The management and monitoring of the campaign can be more consistent, and the implementation process simplified. Against these, however, it can be argued that there are a number of significant disadvantages.

Inevitably, if the brand is at a different stage in its development, it may be less responsive to a marketing communications campaign developed for all markets, than to one specifically designed to deal with its own particular needs. We have already seen that different objectives, such as creating awareness, stimulating repeat purchase and so on, will require different motivations and, hence, different messages. Similarly, in order to ensure universal appeal and comprehension, the resultant execution may be bland and boring, and satisfy none of the individual requirements satisfactorily. This may, in turn, inhibit the opportunity to generate sales volume and result in management frustration.

Indeed, the problem is often one of motivation for staff, both within the company and the agencies it uses. As they may not be involved with the development of the marketing communications programme, they may perceive it as being irrelevant to their needs. And they will often feel no commitment to its successful implementation. As multinational campaigns take a long time to create and produce, this may reduce the ability, on a local level, to respond rapidly to local pressures.

Understanding the international consumer

If marketing communications demand a thorough understanding of the consumer and the environmental factors which surround them, this is even more true of marketing communications in an international context. Where we can reasonably expect to understand the important facets of consumer behaviour in a domestic context, this is far less likely to be the case in different and separate markets where culture, tradition and other factors may result in vastly different meanings being attached to the communications message. Market research will play an important part in identifying areas of similarity in order to allow for the development of a single consistent message, if that is the objective.

Activity 3.13

What are the key issues to be addressed in the development of an international marketing communications programme?

What approaches should be used to minimize the potential difficulties?

It should be clear that, in order to develop an effective multinational or global communications strategy, a number of 'new' dimensions will have to be considered, beyond those, which would be appropriate for a single-market communications strategy.

- o Language
- o Culture and tradition
- o Legal and regulatory requirements
- o Buying habits and motivational factors
- o Standards of living
- o Media availability and usage
- o The competitive environment.

Language

Multinational communications campaigns often fail because the message is simply translated rather than *re-interpreted*. This is not merely a semantic difference. Not only is it true that specific words often will not have a corresponding word in another language, sometimes the true translation will have a negative impact on the target audience. Furthermore, the same principles apply equally to body language and gestures. As we move increasingly towards non-verbal communications, it is vitally important to ensure that the visual imagery we employ communicates positively rather than negatively.

Culture and tradition

Arguably, this is one of the most difficult areas of multinational communications. Perceptions which are based on tradition and culture are extremely difficult to overcome. Fundamental areas, such as pack colours or symbols, may have totally different meanings resulting from cultural interpretation. White may indicate purity in many markets, but in others it is a symbol of death. Certain numbers may be symbols of good luck in some countries, but have opposite meanings in others. More significantly, the cultural values sometimes derived from religious views, result in markedly different attitudes towards products and services. For example, it would be an anathema to show pork or shellfish ingredients in a product intended for a predominantly Jewish market, the same would apply to beef in Hindu communities, or alcohol for Muslims.

 Activity 3.14

> Find examples of packaging and advertising campaigns which, in their current form, would be inappropriate for other markets. Identify the reasons for this and decide how you might change them to make them more acceptable.

While the specific advertising message might avoid such obvious errors, it is important to remember that the surroundings in which the message is set (a home, a retail outlet, etc.) may, similarly, contradict existing cultural beliefs in some markets. In some markets, for example, it would be inappropriate to depict a woman wearing Western clothes; in others, a commonly used motif of a man stroking a woman's skin to connote smoothness would be regarded as a taboo.

Legal and regulatory requirements

There are few common standards for marketing communications across all markets – although there are progressive moves towards harmonization is some areas, such as the EU. Yet tobacco advertising, for example, is still commonplace in many parts of Europe, while limited or totally prohibited in others. Most countries now see condom advertising as part of the global campaign to control AIDS. However, in certain countries, such advertising would be unthinkable due to strong religious beliefs. Sales promotion techniques which are commonly accepted and widely used in some markets are not allowed in others.

Buying habits and motivational factors

The patterns of purchasing frequency differ markedly between countries, sometimes resulting from differences in income levels and on other occasions being the results of patterns of usage. In some parts of the East, for example, fresh produce is bought on a daily basis; whereas in the West, shopping even for fresh ingredients may be carried out weekly and the purchases stored in the fridge or freezer. Motivational factors and aspirations are, similarly, different from one country to another, leading to difficulties in communicating aspirational 'norms' where such values either do not exist or have different parameters.

Standards of living

Products which are consumed on a daily basis may be considered as luxuries in others, particularly if the relative cost is high. Cigarettes, for many purchased in packets of 20, are sold singly in some African markets, with the resultant difficulties of the lack of packaging to communicate brand values. Elsewhere, the incidence of fridges may preclude the sale of some packaged convenience foods and so on.

Media availability and usage

A primary consideration, especially in the context of global campaigns, is the need to access constant media outlets. After all, if a major aim of standardization is to eliminate costly production, then the same media must be available in all markets. However, not only are certain media not available to the marketer in some areas – certain countries, for example, have only limited television penetration, while others do not allow advertising – the patterns of usage may also differ. In some countries, spot advertising throughout the day is commonplace. In others, all advertising is grouped together and broadcast at set times of the day.

 ## Activity 3.15

> Consider the implications for marketing communications of the growth of multinational media such as satellite television, international newspapers, transnational radio broadcasts and so on.

Other aspects of media are equally important. In different markets, different media have a different status, such that advertising placed in them have greater or lesser credibility. This is particularly the case in those markets where media have a distinct religious or political orientation.

The competitive environment

Just as consumers differ between markets, so do the brands available to them. Identifying the aspirational values of a brand, in order to define a unique positioning, becomes more difficult as the number of markets increases and the competitors differ in their stances. Often, a desired positioning is already occupied by another brand in a particular market. As we have seen, the relative position of a brand – leader or follower – will have important implications for communications strategy determination. It is extremely unlikely that all but a very few brands will occupy the same position in all of the markets in which they are available.

It is clear from the above that the task of developing a singular marketing communications strategy, while not impossible, is an extremely difficult one. Many companies have accepted that, in order to achieve their communications objectives, they must adopt a somewhat different stance. Indeed, such consensus as exists suggests that the policy towards multinational marketing communications campaigns should be based on the statement: 'Think globally, act locally.' Inherent in this statement is the acceptance of the fact that common communications strategies can be developed across all markets, but that their implementation must be effected on a local basis in order to reflect the multitude of differences which, despite convergence, continue to exist.

Controls and regulations (Syllabus 4.7)

In the UK alone there are many different forms of regulations which attempt to control the use of communications for business and marketing purposes, for those organizations operating internationally or globally, the burden of keeping track of all different variations is huge. In many instances this is a job for the lawyers! However, it is important to have a knowledge of the main forms of regulation and control in order to effectively manage communications activities. It is not within the scope of the coursebook to detail every piece of legislation or other forms of regulation and control but to provide a broad understanding of key aspects and where to go for further information. The scope also is concentrated largely on UK principles and practice.

One of the key aspects to note is that controls, in many cases, are a mixture of legislation and voluntary industry self-regulation. These range from official parliamentary acts, such as the Office of Communications Act of 2002 (Ofcom) and the Electronic Communications Act of 2000, to the Codes of Practice operated by bodies, such as the Advertising Standards Authority (ASA) and the Direct Marketing Authority (DMA). The Ofcom Act has led to the creation of a new regulatory office, Ofcom, which has taken over much of the monitoring of marketing communications work formerly undertaken by the Independent Television Commission and the Radio Authority, which are discussed below.

From 1st November 2004, the ASA has taken over responsibility for handling complaints about TV and radio advertising from Ofcom. They will, however, continue to enforce existing advertising standards which had been applied by Ofcom.

Codes of practice

Advertising Standards Authority (ASA)
The ASA is responsible for implementing the code of practice drawn up by the advertising industry via the Committee of Advertising Practice (CAP), the CAP code. The main trade and professional bodies in the communications industry, advertisers, agencies, service suppliers and media owners are members of CAP and agree to enforce the code. The 11th edition of the code was launched on 4 March 2003.

The CAP code principles for advertisements, sales promotions and direct marketing are that they should be:

- Legal, decent, honest and truthful
- Prepared with a sense of responsibility to consumers and society
- In line with the principles of fair competition, generally accepted in business.

The ASA regulates advertising in the following media: press, outdoor, direct mail, leaflets, brochures, catalogues, circulars, inserts and facsimiles, cinema, sales promotions and the

Internet (banner ads, commercial e-mails and online sales promotions). There are around 30 million press advertisements published each year which are monitored via ASA researchers who spot check some 6000 ads per week. Complaints made to the ASA number approximately 13 000 per year, mostly from the general public. The ASA has a number of 'powers' if communications are seen to be out of line with the CAP code. These include refusal of further advertising space, generate adverse publicity, withdraw trading privileges such as financial discounts and ultimately refer cases to the Office for Fair Trading (OFT) for possible legal proceedings. The ASA is funded by the advertising industry via levies on display advertising and direct mail expenditure.

Case study

Smirnoff Ice in the clear

A case recently investigated by the ASA involved complaints received about advertising for the Black Smirnoff Ice brand. The advertising involved posters on the sides of black London taxis. These featured the headline 'I've nothing against cyclists' with an asterisk referring to further copy 'Crystal Clear' over a picture of a bottle of the Smirnoff drink. The complaints were based on the grounds that the ads were irresponsible, encouraging inconsiderate behaviour by drivers towards cyclists. The advertisers stated that the ads were intended to be a humorous reflection on the perceived attitude of taxi drivers to all other road users. They were not intended to infer or demonstrate irresponsible behaviour towards consumers and society.

The ASA did not uphold the complaint taking the view that it was a humorous attempt to portray the taxi driver stereotype and that it did not legitimize or encourage drivers to behave inconsiderately to cyclists.

Source: ASA Adjudications: February (2003) – www.asa.org.uk.

Activity 3.16

Go to the websites of the ASA www.asa.org.uk, the DMA www.dma.org.uk, and Ofcom www.ofcom.org.uk – familiarize yourself with further details of their various codes and regulations.

Television and radio codes

Broadcast advertising was formerly regulated by the Independent Television Commission (ITC) and the Radio Authority (RA). These bodies published their own Codes of Advertising Standards and Practice, and also had guides covering Programme Sponsorship and Scheduling. The ASA offer a pre-vetting service for advertisers to check acceptability where there is a degree of uncertainty. For TV and radio, however, pre-vetting is mandatory. Scripts and planned schedules were vetted by the Broadcast Advertising Clearing Centre (BACC) for TV and by the Radio Authority Copy Clearing Centre (RACC) for radio.

Programme sponsorship and product placement (the use of commercial products in TV programmes) are growing areas in marketing communications. These aspects were also monitored by the ITC and the RA.

As indicated above, the creation of Ofcom has led to much of this work being transferred to the new regulator.

Ofcom mission

Ofcom exists to further the interests of citizen-consumers as the communications industries enter the digital age. To do this Ofcom shall:

1. Balance the promotion of choice and competition with the duty to foster plurality, informed citizenship, protect viewers, listeners and customers and promote cultural diversity.
2. Serve the interests of the citizen-consumer as the communications industry enters the digital age.
3. Support the need for innovators, creators and investors to flourish within markets driven by full and fair competition between all providers.
4. Encourage the evolution of electronic media and communications networks to the greater benefit of all who live in the UK.

This remit (www.ofcom.org.uk) obviously encompasses a wide range of communications related issues, much more than the control of marketing communications. It is, however, indicative of the influence of communications, in a wider context, on society as a whole. As the lines between commercially sponsored communications and those embedded in media of all forms becomes increasingly blurred, the need for controls such as those maintained by Ofcom will have increasing significance.

Organizations such as the Direct Marketing Association (DMA), Institute of Sales Promotion (ISP), Institute of Public Relations and other communications trade bodies have developed their own guidelines and codes as well as following those of the ASA and Ofcom. The DMA manages a series of what are called 'Preference Services'. These provide individuals the opportunity to 'opt out' of receiving various types of communications. By providing personal details to one or more of the services, these details will be used to profile against lists which are to be used for marketing purposes. Currently there are Preference Services covering mail, telephone, fax and e-mail.

The European Advertising Standards Alliance currently consists of members from 28 countries which co-ordinates cross-border complaints. On a broader scale, there is self-regulation in the US, Canada, Australia, Japan and parts of South America. In some Scandinavian countries, legislation plays a stronger role than self-regulation.

Legislation

The types of voluntary codes and self-regulations discussed above, to a large extent, 'operationalize' matters in terms of communications' production and content. There are, of course, a number of areas where legislation plays a role in determining the acceptability and use of marketing communications as well as other marketing activities, product controls, pricing and distribution.

In addition to the Ofcom Act and Electronic Communications Act referred to above, some of the other major legislation which affect communications include:

o Consumer Protection Act (1987)
o Control of Misleading Advertisement Regulations (1988)
o Trade Descriptions Act (1968)
o Sales of Goods Act (1979)
o Data Protection Act (1984).

The Data Protection Act, of course, has significant implications for those involved in database marketing activities, and using direct mail and telemarketing. The Act is fundamentally aimed at protecting consumers from misuse of their personal information and intrusion into their privacy. There is now a need for customers to have expressed a wish for details to be stored and used for marketing purposes by virtue of having 'opted in' to doing so. This is done usually by means of tick boxes on advertisements or direct mail responses and now on e-mail or website contacts.

Summary

This chapter has examined the use of external agencies by organizations to manage varying parts of their communications requirements. There are many types of agency in terms of structure and specialisms. Selection, briefing and managing are the key aspects of these kinds of relationships for maximizing effectiveness. For those organizations operating on an international or a global basis, these aspects are even more complex when considering the wider role that marketing communications play in an international and global context. Having in place regulatory and voluntary codes of practice, to control marketing communications practices, and those who practice, is an important aspect of the marketing communications industry.

Further study

The essential texts will elaborate on most of the issues discussed here. Both editions of *Excellence in Advertising* (Butterfield, 1997 and 1999) and the excellent *Handbook of Advertising* by Brierley, 2nd edition, provide a range of insights into the communications agency world with contributions from many experienced leading agency personnels. The contributions, whilst focusing primarily on advertising, also cover important communications issues including media, evaluation and total communication strategy.

Typical exam questions

In this section, references are given to specific examination and assignment questions from the June/July 2004 assessments. The questions are set out in Appendix 5. Detailed feedback on these questions from the CIM Senior Examiner and specimen answers can be obtained from the CIM website. Also included are some general examples of question types, briefings on which are included in Appendix 3.

June 2004 Examination Question 5a, b and c. July 2004 Assignments Question 4, part 3.

Question 3.1

Write brief notes outlining the processes and procedures used by agencies to manage a client's campaign.

(10 Marks)

Question 3.2

Evaluate some of the key issues facing the marketing communications industry in a country/region of your choice.

(10 Marks)

Hints and tips

The best sources for keeping an eye on what is happening in the agency world is to regularly consult the communications trade press, *Marketing, Marketing Week, Campaign, PR Week and Precision Marketing*. Whilst not providing great depth, they do provide wide coverage of communications events, new agency appointments, new campaigns, budgets, people movements and so on – including industry gossip!

References

Butterfield, L. (1999) *Advertising Excellence*, Oxford: Butterworth-Heinemann.

Caetora, P.R. (1993) *International Marketing*, 8th edition, Hemel Hempstead: Irwin.

Crimmins, J. and Horn, M. (1998) 'Sponsorship: From management ego trip to marketing success', *Journal of Advertising Research*, July/August, 11–21.

FT Creative Business, 13 August 2002.

Kotler, P. (2000) *Marketing Management*, New York: Prentice Hall.

Levitt, T. (1993) *Harvard Business Review*, **61**, 92–102.

White, J. (1999) 'Can agencies survive clients' global expansion', *Campaign*, 27 October, p. 24.

www.asa.org.uk
www.dma.org.uk
www.ipa.co.uk
www.itc.co.uk
www.mmo2.com
www.wpp.com

unit 4

relationships and marketing communications

Learning objectives

Few businesses today can afford to rely on single customer transactions for ongoing commercial success. Long-term relationships with customers from whom higher levels of sales and profitability can be derived is an essential aspect of marketing, and the role that communications play in this process is significant. In a wider context, other stakeholders are also of concern in maintaining longer-term viability.

After completion of this section you will be able to:

o Explain the shift in balance from activities centred on acquiring new customers to those based on retaining existing ones

o Describe the types of relationships that can be formed between the firm, the customers and the other stakeholder groups

o Understand the differences between satisfaction and loyalty

o Explain the importance of creating and maintaining trust in relationships

o Demonstrate how marketing communications can be used to develop relationships effectively with customers and other stakeholder groups including internal stakeholders

o Explain the characteristics and role of key account management (KAM) in developing and sustaining relationships.

Syllabus references: 2.10, 2.11, 2.12 (See also Unit 2), 4.1, 4.2, 4.3.

Definition

Relationship marketing – has been an increasingly important topic for both business and academic research from a number of different perspectives. In a business context, the availability of volumes of customer information made possible via developments in computer hardware and software has made the task of identifying and managing valuable customers much more straightforward. Academics have become interested in the types of relationships that exist and the ways in which they can be developed.

Relationship marketing is to establish, maintain and enhance relationships with customers and other parties at a profit so that the objectives of the parties involved are met. This is done by mutual exchange and fulfilment of promises (Gronroos, 1994).

Relationship marketing refers to all marketing activities directed towards establishing and maintaining successful and relational exchanges (Morgan and Hunt, 1994).

Relationship marketing is marketing seen as relationships, networks and interaction (Gummesson, 1999).

Customer relationship marketing (CRM) is a business process which integrates individual customer data from multiple sources in order to create a mutually valuable proposition (Smith and Clark, 2002).

These are just four of the many definitions that have been created. The fundamental principle, upon which relationship marketing is founded, is that the greater the level of customer satisfaction with a relationship – not just the product and service – the greater the likelihood that the customer will stay with and be retained by the organization.

For relationship marketing to succeed in any organization, there will need to be a cultural shift away from the old transactional style of marketing to the more dynamic and rewarding basis of relationship marketing.

Introduction

There are a number of reasons why organizations are seeking to develop a relationship-based approach to their marketing and specifically to their marketing communications activities. These include the high costs involved in continually needing to acquire new customers. The communications effort required to persuade a customer to purchase for the first time is considerably higher than that required to gain second and subsequent sales. This would also be true in 'replacing' customers who have made purchases but who decide for some reason to switch to another supplier.

There are now a wide range of systems available that allow 'customer relationships' to be more effectively managed including those aspects involved in marketing communications. Information about customers can be relatively easily collected, analysed and used. Tesco hold data on over 10 million customers and can produce over 100 000 different variations of offers based on purchasing patterns. Effective relationship development can lead to positive WOM communications and business referrals. Good internal relationships within firms can also have a positive effect on relationships externally. Relationships of any kind rely on effective communication if they are to survive and develop. Therefore, marketing communications play a central role in providing consistent and co-ordinated messages.

In the majority of situations, the basis of any type of relationship that is established is due to the way in which the supplier creates expectations. In creating expectations, it is possible to determine the nature and tone of the relationship, and essentially form and define customer behaviour in response to the organization and its product or service offerings. It is also important to have a good understanding of the purchase decision-making processes and the influences that can be brought into play when considering both the nature of the relationships and how communications can be used. These were considered in Unit 1.

From transactional to relationship marketing (Syllabus 4.1)

The conventional approach to marketing has been that of transactional marketing, whereby the functions of marketing, customer services and quality have been separate entities within the organization. However, the disintegrated approach to marketing meant that the potential to optimize marketing relationships was being lost, as the lack of co-ordination between the three functions gave way to a fragmented approach to achieving customer satisfaction. Ultimately, and in many instances, this started to prove problematic with many organizations, as they found they were suffering lack of market share compared with the more relationship-focused businesses.

There are, therefore, a number of significant differences between the concepts and contexts of transactional and relationship marketing, as illustrated in Table 4.1. These differences also highlight the benefits that can accrue for both the organization and the customer. A more customer-focused approach reduces the costs associated with high turnover of customers, 'churn rates', and the customers receive better service based on their real needs which are understood by their supplier.

Table 4.1 The shift in relationship marketing

Transactional focus	Relationship focus
Orientation to single sales	Orientation to customer
Discontinuous customer contact	Continuous customer contact
Focus on product features	Focus on customer value
Short timescale	Long timescale
Limited emphasis on customer service	High customer service emphasis
Limited commitment to meeting customer expectations	High commitment to meeting customer expectations
Quality is the concern of production staff	Quality is the concern of all staff

Source: Peck *et al.* (1999)

Principally, the key difference in the management of the relationship is that the basis of it will be a long-term relationship, a long-term view achieving long-term customer loyalty.

For an organization to succeed, it is of course essential that the value proposition meets the expectations of the customers, that the expectations in their minds meet those in the mind of the supplier and that there is little scope for customer uncertainties, a concept that you will come across in selling. Therefore, the value proposition needs to fill any gaps in expectations.

The more closely defined are the target markets, the more is the likelihood of success. The more you know and establish in the relationship with customers, the closer to delivering what they really want can be achieved, again closing the expectations gap.

Defining the value proposition: establishing values, core values and peripheral values is an essential starting element in the relationship building process. For relationship management to work, defining the method of actually delivering that value is essential. This includes a range of delivery systems and channels, including communications and these should be appropriately tailored to the customer needs. Of course, with the growing influence of digital marketing and service technologies, it will make it far easier to support a diverse range of customers. However, a word of warning, it is necessary to be aware that while it provides strength to manage customers, so too does it give a competitor strength. The switching process from one company to another can often be fast and painless. For example, switching from a financial services provider used to be a complex process. With the advent of 'Internet banking', this is now much more straightforward and more customers are being persuaded with incentives to switch accounts, in some cases on a regular basis.

Because the quality and strength of customer relationships is vital to the survival and profitability of all organizations, it is essential for competitive advantage to be sustained, customer loyalty to be achieved, and the process of delivering customer satisfaction to be clearly defined, to avoid any potential gaps in customer perception of the value proposition and their expectations.

The shift from transactional to relationship focus has been embraced by many organizations including fmcg producers. Firms such as Heinz, Kellogg's, Nestlé, Coca-Cola have been developing ways of getting closer to customers. These have included formation of 'shopping clubs', shifts from advertising to direct marketing, customer telephone helplines and other below-the-line activities. Communications have taken on a more strategic and longer-term focus rather than looking at ways of encouraging brand switching as short-term tactics.

Activity 4.1

Make a list of those organizations with whom you have some relationship as a customer. Note the nature of the relationship you have with them.

Gummesson suggests a shift from the 4Ps' view of marketing to one based on managing around a range of 30 different types of relationship. These are grouped into four classifications – Classic, Special, Mega and Nano (Gummesson, 1999).

Table 4.2 General properties of relationships

Collaboration
Commitment, dependency and importance
Trust, risk and uncertainty
Power
Longevity
Frequency, regularity and intensity
Closeness and remoteness
Formality, informality, openness
Routinization
Content
Personal and social properties

Source: Gummesson (1999)

The balance of optimizing customer relationships when considering such a wide range of properties is a difficult one to manage. Quite often concentrating efforts on one customer or group of customers or stakeholders means that another customer might be neglected, ultimately to the detriment of the organization.

Pleasing the customer and creating customer satisfaction seems to become a greater challenge almost daily, as organizations strive to achieve some form of competitive advantage. Customers become more demanding, assert their buyer power, and their expectations are continually rising, all the time making the value proposition more difficult to achieve.

With the growing influence of a number of key driving forces through SLEPT factors in the market, managing the marketing relationship is becoming a more turbulent affair. The role of stakeholders, the growing influence of social responsibility and ethics, and internal marketing factors are now squeezing organizations from every angle in order that they please all of the people all of the time.

The emphasis is now on knowing markets, knowing individual customers, being able to address them directly. Thus, having 'an electronic footprint' of them is essential if a robust long-term relationship is to be established. This 'customer knowledge' also extends to knowing when and how to communicate with them for maximum response. Ignoring the issues of managing relationships will ultimately leave organizations and marketers in a very vulnerable position.

One of the main reasons that organizations will, however, start to make positive moves towards managing marketing relationships is in order to maximize their effectiveness by retaining existing customers rather than focusing consistently on acquiring new customers. Long-term relationships provide the basis of consistency, synergy and achieving satisfaction. The long-term profitable benefits to the organizations will be considerable. For example, a 5 per cent reduction in customer defections can improve profitability by an excess of 25 per cent.

Marketing literature and business media make increasingly wide reference to customer-relationship marketing/management. The CIM's *Marketing Business* magazine regularly includes articles which relate to the topic and provides numerous applications of use. In a recent issue, one of the leading protagonists of CRM, Dr Martha Rogers, discussed the diminishing returns that are being obtained from traditional mass marketing approaches compared to those obtained from developing a real understanding of CRM and internalizing its application (Rogers, 2002). She suggests that CRM is a misused term and many firms do not know how it should be used to build relationships.

Moving customers from a position of satisfaction through to what might be considered to be loyalty requires a series of stages, highlighted in Figure 4.1. This suggests bonding with customers and entering into a more personal dialogue. Demonstrating a strong understanding of the customer is a key factor in this process, recognizing their changing situation and communicating at significant points. Demonstrating a targeted awareness means customers become more receptive. In research conducted by the Henley Centre and Royal Mail in 2001, the preferred form of contact for most people is direct mail. Seventy-five per cent of B2C direct mail is opened and 61 per cent of customers like to receive special offers via the post. This report also suggests that acting effectively to customer complaints can turn vociferous complainers into loyal customers.

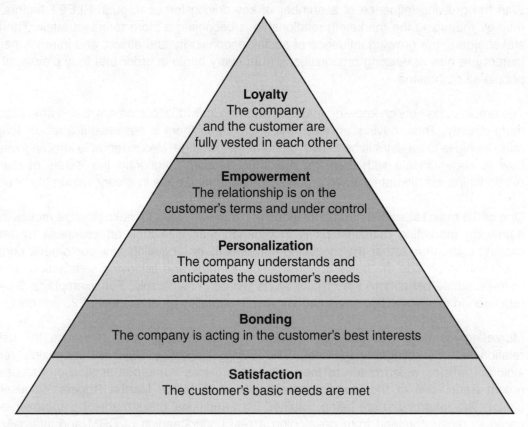

Figure 4.1 From satisfaction to loyalty
Source: Royal Mail Information Pack (2002), www.royailmaiol.co.uk

The scope of marketing relationships (Syllabus 4.2)

The scope of the managing marketing relationships is significant (Figure 4.2), stretching as it does across four key groups: customers, suppliers, internal markets and stakeholder markets, each defined in terms of relationship marketing partnerships.

In addition to this, the scope broadens once more, as the extent of managing marketing relationships in the broader context of business sectors becomes apparent:

1. Organizational markets
2. Service markets
3. Not-for-profit markets.

Each of these particular elements is the focus of other units in this text, where some issues pertaining to relationship management are discussed.

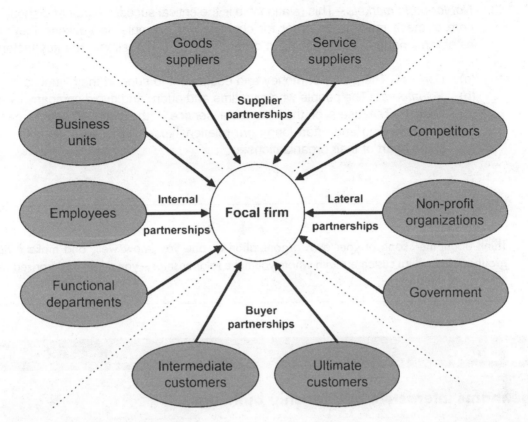

Figure 4.2 The scope of relationships
Source: Adapted from Morgan Hunt (1994)

However, in brief, the critical issues relating to each market sector are:

1. *Organizational markets* – Require high levels of relationship management due to the intensity and time dimensions of the process of purchase. The market is essentially less fickle and more rational, which provides the basis of establishing closer links. Closer links mean working towards gaining preferred supplier status. The basis of achieving this will ultimately mean long-term supplier/buyer relationships, effectively putting a relationship on a strong footing. Essentially, relationship marketing is about collaborative relationships, working together optimizing opportunities and maximizing potential.

2. *Service markets* – Relationship marketing in the context of services is the major imperative, as at the core of any successful services delivery will be the relationship between the service provider and the service consumer. Never before has the power and strength of that relationship become so relevant. The whole basis of its success is upon the key factors of relationship marketing, as defined in Table 4.1:

   (a) Continuous customer contact
   (b) Focus on customer value
   (c) Long timescale
   (d) High customer service emphasis
   (e) High commitment to meeting customer expectations
   (f) Quality as a concern to all staff.

3. *Not-for-profit markets* – This relationship is the critical success factor and should be the core of these markets. In order for charities, for example, to succeed they need to establish long-term relationships in order that they can sustain three key factors:

    (a) *Donors* – The givers of money and equipment to support their work
    (b) *Volunteers* – The people who give time and effort, and avoid company overheads
    (c) *Client* – The users of the charitable service – the charity need to gain trust, understanding and often long-term relationships in order to undertake the work at the heart of their organizations.

Activity 4.2

Think about the scope of your own organization or one you know well, and make a list of groups of individual customers with whom you have relationships – you might be surprised at the balance of the group.

Case study

Debenhams interactive relationship building

Debenhams, the department store chain, launched a multi-channel CRM system in 2003. The system uses software provider Blue Martini's Intelligent Selling System which incorporates merchandising and marketing tools to present customers with personalized information each time they visit the company's website. Tailoring product information and promotional campaigns to the individual lifestyles of customers assists customer retention and increases wallet share both online and in-store. Online usage has also had a beneficial effect on driving store traffic. e-Commerce–generated revenue increased by 100 per cent in the first year.

Adapted from: An article by David Murphy in *Marketing Business*, February 2004.

Planning for relationship marketing (Syllabus 4.3)

The development of marketing relationships has to be planned. As with all other aspects of marketing, it requires a structured approach to ensure that relationship marketing does maximize business potential, provide the basis of profitability, and create sustainable competitive advantage, through robust and long-term customer, supplier and stakeholder relationships.

In order to plan for relationship marketing, there needs to be an understanding of some key factors: customer loyalty, the dimensions of quality, building trust and the basis of continuous improvement.

Whilst the emphasis in this unit is on the use of marketing communications to support relationship building (retention), it should not be ignored that relationships begin with a 'first meeting' (acquisition). Some of the examples in this unit, BT and Lancôme, explain both how new customers were targeted initially and, then, how the relationships were developed over time.

'New' customers may be acquired from a number of different sources. They may arise as a result of response-driven advertising, direct mail, telemarketing and so on. They could be customers the firm has never dealt with or could be customers with whom they used to do business before defaulting to competitors. Customers switch their allegiances for all kinds of reasons. Companies should not lose sight of these groups as it is possible that over time the reasons for leaving might be changed. Subsequent contact might encourage them to return. This is probably most significant in BTB markets but can also be apparent in consumer markets by adaptations to different elements of the marketing mix.

The process of segmentation, targeting and positioning will determine who and on what proposition customers will be approached. Similar communications methods may be used for both acquisition and retention but the ways in which they are deployed (and co-ordinated) will exhibit significant differences.

Customer loyalty

To achieve customer loyalty is highly challenging, as it looks at the loyalty of all customer and other stakeholder groups that are involved in the relationship marketing process. For relationship marketing to be truly implemented and part of the business culture, it has to focus on all customer groups.

We have already established that relationship building is a long-term process, and in order for customer loyalty to be achieved, there are a number of key identifiable stages that the relationship moves through. This is more formally known as the 'Relationship marketing ladder' of customer loyalty (Figure 4.3).

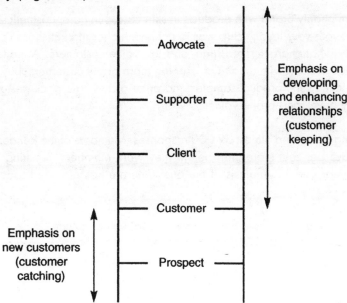

Figure 4.3 The relationship marketing ladder of loyalty
Source: Peck, Payne, Christopher and Clark (1999)

The ladder highlights the process from targeting the customer, to adoption, to developing the relationship from customer to long-term client. From here, it is then essential to encourage them to become both a support and advocate of the company in order that they can become marketing tools. Thus you not only retain them, but also use them to grow market share.

A more recent 'step' to the ladder has been added, that of 'partnership'. In the organizational marketing context, partnership is a very positive stage to move towards in order to secure optimization of opportunities to be exploited, to the benefit of both the supplier and the buyer organizations.

Customer loyalty, however, has two dimensions: long-term loyalty, which is the basis of a true relationship marketing scenario, and false loyalty. This will essentially be driven by a number of key factors:

1. Limited completion of the task
2. High switching costs
3. Proprietary technology
4. The attraction of some loyalty scheme.

The key objective in this context, therefore, will be to switch the power base of loyalty to a more long-term relationship and indeed partnership. Customer loyalty is strongly interlinked with brand loyalty. Different forms of communications can be used to move customers up the ladder as relationships develop. The types of communications may be the subject of formal agreement between the organization and the customer at the higher levels of the ladder.

Royal Mail have provided some interesting content on their website which considers relationship marketing issues and uses some case studies to illustrate differing perspectives.

Case study

Lancôme's Rendezvous-vous club

Lancôme is a premium beauty brand with products in skin care, sun care, cosmetics and fragrances. The concept of the Rendezvous-vous loyalty club was to achieve higher market share in a highly competitive sector, and to identify what characterized high- and low-value customers. A leaflet and questionnaire was mailed to 300 000 women with an aim of learning more about customers' buying habits. Response incentives included make-overs, product samples and prize draws. The pack design was set to emphasize Lancome's newly developed brand values.

The recruitment mailing generated almost 32 000 responses. Members of the Rendezvous-vous club have gone on to spend 13.5 per cent more than before they were members, resulting in over £1.7 million extra sales over a 2-year period. Analysis of the questionnaire has provided Lancôme with significant customers' data.

Source: Adapted from Royal Mail Case Study – www.royalmail.com/cmr.

 Activity 4.3

> Go to the Royal Mail website and access the section on Customer-Managed Relationships (CMR). Make a request to receive the further information packs. These contain some valuable articles on relationship marketing and examples of how communications are effectively used – www.royalmail.com.

The key elements of relationship marketing

There are some key elements of relationship development.

Reliability – Ability to perform the promised service dependably and accurately
Responsiveness – Willingness to help customers and provide prompt service
Assurance – Knowledge and courtesy of employees and their ability to inspire trust and confidence
Empathy – Caring, individualism and attention the firm provides it customers
Tangibles – Physical facilities, equipment and appearance of personnel.

These elements can also provide the basis for positioning messages. In order for the relationship to be established, the basis of what might be called the 'quality gap' must be filled, that is the difference between the customer expectations and the organizational perception of what is being delivered.

A relationship based upon trust

Morgan and Hunt (1994) suggested there are three dynamics to trust within a relationship (Figure 4.4).

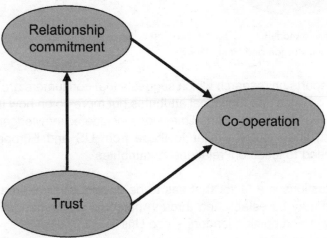

Figure 4.4 What builds trust?
Source: Morgan and Hunt (1994)

These are three quite simplistic components that would form the basis of any relationship, personal or business. The basis of trust provides the opportunity to develop a relationship that includes co-operation, leading to relationship commitment. While principally they should be the basis of relationship marketing aims and objectives, typically these three components can often be overlooked, perhaps assumed or even ignored. However, in Figure 4.5 it is possible to see the benefits of building a relationship on trust, as relationship termination costs can be avoided, and look towards a relationship based on shared values. Opportunistic behaviour will be a great benefit of partnerships in a relationship management context.

The more the inward- and outward-bound communication exists, so the more knowledge about customers can be gained, their needs, wants and perhaps their competitive experiences, all of which serve to strengthen the basis on which to operate.

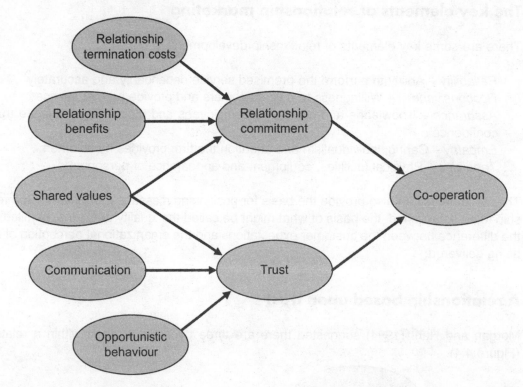

Figure 4.5 Relationship model
Source: Adapted from Morgan and Hunt (1994)

Mitchell (2003) reports on research which suggests that consumers are increasingly measuring brand value, not on price and functional attributes but more so on how they are being treated in interactions with the brand. Important dimensions include acknowledgement, respect and trust. The UK research findings are similar to those from US and European surveys. This shift suggests firms need to focus on 'relationship attributes'.

Trust in most situations is a factor that has to be developed over time through a relationship. Initial confidence may be established through personal recommendation or via endorsement via opinion formers and opinion leaders – see Unit 1.

Customer retention management (Syllabus 2.12)

The most simplistic view that any organization could take of customer retention management is that the best way to keep customers is to keep them satisfied. While some organizations think that this means zero defects, others are realizing the increasing importance of this and are really looking at ways in which retention is not just a concept but a reality.

Peck *et al.* (1999) have developed a number of techniques for measuring customer satisfaction and linking them directly to profitability. Principally what they are doing is measuring customer retention, where customer satisfaction is measured at the rate at which customers are kept.

Peck *et al.* suggest that a retention rate of 80 per cent means that, on average, customers remain loyal for 5 years, whereas a rate of 90 per cent pushes the average loyalty up to 10 years. As the average life of a customer increases, so does the profitability to the firm.

They go on to suggest that long-term established customers are more profitable for six reasons:

1. Regular customers place frequent, consistent orders and, therefore, usually cost less to serve.
2. Long-established customers tend to buy more.
3. Satisfied customers may sometimes pay premium price.
4. Retaining customers makes it difficult for competitors to enter a market or increase their share.
5. Satisfied customers often refer new customers to the supplier at no extra cost.
6. The cost of acquiring and serving new customers can be substantial. A higher retention rate implies fewer new customers need to be acquired, and they can be acquired more cheaply.

Therefore, a relationship based on trust can increase commitment and co-operation with all of the other add-ons as previously discussed.

Customer retention in business-to-consumer markets

In consumer markets, customer retention schemes are, in the main, focused around loyalty cards. Many retailers such as Sainsbury and Tesco have implemented schemes based around rewarding customers with points for the level of purchases made. This is not always a good identifier of loyal customers as research has shown that most people on average will have at least five loyalty cards at any one time. For some consumers, the benefits are very worthwhile. Other supermarkets have either rejected the loyalty card idea, or tried it and withdrawn. The Safeway ABC card scheme, for example, was ultimately withdrawn in favour of a more traditionally based promotional programme.

Loyalty cards became highly popular in the mid- to late 1990s as the intensity of competition began to rise in the supermarket wars, closely followed behind by banks and credit card companies. For example, the American Express Blue Card gives you a penny back for every pound you spend on their card, at the end of the year. Boots followed suit with their Advantage loyalty card, which proved to be very beneficial to the customer. With double points and special offers, the Boots card has been branded as a success by its customers.

Case study

Loyalty cards

A more recent development in the loyalty scheme sector has seen the launch of a scheme based on the 'partnering' of members. The Nectar programme was launched at the end of 2002 and is owned by Sainsbury's, Barclaycard, BP and Debenhams. This collaboration has meant that for some of the participants, they have withdrawn their individual schemes such as the Sainsbury's Reward Card. Nectar aims to have the card held by 70 per cent of UK households. This approach means that the partners share the risks and costs of operating the scheme. With potential membership of over 15 million, the costs of managing the scheme are considerable. When first launched, such was the demand for membership that the Nectar computer system was overwhelmed. These problems were quickly overcome and new partners will be added over time.

The benchmark loyalty scheme, the Tesco Clubcard, continues to grow in both terms of numbers of card holders and effectiveness. In addition to providing Tesco with customer data, major brand producers such as Unilever, Procter & Gamble, Coca-Cola, Nestlé and Gillette share the intelligence gathered. The scheme identifies every item purchased and records date and time and how you pay. Purchase of products in the Tesco Finest range, classifies the customer as 'upmarket', whilst buying Tesco Value products will mean a classification as 'price sensitive'. The data gathered can also be used to analyse the effectiveness of advertising response by customer group.

Tesco information, adapted from: An article by Richard Fletcher in the *Sunday Times*, 19 December 2004.

 ### Activity 4.4

What kind of communications activities are used by companies who utilize loyalty schemes compared to those who do not?

This would involve looking at how above- and below-the-line tools are used. Loyalty schemes are based on accessing information from customer databases and making use of direct response media such as direct mail and telemarketing. Point-of-sale activity and in-store recruitment is used to support advertising-based acquisition. Product-based sales promotion advertising is more widely used by retailers who do not use loyalty schemes. If you have loyalty cards, identify what type of communications are being used.

Customer retention in business-to-business markets

There are five basic principles that an organizational market should consider in relationship development:

1. *Technical support* – Providing added value to clients in industrial markets.
2. *Technical expertise* – Providing expertise in design and engineering can be a unique selling point (USP) of the organization, and add to the value proposition.
3. *Resource support* – Ensure that a range of versatile resources are available to support the relationship, that are cost-effective and efficient, and that could ultimately see the development of an alliance when business opportunities are presented (the basis of partnerships).
4. *Service levels* – These appear to be of growing importance and will relate in particular to time, delivery and product quality.
5. *Reduction of risk* – Giving as much insight into the product proposition as possible through exhibitions, trial use and product delivery guarantees.

 ### Activity 4.5

Why do you think customer-relationship marketing is so important in organizational markets?

Customer retention in not-for-profit markets

One of the key considerations in the marketing activities in not-for-profit markets is the need to be very focused on each of their customer groups, as we ascertained earlier, those being donors, volunteers, client/users.

It will be essential that the charity understands their target markets and segments them exactly, as each of them will manifest different customer retention characteristics, particularly as their personal reasons for charitable involvement will be very diverse.

Key relationship marketing issues will include:

1. Analysing acquisition and retention costs
2. Managing customer retention and customer acquisition activities concurrently
3. Recognizing how emphasis needs to be placed on all markets in order to achieve the success the objectives demand
4. The need to have adequate information sources about each of the customer groups.

Within the not-for-profit sector there are some far broader strategic issues that typical organizations will grapple with, such as the challenges of the functions of management and marketing, developing and understanding the basis of market segmentation strategies, and finally the scope of their mission, which in many instances can be huge.

Internal marketing communications (Syllabus 2.12)

The internal audience, comprising management, other executives and the workforce are, similarly, the recipients of messages from the organization. Importantly, how they interpret messages will have a bearing on the way in which they deal with and respond to outside audiences.

Organizations, it may be argued, communicate through the behaviour of their managers and employees as well as through the tools of the communications mix. This is particularly significant in service businesses where there is a high level of contact between employees and customers. There is a need to account for the degree to which employees believe in the organization, its values and how they communicate with others outside the organizations. In addition, there is a need to account for the financial resources and understand the broad amount of funds that are likely to be made available.

Employees constitute an internal market, and in that sense need to be communicated with just as much as external (or non-member) stakeholders, through effective marketing communications. Marketing communications should be used to differentiate, remind/reassure, inform and persuade (DRIP) employees, just as much as any other target segment.

 ### Activity 4.6

Apply each of the elements of the DRIP roles of marketing communications to employees.

Organizational identity is concerned with what individuals think and feel about the organization to which they belong. When their perception of the organization's characteristics is in balance with their own self-concept, organizational identity is said to be strong. These shared perceptions and feelings (with other employees) form a collective sense of organizational identity.

There may well be variances between the perceptions of employees and those held by external stakeholders, and this may be a cause of confusion, misunderstanding or even conflict. In general, the closer the member/non-member identification (the smaller the gap), the better-placed the organization will be to achieve its objectives.

There are a number of occasions when identity is critical. These may be during periods of rapid growth or decline, during merger and acquisition or when a major part of the organization's identity 'kit' is lost (e.g. when a founder member retires or leaves the organization).

The strength of organizational identity is a reflection of the culture that binds (or not) the organization together. Although it is possible to see various levels of organizational culture it is really the basic beliefs, values and assumptions that are shared by members of an organization, that define an organization's view of itself.

Culture and communication

Organizational culture is not static; the stronger the culture, the more likely it is to be transmitted from one generation of organizational members to another, and it is also probable that the culture will be more difficult to change if it is firmly embedded in the organization. Most writers acknowledge that effective cultural change is difficult and a long-term task.

The focus of internal marketing communications has evolved through noticeboards, and training and development programmes to one that is more frequent, informal and often based around new technology. Videoconferencing, internal television, e-mail, intranets, bulletin boards, newsletters and magazines constitute an array of appropriate communication devices. External communications need to take account of staff reaction, get their co-operation and support, and depict them in a positive and motivating manner. Major TV advertising campaigns from organizations such as B&Q, the DIY retailer, and the Halifax Bank have featured company employees. This is seen as a motivator in the sense that all employees can associate themselves with the campaigns and as attempts to add credibility to the messages being delivered.

The development of CMC has to be based on internally generated communications blending and reinforcing externally orientated communications. An understanding of organizational identity and culture is the foundation of profile-based communication strategies.

It is essential to understand and manage organizational identity to minimize any discrepancy between members' and non-members' perceptions of what is central to and distinctive about the organization. If you think about your own experiences buying clothes, music or food, part of your perception of the organization you are buying from is influenced by how staff treat you and how attentive or caring they appear to be. The quality of the service encounter (or point of interaction) between staff (members) and customers (non-members) is a reflection of the degree to which their marketing communications are integrated.

Remember, organizations communicate with customers and other external stakeholders through their employees. Marketing communications are more likely to work when the behaviour and signals delivered by employees reinforce the messages delivered through the promotional mix to external audiences.

Case study

Customer care culture pays off for brewer

Adnams is traditional brewer based in Southwold, Suffolk and they have been winning awards for their approach to handling customer complaints. They came top in the 2004 National Complaints Culture Survey. The report is compiled by the TMI consultancy, which also shows that 54 per cent of customers are willing or mostly willing to complain. Half of the those sampled belived businesses were getting worse at handling customers problems.

Adnams provides extensive training programmes for staff in their customer service teams, including psychometric testing to identify the right people and have regular appraisal checks. There is a focus on three key issues. Making sure customers were given access and that the complaint was dealt with at a single point of contact, making sure staff felt confident that their decisions would be supported by management and that the culture had to recognise the true value of customers and the significance of retention.

Adapted from: An article by Roger Elgin in the *Sunday Times*, 3 October 2004.

See also the section on Internal PR and the Case study on SEEBOARD which is relevant to this discussion (Unit 2).

The relationship marketing plan

It is essential that an organization manages the scope and range of relationships within the marketing environment in order to achieve all-round success.

As the management of relationships in each of the markets we have defined is critical to the achievement of the overall customer retention objectives, there must be crystal-clear linkages that bridge the objects and the markets (Figure 4.6).

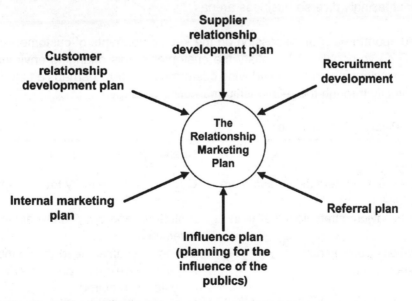

Figure 4.6 The relationship marketing plan
Source: Adapted from Payne, Christopher, Clark and Peck (1998)

In order to achieve a meaningful relationship marketing plan, you have to consider the needs of each of the individual markets in order for it to be successfully developed and implemented. The linkages between each audience should be clear, and they should all be directed towards the same overall purpose. The successful implementation of such a plan will most likely impact upon the achievement of retention goals.

Key account techniques to aid customer retention management (Syllabus 2.11)

Key account management is growing in importance as a tool to retain customers, particularly in the organizational sector of the marketing environment. This follows from the well-worn marketing adage that 80 per cent of profits come from 20 per cent of customers based on the Pareto principle. Profitability is obviously an important factor but firms also need to look at other aspects of the business relationship in making judgements as to the long-term value of customers. Sales volumes, regularity of orders, payment structures and growth potential will aid decision-making in key account relationships.

On the basis that key accounts are usually large customers, the main form of marketing communications is based on personal sales but not wholly in face-to-face situations. This would involve co-ordination of meetings, mail, telephone and various electronic communications. Organizations will use different terms to describe their key accounts; house accounts and national accounts are commonly used.

Typical symptoms of change that have led to an increasing focus on identifying and managing key accounts, as suggested by Mc Donald, Rogers and Woodburn (2000) in *Key customers – How to Manage them Profitably* are:

1. Compressed time horizons
2. Intensity of competition
3. Shorter product life cycles
4. Shorter technology-based life cycles
5. Transient customer preferences
6. Increasingly diverse business arenas.

So, based upon the earlier discussion on the key components of customer retention management, how do you continue to satisfy the customer in this changing environment? Table 4.3 provides an insight into the issues driving customers and how perhaps a company can respond to them directly through the relationship marketing strategy.

Table 4.3 Pleasing the customer

Symptoms	Challenge
Customers are more demanding and more knowledgeable	Quality and traceability favour supply chain partnerships
Purchase behaviour strategic rather than tactical	A strategic and sympathetic approach to selling is required
Concentration of buying power	Selling companies need to add more value
Higher expectations	A greater investment and closer relationship to the customer required
Customer identity and role more complex	Need to better manage the complexities of multiple market channels

Source: Mc Donald, Rogers and Woodburn (2000)

From a key account perspective, understanding the relationship between the buyer and the seller, and the two organizations will be extremely important (Figure 4.7). While typical marketing mix factors are highly relevant, the relationship goes beyond these dynamics to the need to understand the strategic intent. Strategy development as the basis of the relationship may provide new business opportunities and business development. Therefore, it is essential when pursuing relationships and indeed managing relationships that the organizations have a good understanding of each other.

There are risks and implications of KAM that all organizations should always consider in order to plan the relationship sensibly to optimize it, and grasp potential opportunities that are affordable and not damaging.

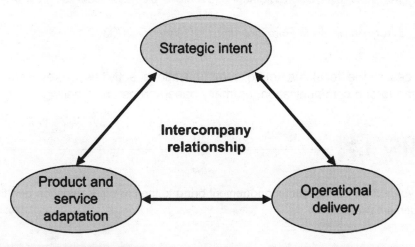

Figure 4.7 Intercompany relationship
Source: Mc Donald, Rogers and Woodburn (2000)

The risks associated with key account relationships include:

1. The risk of being vulnerable to opportunism and not obtaining a satisfactory saving or return on investment in the relationship
2. The risk of committing to one partner at the exclusion of others
3. The risk of misunderstanding the relationship and failing to achieve reciprocal security.

While risk is something that all organizations should be aware of, there is also a group of limitations that can hinder the profitability of a customer relationship:

1. Close relationships with key accounts have sustainable cost implications
2. The mismanagement of just a few large accounts can be potentially loss-making and even catastrophic
3. Customer relationships should be carefully selected and prioritized for prudent investment of scarce resources.

Case study

Changing customers

These kinds of limitations have prompted many firms to reassess the type of customers they are targeting. Connect Support Services, a London-based computer support company was dependent on a small number of large corporate clients for 95 per cent of turnover. These customers were becoming expensive and difficult to manage. One client contract was worth £600 000 a year but cost £100 000 to negotiate and lasted only for 2 years. Connect has now switched from this type of costly account to targeting of small to medium size businesses who pay a fixed price depending on the number of computers being managed. They now have over 300 customers and there is plenty of room for growth.

Source: Adapted from an article in *Financial Times*, 30 January 2003.

In most cases, the focal marketing communications activities in key account relationships involve one-to-one communication, normally based on personal selling.

Activity 4.7

What value does key account management bring to the customer retention and the relationship management process?

Co-ordinating communications in key account management

The communications emphasis in KAM is usually personal selling, given the usual B2B situation. As personal selling costs can be significant, many organizations are seeking alternative communications tools to support it (and in some cases replace it) – by using telemarketing, direct mail, online, trade promotions, exhibitions, corporate hospitality and similar activities. The balance required may depend to a large extent on how the customer wishes to be communicated with. Such channels can be established by agreement.

Summary

Understanding and meeting customer needs is, of course, a fundamental aspect of marketing philosophy. Segmentation and targeting have long been identified as key marketing tools for identifying customers with similar characteristics which offer the firm potential sales and profitability. One of the factors that has led to the shift from transaction to relationship approach has been the need to look at customer retention on a long-term basis. In essence, the relationship concept is not a new one, but having recognized the potential benefits to be achieved by retaining existing customers, many firms are adopting the principles involved.

This section has looked at the ways in which relationships are developed and managed, internally and externally for profitable growth. The continued developments in technology will enhance this process and continue to smooth the communications involved at all stages.

A wide range of marketing communications tactics will be employed to ensure that relevant and consistent messages are delivered over time to facilitate the relationship development.

Further study

As it has been identified, relationship marketing and associated issues are increasingly significant areas for business and academic research. A number of writers have been identified and some of their ideas briefly discussed. It would be worthwhile obtaining one of the key texts in order to substantiate your knowledge in what is a key marketing communications field. Academic marketing journals regularly publish articles covering different aspects, and the business press also considers relationship issues on a regular basis.

Typical exam questions

In this section, references are given to specific examination and assignment questions from the June/July 2004 assessments. The questions are set out in Appendix 5. Detailed feedback on these questions from the CIM Senior Examiner and specimen answers can be obtained from the CIM website. Also included are some general examples of question types, briefings on which are included in Appendix 3.

June 2004 Examination Questions 1c, 2b, 3b and 4c. July 2004 Assignments Question2.

Question 4.1

Describe the main stages associated with the development of key accounts.

(5 Marks)

Question 4.2

Recommend ways in which business relationships can be developed through marketing communications.

(10 Marks)

Hints and tips

Identify several examples of relationship building strategies in different market sectors. These will provide you with the type of information required in supporting examination questions on this topic.

References

Elgin, R. (2004) 'Customer care pays dividends', *The Sunday Times*, 3 October, p. 7.

Financial Times, 30 January 2003.

Fletcher, R. (2004) 'Tesco's success puts Clubcard firm on the map', *The Sunday Times*, 19 December, p. 7.

Gronroos, C. (1994) 'Quo vadis, Marketing? Toward a relationship marketing paradigm', *Journal of Marketing Management*, **10**, 347–360.

Gummesson, E. (1999) *Total Relationship Marketing*, Oxford: Butterworth-Heinemann.

Mc Donald, M., Rogers, B. and Woodburn, D. (2000) *Key Customers: How to manage them profitably*, Oxford: Butterworth-Heinemann.

Mitchell, A. (2003) 'The feel-good factor', *Marketing Business*, p. 17.

Morgan, R.M. and Hunt, S.D. (1994) 'The commitment-trust theory of relationship marketing', *Journal of Marketing*, **58**, July, 20–38.

Murphy, D. (2004) 'The truth about CRM', *Marketing Business*, February, pp. 29–30.

Peck, H., Payne, A., Christopher, M. and Clark, M. (1999) *Relationship Marketing*, Oxford: Butterworth-Heinemann.

Rogers (2002) 'The customers champion', *Marketing Business*, November/December, pp. 14–16.

Smith, B. and Clark, M. (2002) 'Beyond the hype', *Marketing Business*, April, pp. 29–31.

www.royalmail.com
www.royailmaiol.co.uk

unit 5
marketing channels

There is an increasing level of B2B marketing and associated communications activities. Very often, this is an understated part of promotional work but is a large, growing and vitally important part of the marketing communications range of activities.

This unit focuses on a particular part of B2B marketing, namely the marketing channels. Knowledge and skills relating to channel-based communications is applicable to Small and Medium Enterprises (SMEs), large blue chip organizations operating in the fmcg sector and those high-tech companies working at the edge of technology. Regardless of the context, the principles remain the same, only the tools, messages, media and resources are adapted.

This unit is designed to cover issues relating to the structure and characteristics associated with marketing channels. In addition, it considers the characteristics and roles that marketing communications plays in developing and maintaining relationships between channel members.

After completion of this section you will be able to:

o Understand the reasons why organizations use intermediaries

o Explain the different channel configurations and the benefits of multichannel systems

o Understand the nature and principal causes of channel conflict

o Appreciate the interrelationship between relationship marketing concepts, marketing channels and marketing communications

o Evaluate the role of the promotional mix in the channels, and make judgements about the best tools and media to use in different channel contexts.

Syllabus references include: 2.1 (See also Unit 2), 3.1, 3.2, 3.3, 3.4, 3.5, 4.1 (See also Unit 4).

Channel structures (Syllabus 3.2)

Marketing (or distribution) channels are an integral part of the marketing mix. They provide the means by which products and services are made available to end-user customers for purchase and consumption. They provide the means by which manufacturers become linked with their target markets. More importantly and more pertinently, marketing channels are the means by which customers can access the products and services that they want, at a time that they prefer and at their convenience.

Manufacturers use channels of different designs and configurations in order to reach different markets. The most simple and straightforward channel is a direct channel whereby customers buy products directly from the manufacturer or producer. However, this arrangement places limitations on the scope and breadth of each producer. In order to reach each customer and complete a buy/sell transaction, the manufacturer must replicate all the necessary business processes and procedures with each customer. These processes are referred to as exchanges (Figure 5.1).

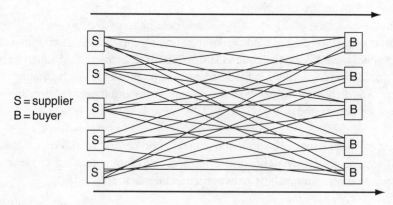

Figure 5.1 Exchange efficiencies

However, Figure 5.2 shows the impact on the number of exchanges the manufacturer needs to undertake, when an intermediary is introduced to the channel structure and the direct channel becomes an indirect channel.

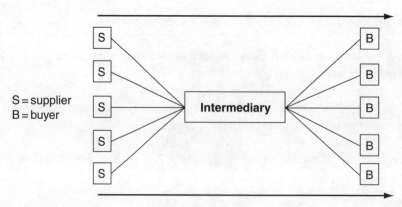

Figure 5.2 Exchange efficiencies

Marketing channels consist of a number of different organizations, each of which fulfils particular roles in the channel. Typically, a channel will consist of a manufacturer, a wholesaler, a retailer and an end-user customer. This is referred to as a conventional channel and is depicted at Figure 5.3.

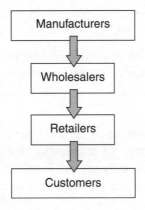

Figure 5.3 A conventional marketing channel

These different organizations, those who populate marketing channels, are known as intermediaries. Their primary task is to provide added value by meeting and exceeding end-user expectations. This will be looked at later.

Activity 5.1

Make a list of the tasks that you think might help a wholesaler add value for their retailers.

So far, reference has been made to products moving towards the ultimate customer, a downstream movement. However, marketing channels manage more than products. In order for a successful buy/sell transaction or an exchange to occur, a host of other ancillary activities need to take place. These ancillary activities may relate to orders, payments, negotiation or promotion and are referred to as flows (an order flow, payment flow, etc.).

It should be understood that there is a difference between the marketing channels and supply chains. Supply chains extend from the customer to the individual suppliers and are concerned with the physical aspects of distribution. The physical aspect of distribution is commonly known as logistics management, and is really concerned with the efficiency and timeliness with which stock is moved and stored. This is not the concern of marketing channel management. Their concern is with the management of customer behaviour in order to achieve their marketing goals.

Membership – independence and interdependence

Membership of a marketing channel will vary according to a range of factors but intermediaries play a key role in enabling manufacturers to reach their end-user markets. In order for this to happen, each individual intermediary engages in an act of compromise.

Each organization wishes to be independent of all other organizations and to be free to make decisions free of the wishes of others. However, in most cases, a purely independent state is not achievable for the simple reason that in order to survive it is imperative that the organization works, that is collaborates and co-operates, with other organizations. This represents a degree of interdependence, the antithesis of independence.

Activity 5.2

Select an organization with which you are familiar and prepare notes explaining why and how it co-operates with both a supplier and a customer organization.

Therefore, an independent organization is one that is unhindered by ownership, finance or other undue economic, regulatory or marketing restrictions so that they are free to form voluntary relationships with whom they prefer. These organizations prefer to act independently of others and only work with others on a transactional and often temporary basis.

Organizations that are interdependent are those that either through ownership, regulation or voluntary deed recognize the necessity to co-operate and collaborate with other specific organizations if their goals are to be achieved. They collaborate willingly and often seek to establish longer-term working relationships. This may involve collaborating in many different ways in order to help fellow channel members achieve their goals, for example, through product development, joint promotion activities and preferred financial arrangements. It is the organizations that embrace the need to be interdependent that are more likely to be willing and able to enter into inter-organizational relationships and be a contributor to the workings of a marketing channel.

Case study

Cisco systems announced that they are to reduce the number of European distributors from 17 to 7. The new structure will consist of Cisco Distribution Partners (large distributors) and a series of smaller ones Cisco Accredited Distributors. The aim is to improve stock handling, the mix of stock available to resellers and speed to market.

Intermediaries assume different roles according to their position in a channel. There are many different types of intermediary ranging from wholesalers, merchants, agents, manufacturers, representatives and distributors to dealers, retailers and value-added resellers. See Figure 5.4 for a visual interpretation about how these can be configured.

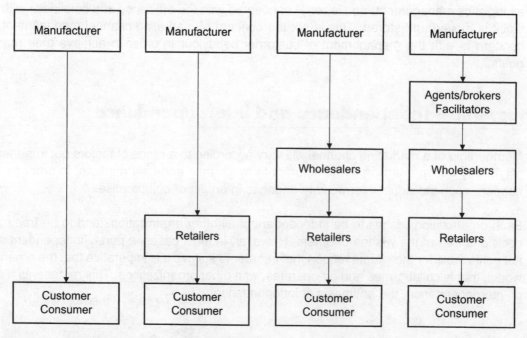

Figure 5.4 Typical range of channels of distribution

The detail concerning the operations of each of these different types of intermediary and how they each contribute to the marketing channel is not of prime concern in this unit. However, the role of both wholesalers and retailers will be examined because their contribution is different, interdependent and the basis for much of the marketing communication activities that occur in the channel.

Wholesalers purchase products from a range of different manufacturers, store them, develop new assortments and market them to retailers. Their principal contribution rests with breaking bulk and reassembling (accumulating) the different goods that they buy from all the manufacturers they deal with (in a category). Breaking bulk refers to the purchase of large quantities of stock from producers and then breaking this down into smaller manageable collections that retailers are willing and able to buy. This enables them to assemble different assortments that meet the needs of retail customers. Retailers do not have the storage space for a lot of stock so rely on wholesalers to hold stock for them and to deliver promptly as required. The price paid by retailers to wholesalers for this stockholding operation is a higher price than if they had the whole lot delivered immediately.

Retailers provide wholesalers with sales contacts and outlets. This enables stock to be transferred to consumers for consumption. It is more efficient for retailers to undertake this operation than for wholesalers. Retailers help wholesalers by purchasing small quantities of stock on a regular basis. Retailers focus on end-user consumers and consider their buying motivations.

Both wholesalers and retailers seek to add value in their contribution to the channel effort so that their respective customers perceive a high level of service, and hence value in the goods and services they purchase.

Activity 5.3

Why might the concept of customer value be different to that expected by a consumer?

All intermediaries assume particular roles. These may be to act as a wholesaler or as a retailer but it is the set of accepted tasks that each perform, that establishes their contribution and responsibilities to the other members of the marketing channel. By enabling each member of the channel to assume a set of discrete tasks, each channel member is able to concentrate on their core activities and to become more efficient and more effective at what they do best.

The breadth of the roles undertaken is summarized in Table 5.1.

Within marketing channels, it is possible to identify that it is not only products that flow downstream from producers to customers but that there are other flows necessary to make the system operate properly to everyone's benefit. In order that transactions are completed properly, there needs to be a flow of information up and down the channel, a flow of finance, either in terms of investment or purchase, usually up the channel, a flow of orders and a negotiation flow (both ways). However, one of the most important flows is the promotional flow. This refers to the marketing communications information necessary to differentiate, reinforce, inform and persuade all members of the marketing channel. Understanding the significance of these different flows can affect not only the balance but also the relationships between the members. Marketing communications can oil the relationships between channel members and is therefore an important aspect of marketing channel management.

Table 5.1 Breadth of channel member roles

Category of marketing activities	Possible activities required
Marketing information	Analyse information such as sales data, carrying out research studies
Marketing management	Establish objectives, plan activities and manage, co-ordinate financing, risk-taking, evaluate channel activities
Facilitating exchange	Choose and stock products that match buyers' needs
Promotion	Set promotional objectives, co-ordinate advertising, personal selling, promotions and so on
Price	Establishing pricing policies, terms and sales
Physical distribution	Manage transport, warehousing, materials handling, stock control and communication
Customer service	Provide channels for advice, technical support, after-sales service and warranties
Relationships	Facilitate communication, products, parts, credit control and so on. Maintain relationships between manufacturer and retail outlets, and customer/consumer

Adapted from: Dibb *et al.* (2001)

Vertical channel structures

There are a number of variations associated with the conventional channel mentioned earlier. These are based on the degree to which two or more intermediaries are linked other than through voluntary arrangements. These are referred to as vertical marketing systems (VMS) and vary from contractual arrangements commonly associated with franchise operations (e.g. Burger King) through to a situation where one organization owns all the other channel members. This is known as a Corporate VMS and was regarded as an optimal channel structure. This was because the owners were able to control their own policies across the channel and derive profits across all aspects of the operation. However, this structure has inbuilt inflexibility and has fallen from favour in recent years.

 Activity 5.4

Try to identify a corporate VMS. List the companies owned in the group. Note any special characteristics.

More recently, the trend has been for organizations to become associated with loose alignments referred to as value networks. These consist of organizations who choose to work together collaboratively, who come together to work on a particular project and then may disband once the project is completed. The value rests with the network and no one single organization.

Multichannel Marketing

In reality, organizations do not use a single marketing channel. The trend is to use multiple channels in order to reach different target audiences. Increasingly, customers prefer to use a variety of channels, because this fits better with their changing lifestyles. Therefore, in order to be competitive and deliver superior value, it is incumbent upon organizations to use the right mix of channels to reach their target markets.

Activity 5.5

Select a market sector (e.g. cars, perfume, bottled water, etc.) and try to determine how many different channels exist to reach end-user consumers.

Internet and digital technologies to support marketing channels (Syllabus 3.5)

The development of the Internet and related digital technologies has enabled organizations to revert to a direct channel approach, and in doing so restructure their distribution strategies. The AA (Automobile Association) closed 140 high-street sites when they concluded that their customers preferred to use the telephone, fax or the Internet when they wanted to communicate with the AA. Abbey National developed a new brand, Cahoot, only available online, which appealed to a target audience that previously they had been unable to reach through traditional offline channels.

Case study

WH Smith

Developing an online marketing channel to parallel with an established off-line trading format is a frequent source of tension and internal channel conflict. The UK based high-street retailer, WH Smith suggests that online profitability can threaten the off-line format even though the online format demands a substantial level of resources in terms of marketing communications. However, WH Smith recommends that a multi-channel strategy is required in order to meet the needs of different segments and use marketing communications to build the brand name and start to associate it, in the minds of consumers, with the online channel.

Source: www.csd.abdn.ac.uk/ – accessed, 07 March 2003.

One of the major developments resulting from the use of Internet technologies has been the impact on established marketing channel structures. Decisions to provide a direct only or to add a direct channel, impact on current channel members and often results in the elimination of various intermediaries. The very decision to go direct is an attempt to reduce costs, to become more competitive and to provide increased customer value. It is inevitable that the services of some intermediaries will no longer be required. This process is popularly referred to as disintermediation – a depopulation of a marketing channel.

However, the development of many direct channels has also resulted in the emergence of new types of service providers for both B2B and B2C markets. These new types of intermediary provide services that are necessary to either directly support the new channel or to provide services across a sector or a number of similar channels. At the same time, advances in digital technology have enabled the development of new types of business models and a reworking of the value chain concept to one that emphasizes *virtual* integration, rather than *vertical*

129

integration. All of this activity leads to the development of new forms of intermediary and this process is referred to as reintermediation – a repopulation of marketing channels.

Channel conflict (Syllabus 3.4)

It is inevitable that there will be some conflict between channel members, so the main issues concern the frequency, intensity and duration of the conflict when it emerges. Channel conflict can be interpreted as a breakdown in the levels of co-operation between channel partners (Shipley and Egan, 1992). As mentioned earlier, co-operation is important because members of any channel are, to varying degrees, interdependent; hence their membership in the first place.

 Activity 5.6

Make a list of four reasons why conflict can occur between members of a marketing channel.

Channel conflict occurs in established offline channels, in new online channels and in multi-channel situations, either vertically or horizontally. It is generally accepted that conflict occurs for one or more of the following three broad reasons.

1. Competing goals
2. Differences over domains
3. Perceptions of reality.

Competing goals

This is a common form of conflict and typically occurs when one upstream member changes strategy so that their goals become difficult for other downstream members to support. For example, a manufacturer of office furniture may decide that it wants to reach new market sectors, perhaps the home working market. Current dealers might resist this as it is not in their interest to supply other (new) channels with these products. Indeed, if actioned it might give rise to increased channel competition and then impact on dealer revenues and profits.

Another example of competing goals can be seen when retailers try to increase performance by lowering their stock levels. Conflict is likely as the manufacturer's goal is to increase the level of stock in the channel.

Domain differences

Domain refers to an area, field or sphere of function. Disputes can arise because one channel member perceives another member operating outside of the previously designated (agreed) area, perhaps geographically, or in terms of its role.

So, a wholesaler who starts to sell directly to end-user consumers, or retailers who begin to sell to other retailers are blatantly adopting a new role and this may infringe upon another member's role and prevent or impede them from achieving their objectives.

A more common example exists when the furniture manufacturer mentioned earlier decides to sell through a dealer's competitors, even breaking an exclusivity arrangement. The reverse of this intrachannel type of conflict can also cause conflict, when a manufacturer perceives an intermediary selling another office furniture manufacturer's products (a competitor) at the expense of its own range of products.

The emergence of multiple channels is often a cause for domain conflict as an intermediary might feel threatened by increased competition and reduced financial performance opportunities.

Case study

Channel conflict

Vidal Sassoon originally sold its haircare products through professional hair salons. This enabled them to earn higher margins and retain control over the way in which its brands were presented and delivered. The positioning for the brand, upmarket, elite and aspirational was reinforced through these marketing channels.

However, the brand became available through Target, a US-based chain of retail outlets that operated with high-quality merchandise and very low prices. The Sassoon brand was diluted and retail prices (and margins) fell by over 60 per cent. Conflict arose because the marketing channel strategy had been damaged.

Source: http://www.reshare.com/managingcc.htm – accessed, 05 February 2003.

Disagreements about pricing, sales areas or sales order processing, for example, are sensitive issues that can lead to channel conflict. Once agreement has been made about policy or terms operational formats, any changes need to be negotiated and managed in a co-operative, considered way. Indeed, some channels often stipulate the way in which changes to key domain-based issues should be managed.

Perceptions of reality

As each member organization perceives the world differently, their perception of others and their actions may lead to tensions and disagreements. So, an action taken by member X, might be perceived differently by member Y, to that intended. Any action that Y takes as a result of this perception may result in conflict. Perceptions about a product attribute, its applications and appropriate segments can all give rise to perceptually based conflict.

The main reason for this tendency to see different information or actions differently to that intended may arise because, in the absence of a strong co-operative relationship, different channel members are focused on different business elements (Coughlan *et al.*, 2001). A manufacturer might be focused on products and processes, and a dealer may be focused on their customers and the functions and processes necessary to meet their needs. Differences in perception may arise because member focus is culturally driven. What may be an appropriate behaviour in one culture may not be understood, known or be just different to that in another. This can obviously be a problem for internationally based organizations.

Activity 5.7

Find examples of the three main types of channel conflict.

Resolving channel conflict

Channel conflict cannot be stopped but it can be managed. Through adequate proactive strategies and methods, conflict can be reduced in frequency, intensity and duration but it cannot be totally prevented. There are a number of methods that can be used and at the root of them are two main factors, the strength of relationship between channel members and quality of (marketing) communications.

These two factors are now examined.

Strength of relationship (Syllabus 3.3)

Marketing channels are a part of the wider B2B sector and one of the principal factors leading to successful channel performance has been found to be the form and strength of the relationship that develops between buyers and sellers in the marketing channel and across the membership of the whole channel.

There are a number of factors that contribute to the development of strong relationships but linking them all are ideas concerning trust and commitment.

Trust and commitment

The interdependence of channel members and indeed of most strong and longer-running relationships, including those between clients and agencies, is founded on a degree of trust between parties. In a channel context, trust is the confidence that one channel member has interacting with another member with respect to their reliability, integrity and predictability regarding desirable outcomes.

Commitment within a relationship can be interpreted as the desire to continue and maintain a valued relationship. Therefore, a strong relationship requires that trust be established between channel members. Once trust is formed, the opportunity arises for relationship commitment and it is through this co-operation that a major outcome might be end-user satisfaction.

As discussed in Unit 4, Morgan and Hunt (1994) proposed that building a relationship based on trust and commitment can give rise to a number of benefits. Some of these include developing a set of shared values, reducing costs when the relationship finishes and increasing profitability as a greater number of end-user customers are retained because of the inherent value and satisfaction they experience.

Case study

HP and channel conflict

HP reported that their first quarter profits in 2003 were down, mainly as a result of (internal) channel conflict. Conflict emerged between their direct and indirect sales channels as the sales force tried to (aggressively) achieve their growth targets. The HP CEO Carly Fiorina said they had damaged their own channel relationships and 'opened the door for their competitors' as intermediaries became suspicious.

Source: http://www.vnunet.com/News/1118093 – accessed, 16 March 2003.

The unit on Relationship Marketing explores the work of Morgan and Hunt in more detail. However in terms of conflict, the development of trust is important in preventing it developing in the first place and if it does, the presence of trust should go some way towards reducing the intensity and duration. If there is a high degree of commitment, then the fact that both parties value the relationship will go a long way to preventing the issue, which could give rise to conflict, from emerging in the first place.

Marketing communications (Syllabus 3.1)

The second method of resolving conflict concerns the communications used between members. It seems clear that communication is an important co-ordinating mechanism for all members of a marketing channel. Its absence or failure will inevitably lead to behaviour that is not in the best interests of the whole channel. Undoubtedly, inadequate communications between channel members will be a major cause of conflict in its own right but it is also a part of each of the three main reasons why conflict occurs.

Activity 5.8

Write notes explaining why communication is important between channel members.

There are three broad issues that need to be considered: the strategy and direction of the channel strategy, the timing of the communication and the degree to which parties in the channel share common attitudes. These are looked at in turn.

Strategy and direction

Marketing communications is an audience-centred activity and when directed at members of a marketing channel, it is said to be a push strategy. Push strategies can encompass a range of marketing communication activities and events and some can be specific to the needs of different groups of intermediaries. The flow of communication would typically be represented by a manufacturer communicating first with a wholesaler, who then communicates with a retailer, who then communicates with end-user consumers. This is represented at Figure 5.5.

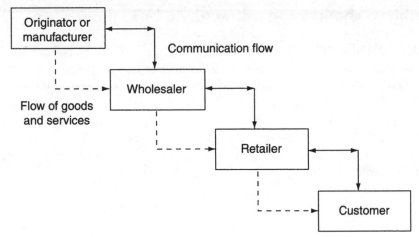

Figure 5.5 A push communication strategy
Source: Fill (2005)

The objective is to stimulate demand by encouraging channel partners to take and sell stock, to allocate scarce resources such as shelf space and to become product advocates. The flow need not be orderly and systematic as the diagram suggests and the emphasis of any single communication activity may focus on a single level within the channel, namely retailers or agents.

133

The advantages of a push marketing communications strategy are as follows:

1. Improved control over desired branding and positioning
2. Provides reasons for retailers to stock
3. Opportunity for positive associations between store perceptions and product
4. Opportunities to support, reward, train and motivate channel partners with a view to developing positive relationships
5. Helps prepare for a product (re)launch by creating stock availability
6. May help reduce overall promotional costs by distracting from heavy consumer push.

The disadvantages of a push marketing communications strategy are as follows:

1. Too much channel availability may harm perceptions of quality or exclusiveness, if an important part of the positioning strategy
2. Needs consolidation with product knowledge otherwise service may damage quality perception
3. Could be expensive if there is a large range and diversity of distributors
4. Danger of information deviance and channel conflict.

A planned push communications strategy should contribute to and reinforce channel relationships, and of the many influences on channel strategy, the following should be highlighted.

Power	How is power distributed in the channel equally?
Direction	Is the communication one- or two-way?
Frequency	How often should messages be sent?
Style and content	Should messages be formal or informal?
Distortion	Will information be received, stored, processed and actioned in the way intended?

Case study

Red Bull achieve channel commitment via buzz marketing

Buzz marketing – a mix of e-mail, mobile phone and WoM-generated communications – has been used by a number of companies to gain consumer product interest and thus lead to channel acceptance. Originally developed in Austria, bars refused to stock the energy drink, perceiving it to be a medicinal or health-related product rather than a mixer such as tonic or colas. Interest was stimulated amongst extreme sports participants and clubbers for the boost it gave them. Bars soon began to stock Red Bull, which mixed with vodka became the drink of choice in ski resorts. In other channels such as universities, brand ambassadors were recruited to host parties where Red Bull could be sampled. These activities led to the creation of the energy drink category in relevant channels.

Adapted from: Kumar and Linguri (2003).

Timing
Figure 5.5 suggests that information in the marketing channel passes in a *sequential* manner. That is, a message is delivered to different audiences through successive stages. This may be all dealers first, then all retailers. A more likely approach is to prioritize particular dealers or

wholesalers and to target messages at them successively. So, all A grade dealers receive the message first, then all B grade dealers, and then C grade dealers and so on. The problems associated with this approach are that the messages delivered to the As and Cs may be different to those perceived by the Bs. Such message deviance can have severe implications for channel performance. In addition, there are large costs associated with repeating the messages to different audiences.

The alternative is to use a *simultaneous* approach, whereby all members of the marketing channel are informed at the same time. The benefits are reduced costs, the same information is communicated so little or no information deviance or corruption, and the elapsed management time associated with the marketing communication exercise is reduced creating opportunities to undertake other work.

Sharing attitudes

Following Morgan and Hunt's idea that shared values are important to the development of trust, a sharing of information is important from a communication perspective.

The willingness of members to share information and associated resources is an important factor because it enables an openness between parties through which full information can be exchanged. Extranets engaging distributors and producers allow for fast, accurate, low-cost exchange of information, all intended to provide for customer satisfaction. However, the facility might need existing members to use it (Extranet) in order to realize the benefits. That means, for example, that the producer must be willing to share sensitive information, and the distributor must be willing to share information about themselves, their customers and markets. This concept is referred to as the propensity to share information and different organizations have different propensities in this respect, which will affect the quality of the relationships they have with other channel members.

 Activity 5.9

> Without referring back in this coursebook, write notes explaining the differences between a simultaneous and sequential flow of information.

The promotional mix in the marketing channel (Syllabus 3.1)

The role of marketing communications in the distribution channels is different to that used in consumer markets. So, it should not be a surprise to learn that the configuration of the promotional mix is different as well.

The role of marketing communications is different because the target audience is different (to consumer audiences), and their information needs and disposition are different.

Distributors are businesses and in that sense their buyer behaviour is characterized by group buying, different risks, a smaller number of orders, larger order values, infrequent purchases and purchase consequences that are very different to that experienced by consumers, namely greater visibility and the potential to affect the lives of many other people.

You will recall that the role of marketing communications can be considered in terms of the DRIP acronym. In terms of the channels, the below table shows the examples of possible needs:

Differentiate	Required downstream so that channel members understand how a manufacturer (and or products) adds value and is different from competitors and other products that they carry
	Required upstream to flag attention and to secure stock, support and resources
Reinforcement	Reminding downstream members of superior product features, benefits plus support facilities, reassuring them in terms of continuity, value and reliability
	Reminding upstream members of their needs, problems and required support
	Reassuring them that they are working hard on their behalf, that they have their interests in mind
Information	Provide downstream members with suitable levels of customer support
	Provide upstream members with market and performance information
Persuade	To encourage downstream members to carry (extra) stock, provide facilities and to meet required service levels
	To stimulate upstream members to allocate stock, promotional support and financial conditions in their favour

Source: Fill (2005)

Case study

Lipton offer international channel support with Yellow campaign

Unilever's Lipton tea brand introduced a 'Paint the world yellow' campaign in order to stimulate consumer interest through their various marketing channels. Lipton use a range of channels with different roles. In some, the objectives are to generate sales and in others to create positive brand experiences to communicate fun and vitality.

This involves point-of-sale activities in cafes, kiosks, leisure centres, offices and universities. The campaigns which are tailored to different markets in which the brand operates are targeted to achieve sales against more popular soft drinks. Didier Cumin, Global Channel Manager for Lipton, suggests such support is important to provide consumers with evidence which backs up advertising.

Source: www.unilever.com/brands/casestudies – accessed, 16 February 2004.

 Activity 5.10

Find examples of B2B marketing communications that demonstrate each of the elements in the DRIP framework.

To fulfil these roles, the communication mix needs to be configured appropriately. However, the fundamental principle is that personal selling is the main tool supported by direct marketing, sales promotions, public relations and exhibitions. Advertising often plays a minor role. In addition to this mix, the Internet, which is both a distribution channel and medium of communication, has transformed a large part of marketing communications activities.

Case study

Samsung

In early 2003, Samsung announced that it was planning to reorganize its internal structure in an attempt to change its reseller network. Resellers had apparently expressed some dissatisfaction about the varying incentives and sales promotions. By merging product divisions into a smaller number of super groups and building 10 new Samsung Solution Centres, each one close to major resellers, it was hoped to improve reseller trust and understanding.

Source: http://www.vnunet.com/News/1139317 – accessed, 16 March 2003.

Personal selling remains the main tool because it is through face-to-face encounters between people representing buying and selling organizations that interorganizational relationships are developed and maintained. Direct Marketing has had an increasing impact together with the Internet, releasing the salesforce to undertake more core work. You will recall that the propensity of organizations to share information is crucial to the development of a stronger and enduring relationship. The Internet fosters this propensity and enables organizations to share information.

The promotional mix has to deliver messages that are largely informational and which relate to product features and benefits. Advertising is expensive and relatively inefficient in achieving these aims whereas personal selling – supported with direct marketing and the Internet, plus exhibitions and sales literature – provides a potent and effective promotional mix. See Unit 2 for more details about the characteristics of each of these promotional tools.

Summary

The focus of this unit has been on the structure of the marketing channels, the roles and tasks of the membership plus the nature and form of the relationships that develop between the constituent inter-mediaries. Above all, however, it is the significance of marketing communications in the marketing channel that is the main issue to be considered.

Marketing channels are an important and vital aspect of the way organizations interact with one another. Contemporary marketing thought embraces the relationship marketing approach and this is featured heavily in this unit. In addition to considering the nature and reasons for conflict in the marketing channel, emphasis is given to the importance of relationships (and trust and commitment) plus the role of marketing communications in both preventing and resolving conflict.

Marketing communications activities in the marketing channel are different to those deployed for consumers and, indeed, end-user business customers. The reasons for these differences and the nature of the marketing communications need to be understood in order to operate successfully and develop suitable channel relationships.

Further study

The essential texts for the module provide more depth and breadth of most of the issues covered here. Issues concerning marketing channels and supply chain management are to be found in the business press and specialist academic journals.

Typical exam questions

Question 5.1

Recommend ways in which marketing communications might be used to help improve relationships and reduce levels of conflict among the different stakeholders.

(10 Marks)

Question 5.2

Consider the extent to which marketing communications should be used by a cosmetics manufacturer to develop trust and commitment with their key retailers.

(10 Marks)

Hints and tips

Although knowledge of the different channel structures is important to underpin the subject, students are reminded that their focus should always be on the implications of changes to channel structures for marketing communications. The applications of the Internet and digital-based communications are very significant and have had a major influence on the structure, content and relationships between members of the marketing channel.Keep practical examples of different kinds of channel issues and their related communications activities. Always make your notes relating communications to relationship issues wherever possible.

References

Coughlan, A.T., Anderson, Stern, L. and EL-Ansary, A. (2001) *Marketing Channels*, 6th edition, Englewood Cliffs, New Jersey: Prentice Hall.

Dibb, S., Simkin, L., Pride, W.M. and Ferrell, O.C. (2001) *Marketing Concepts and Strategies*, 4th European edition, NY: Houghton Mifflin.

Fill, C. (2005) *Marketing Communications: Engagement, Strategies and Tactics*, 4th edition, Harlow: Pearson Education.

Kumar, N. and Linguri, N. (2003) *Financial Times*, 8 August.

Morgan, R.M. and Hunt, S.D. (1994) 'The commitment-trust theory of relationship marketing', *Journal of Marketing*, **58**, July, 20–38.

Shipley, D. and Egan, C. (1992) 'Power, conflict and co-operation in brewer–tenant distribution channels', *International Journal of Service Industry Management*, **3**(4), 44–62.

www.csd.abdn.ac.uk/
www.reshare.com/managingcc.htm
www.unilever.com/brands/casestudies
www.vnunet.com/News/1118093
www.vnunet.com/News/1139317

unit 6
communication strategies and planning

Learning objectives

Communication is a significant element of the marketing mix and it is important to recognize that to be used to maximum effect, it should be planned and deployed strategically, and not as a series of *ad hoc* actions to meet short-term goals. A more detailed and in-depth focus on strategies will be at stage 3 of the CIM qualifications. However, it is important to have an appreciation of broad strategic approaches to marketing communications and planning.

As organizations become more result-orientated and demanding of the agencies they appoint, the need for thorough planning becomes more important. Differing communications strategies are used to reflect the ways in which communications are employed to reach different audiences based on achieving different objectives. Some aspects of this are covered in the section on marketing channels where push strategies dominate. Advertising and other forms of communications are used in different ways using different media than those that would be used to reach end-users.

After completion of this section you will be able to:

o Understand the characteristics associated with different communications strategies aimed at different stakeholder groups

o Evaluate the differences between marketing communications aimed at consumers (B2C) and organizations (B2B)

o Explain the importance of planning effectively using appropriate frameworks

o Demonstrate the significance of an integrated approach to planning

o Demonstrate the significance of budgeting and the methods used to determine budget levels.

Syllabus references covered: 1.4, 2.9, 2.13, 2.14, 3.1 (see also Unit 5).

Key definition

Pull strategies have a focus on communicating directly with customers. Push strategies recognize the roles played by intermediaries and other channel members, where communications are aimed at moving goods through those channels. Profile strategies are aimed at maintaining long-term relationships with all the organizations' stakeholders.

Marketing communication strategy – the 3Ps (Syllabus 2.9)

Introduction

In order to accomplish the promotional objectives or goals that have been established, it is necessary to formulate ways of achieving them. Strategies are used to meet the goals that we seek to achieve.

Some people regard marketing communications strategy as simply the combination of activities in the communications mix. The key issues really concern the overall direction of the programme, how it fits in with marketing and corporate strategy, and the targeting of primary messages in order to establish effective positions.

From a 'customer perspective' it is possible to observe three different types of customer needs and from that deduce that there could be three different types of communication objective and strategy to meet those needs. There are customers who are end-users, there are those who do not consume the product or service but add value to it as part of the marketing channel and finally there are stakeholders whose focus is not the product or service but the organization itself.

The first group of 'customers' requires product- service-based messages that aim to increase levels of awareness, build and/or reinforce attitudes, and so motivate them to buy the offering. They expect it to be available when they decide to enquire, experiment or make a repeat purchase. This approach is known as a *pull* strategy as it encourages consumers to pull the products through the channel network.

Members of the marketing channel require messages that encourage them (retailers, wholesalers and dealers) to take stock, to be motivated and committed to their partner organizations or participate in the movement of the product/service so as to make it available to end-user customers. Communication strategies in these circumstances are referred to as *push* strategies.

There are occasions when stakeholders need to understand how or what an organization's position is regarding particular issues. This approach seeks to influence attitudes towards the company and is referred to as a *profile* strategy. These three strategies are considered in turn.

Therefore, the three main types of audience can be identified broadly as customers, members of the marketing channels and all other stakeholders who are connected to the organization or the brand in question. Communication strategy may be referred to as the 3Ps:

Pull strategies to reach customers (consumers and businesses)
Push strategies to reach members of the marketing channel
Profile strategies to reach all relevant stakeholders.

Each of these strategies will now be explored in turn.

Pull strategy

Here the objective is to stimulate demand by encouraging consumers (and end-user businesses) to 'pull' products through the marketing channel network (Figure 6.1). However, a pull strategy requires a core message to support it, to reflect the different opportunities that are available to position a brand.

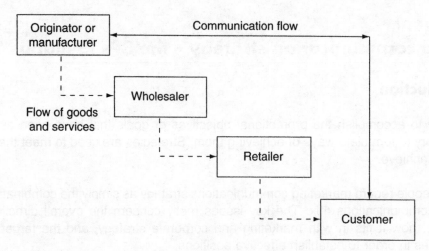

Figure 6.1 Direction of communication in a pull strategy
Source: Fill (2005)

 Activity 6.1

Write down what DRIP stands for without referring back to Unit 1.

You will (hopefully!) have remembered that this means to differentiate, reinforce (remind/reassure), inform and persuade an audience.

A pull strategy might be used to reposition a brand, to *differentiate* a brand from its competitors and to add value so that a customer clearly understands what the brand means and what it can do for them. For example, Thorntons, the chocolate manufacturers and retailers, have recently repositioned themselves so that they now wish to be seen as a part of giving gifts. The message, therefore, is about differentiation and gifts.

A campaign objective might be to *remind* lapsed customers of the brand values and so encourage them to begin buying the brand once again. For example, Specsavers Opticians use marketing communications generically to build association between the need for good eyesight and their brand. In some instances, the strategy serves to ensure that the brand is brought towards the front of the consumer's mind. In others, it will seek to communicate specific benefits or uses of the brand which may have been forgotten. Or, perhaps it will suggest new uses which will make the brand more relevant to the consumer's needs. Alternatively, the strategy might be to *reassure* customers that their recent purchase was a wise one.

Many campaigns aim to keep audiences informed in order to keep a brand alive in their minds. New variants (e.g. tastes, colours, packaging and performance ability) may need to be communicated. Very often, the goal is to build awareness levels so that when a customer thinks of a product category they immediately think of a particular brand. So, dog owners need tinned dog food (product category) and then think of their (dog's) preferred individual brand.

At various times in the life of a brand, it is important to raise the level of awareness among target consumers. Inevitably, this is most often associated with the introduction of a new product. However, either because of competition or other pressures (perhaps a reduction in the levels of marketing communications support), the levels of awareness of a particular brand may fall, and it is necessary to improve these levels. In some instances, although the consumer may be aware of the product itself, they will need information as to where to purchase it (particularly if it is in limited distribution). Advertising will seek to identify stockists of the product.

Many people argue that marketing communications is used to deliberately *persuade* a target audience to *behave* in a particular way. For example, this might be to buy and/or try a product, attend a retailer's sale, telephone for a catalogue, visit a website or to collect tokens or ring pulls with a view to taking part in a sales promotion event. It could also be argued that communication is used to *persuade* an audience to *think* in a particular way.

From time to time, marketing research may reveal a dissonance between the stance of the brand and the desired positioning. Perhaps the image of the brand has become 'old fashioned' or more recently introduced competitor products are seen to have greater relevance to current needs.

 ## Activity 6.2

Identify examples of where advertising has sought to remind customers of a brand or benefit.

Often, the role of advertising is to remind consumers (particularly in the case of routine purchases) of the original reasons why they chose the product. In some instances, such advertising will reassert the original values of the brand either to offset competitive pressures or simply to reassure consumers that those brand values have not been changed. Kellogg's, for example, ran a campaign with the broad theme 'If it doesn't say Kellogg's on the box, it isn't Kellogg's in the packet' to reduce the encroachment of retailer products which might otherwise be confused with the leading brand.

All the tools of the promotional mix, with the exception of public relations, are capable of persuading audiences to buy a brand. However, in consumer markets, advertising and sales promotions are the most often used tools; and in B2B markets, personal selling is the traditional potent force.

The Strong theory of advertising reflects the persuasion view and the Weak theory is reflected in the remind/reassurance strategies. It should also be noted that not only do both these campaign strategies need to inform and make audiences aware but also that a pull strategy may try to differentiate and persuade or inform and persuade or differentiate and inform an audience. Indeed any combination might be applicable, according to the contextual conditions.

Case study

London Eye strategy pulls customers

The London Eye, part of British Airways, developed a range of communications aimed at generating new business. An annual marketing budget of £1.5 million was aimed at increasing passenger numbers via highly focused advertising and other promotional activities.

Londoners were encouraged to take further rides with joint tickets for a 'flight' followed by a champagne meal at a nearby restaurant. Overseas visitors were targeted with an online campaign combined with outdoor advertisements at key points of entry into the UK. Joint student tickets with Tate Britain for the Turner Prize exhibition were offered. This was promoted through student bars and student union mailings, resulting in 300 redemptions.

Other new initiatives included a 45-minute Thames cruise, guide books, trained capsule hosts to answer questions during flights and the relaunch of the website www.Londoneye.com.

The overseas campaign led to an increase of 5 per cent in visitor numbers year on year. Within 3 months, 7800 Londoners had taken up the flight and meal offer. Overall activity has seen an 8 per cent growth in visitor numbers to over 4 million and an increase in gross profit by 23 per cent.

Adapted from: An article in *Marketing Business*, March 2004. The campaigns led to the London Eye winning the CIM Marketing Effectiveness Award for 2003 in the Leisure and Travel sector. For more information see the CIM website – www.cim.co.uk/casestudies.

Frequency of purchase

For products and services which are bought routinely, the fundamental role of marketing communications is to reinforce the values associated with the brand, and to ensure a high level of pack recognition at the point of purchase. Consumers do not spend a long time evaluating the available alternatives. They will possess adequate information on which to make the purchase decision, and advertising must ensure that the brand values are sufficiently well known and 'front of mind' to ensure that the brand, at the very least, is included on the shortlist of products to be considered.

For products and services which are purchased on a less regular basis, the primary task is to provide the necessary levels of reassurance for the consumer that the purchase is an appropriate one. Since the purchase itself is undertaken less frequently, the advertising will need to remind the consumer of the benefits associated with using the brand, and to establish clear advantages relative to the competition. Sometimes, these will be tangible benefits relating to particular attributes of the brand, such as taste, quality, economy and so on. In other instances, these will be emotional benefits, such as good motherhood (caring for the needs of the family), or social values (the type of people who use the product or service).

In the context of products which require more extensive problem-solving – as we have seen previously, these are normally expensive and very infrequently purchased items – the role of advertising will be both to establish the specific values of the brand and to provide much of the necessary information upon which the purchase decision will be made. Sometimes, advertising in such instances will attempt to establish the evaluative criteria which the consumer will use in the making of brand comparisons. It will indicate suggested criteria for choice and, not unreasonably, demonstrate how it performs better than the competition against these given criteria.

Activity 6.3

How does the role of marketing communications differ when the product is a fast-moving consumer good as opposed to a consumer durable?

It is important to make a distinction between the dimensions of purchasing behaviour. Not all products are purchased for rational reasons, although these may be important in the context of justifying the particular purchase to others.

Consumer and business-to-business marketing communications

Business-to-business communications is the promotion of goods and services to organizations rather than individuals. The B2C communications is the domain of communications aimed directly at end-user consumers and most closely associated with pull strategies.

Business-to-business communications are traditionally referred to as 'industrial marketing communications', however, this term fails to recognize the diversity of the products and buyers involved within this area. The importance of the sector is underpinned by the extraordinary development of Internet-based marketing communications in this sector, compared with the relatively sluggish growth in B2C market.

It is also a reflection of the fact that many B2B markets are larger than most consumer goods markets. There are, of course, a number of similarities and differences between the B2C and B2B markets and some of these are depicted in Table 6.1.

Table 6.1 Similarities and differences between B2C and B2B marketing communications

Business-to-business markets	Consumer markets
Use company money	Use own money
Small number of buyers	Large number of buyers
Group buying decision	Individual or family decision
Extended buying timescales	Often short timescales
The similarities	
All buying decisions are taken by people	

It is often believed that, consumers often make emotionally driven buying decisions based on the image dimensions of a brand, whereas organizations base their decisions on a more rational consideration of the information that is available. This, to say the least, is something of an oversimplification. Companies, as such, take no decisions at all. The decision to purchase or not to purchase a particular good or service on behalf of the company is taken by one or more individuals. These, in other circumstances, are the same people who are responsible for buying goods and services on their own behalf or for the benefit of their families. Whatever role they fulfil, they are influenced by the same demographics, personalities, aspirations, lifestyles and so on. Both consumer purchases and B2B purchase decisions are, therefore, influenced by a complicated array of factors, some rational and some irrational.

Activity 6.4

How will the approach to marketing communications differ between a company selling a conventional consumer product and one involved in B2B marketing?

However, it is important to recognize some key differences between the two types of market. First, in the business context, buyers are using the *company's money* and not their own, and this fact may have ramifications for the way in which they consider the purchase.

Not only is it important that they spend the company's money in a way that delivers value for money, it must be perceived as achieving that. For many years, the litany of 'Nobody ever got fired for specifying IBM' dimensionalized this factor. So long as IBM was perceived as the primary source of computing equipment, the purchase decision was unlikely to be challenged, even if it failed to deliver the best value.

A second consideration is, in many instances, the relatively *small number* of potential buyers in B2B markets. Often, the target audience for a company's products or services may be numbered in the hundreds, rather than the many millions of potential consumers in the vast majority of retail markets.

The most important difference, however, is that with only a few exceptions organizational buying decisions are taken by *groups* of people rather than individuals. A key strategic issue may, therefore, relate to the identification of the individuals who comprise the DMU rather than any one person.

The decision-making unit

In many company purchasing decisions, it is unusual that a single person will have the necessary authority to arrange the purchase. Often there will be several people, fulfilling different functions within the organization, who will all contribute to the DMU. Each of them will need to be exposed to the product or service proposition, and it is quite likely that they will require different aspects of the offering to be detailed. Some, for example, will be interested in the performance of the product itself; others in the financial aspects of the proposition; yet others in the technical aspects of integration with existing machinery or materials and so on.

Activity 6.5

What is the role of the decision-making unit? How should the members of the unit be targeted by marketing communications?

Another important distinction between B2B and consumer goods marketing is that the product itself may be *modified* to suit the needs of the individual user, as indeed can other aspects of the specification (Table 6.2). Despite the fact that the product is often more complex than its consumer equivalent, the nature of satisfying the consumer's needs may be dealt with by adaptation to the specific requirements of the customer. Adjustments may be made in the terms of trade, delivery, training of the user's staff, repairs and spare parts to ensure that the offer matches the individual needs of the customer.

Moreover, because the typical B2B market is comparatively small, *personal contact* is the most widely used method of communication. Often the scale of the order, the length of the negotiations and the technical nature of the purchase will demand that the supplier maintains in-depth contact on a regular basis with the potential customer. The role of other forms of marketing communications is often to provide the essential support to the personal selling effort.

Table 6.2 Difference between consumer and business-to-business marketing communications

	Consumer-orientated markets	Business-to-business markets
Message reception	Informal	Formal
Number of decision-makers	Single or few	Many
Balance of the promotional mix	Advertising and sales promotions dominate	Personal selling dominates
Specificity and integration	Broad use of promotional mix with a move towards co-ordinated mixes	Specific use of below-the-tools but with a high level of co-ordination and integration
Message content	Greater use of emotions and imagery	Greater use of rational, logic and information-based messages although there is evidence of a move towards the use of imagery
Length of decision time	Normally short	Longer and more involved
Negative communications	Limited to people close to the purchaser/user	Potentially an array of people in the organization and beyond
Target marketing and research	Great use of sophisticated targeting and communication approaches	Limited but increasing use to targeting and segmentation approaches
Budget allocation	Majority of budget allocated to brand management	Majority of budget allocated to sales management
Evaluation and measurement	Great variety of techniques and approaches used	Limited number of techniques and approaches

Source: Fill (2005)

Marketing communications in the B2B sector have been transformed by technological advances and the Internet in particular. Through the use of extranets and intranets, organizations are able to work together more closely, build relationships and free other resources for more effective work.

In the B2B sector, marketing communications can fulfil a variety of specific objectives which will vary according to the circumstances:

1. To create and maintain awareness
2. To generate sales leads
3. To pre-sell sales calls
4. To contact minor members of the DMU
5. To build corporate and product images
6. To communicate technical information
7. To support the promotional effort.

While personal selling is often the most motivating form of communications, it is also the most expensive technique, and other forms of marketing communications must be used to ensure maximum cost-effectiveness. As with consumer goods marketing, B2B communications will depend on the successful identification of the appropriate mix of communications tools to achieve the objectives.

The *planning process* is, essentially, the same as that for other forms of marketing communications, and it is important to identify the key objectives of the activity at the outset. Inevitably, however, given both the nature of the objectives and the scale of the budgets available, the planning considerations may be somewhat different.

 Activity 6.6

> Prepare an *outline* marketing communications plan for a company involved in industrial cleaning. You have a marketing communications budget of £75 000.

Co-ordinated marketing communications is no less important here than in other areas of business. Indeed, it might be argued that the relative sizes of budgets require an even more careful consideration of the dimensions of co-ordination to ensure that every element of the marketing communications campaign reinforces the others.

Increasingly, organizations are seeking to achieve a balance between their external and internal communications in order that they present the same series of core messages. For example, product literature, direct marketing activity, exhibitions, videos, website design plus all corporate branding materials reinforce the core proposition. Over time these messages need to be reinforced and, where appropriate, altered to reflect the changing perceptions of the organization held by different stakeholders.

Although direct marketing techniques are increasingly being applied to consumer goods and services, they are especially relevant to the B2B area. Indeed, to a far greater degree, B2B marketing relies on the underlying mechanics of direct marketing as a key platform for marketing communications. There are a number of reasons which serve to explain this situation.

The need to create and reinforce awareness

The interval between purchases in B2B sectors may be extremely long and relationships with alternative suppliers may be quite strong. In this context, organizations need to ensure cost-effective contact with potential purchasers over an extended time period in order to maintain an awareness of their company and its products at a reasonable level.

For many organizations, direct marketing represents the most cost-effective solution to their marketing communications requirements. In this context, direct marketing can ensure:

1. Cost-effective-lead generation by maintaining regular contact with potential purchasers and prospects.
2. Corporate and product awareness, by targeting specific messages which are 'tailored' to the needs of named individuals or job functions.
3. A more effective sales visit, by ensuring that prospects have pre-awareness of the proposition and may be motivated to request a sales call.

Push strategy

The objective with a push strategy is to influence members of the marketing channel (intermediaries). The influence is intended to stimulate demand by encouraging these channel partners to take and hold stock, to allocate scarce resources such as shelf space, and to become advocates of the product. As well as a product purchase orientation, there is also a strong need to provide information, support and encourage participation with a view to building long-term relationships (Figure 6.2).

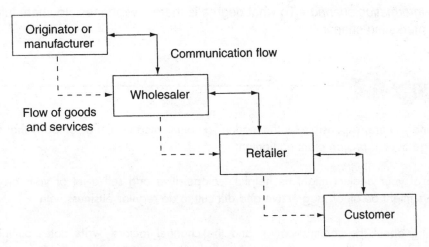

Figure 6.2 Direction of communications in a push strategy
Source: Fill (2005)

Channel intermediaries include dealers, wholesalers, agents, value-added resellers, distributors and retailers. These organizations must co-operate to achieve their own objectives. Communication within networks serves not only to provide persuasive information and foster participative decision-making, but also enables co-ordination, the exercise of power and the encouragement of loyalty and commitment, so as to reduce the likelihood of tension and conflict.

The various channel networks have become even more complex, and the expectations of buyers in these networks have risen in parallel with the significance attached to them by manufacturers. This impacts upon the choice of appropriate marketing communications strategies and tools. Multiple retailers, such as Tesco, have the power to dictate terms to many manufacturers of branded goods. This includes the type and form of promotions.

Communications in marketing channel networks (Syllabus 3.1)

Some of these issues have been covered in more detail in Unit 5 but it is worth further consideration in this strategic context. Communication flows within networks do not usually change radically in the short term. What is more likely is that they become set so that the communication becomes standardized. A planned channel-orientated communications strategy, a push strategy, should contribute to and reinforce the partnerships in the network. There are many factors that can influence channel communication strategy but most notably the following need to be highlighted.

1. *Power* – Are some organizations more important than others (including your own organization)?
2. *Direction* – Are communications one-way or two-way?
3. *Frequency* – How often should messages be sent?
4. *Timing* – Should messages be sent to all members simultaneously or serially?
5. *Style and content* – Should messages be formal/informal? What must be included?
6. *Distortion* – Will messages be received, stored and acted upon as the originator intends?
7. *Information sharing* – To what degree is there a willingness to share information in the marketing channel?

 Activity 6.7

Imagine you are responsible for the marketing communications of a company that manufactures a range of construction plant equipment.

Some of your dealers might be helpful, co-operative and sell a lot of your products. Other dealers might be aloof, aggressive and difficult to do regular business with.

Thinking about the communication and the channel factors, write notes outlining how the communications with these different types of dealers might be different.

The development of electronic communications and extranets in particular has helped organizations develop stronger, closer relationships in the marketing channel. These serve to not only bind organizations together but they also represent switching costs which may deter organizations from leaving the channels in which they currently participate.

A push strategy is not complete unless supported by a core message. The *DRIP* acronym is equally applicable here as:

1. Differentiation is required in order that intermediaries understand how a manufacturer differentiates an offering and what is of added value, in other words positioning is equally important.
2. Reminding and reassuring dealers about the quality or utility of the products or the manufacturer.
3. Information is constantly required by distributors and retailers in order that they provide suitable levels of customer service.
4. Persuasion is always necessary to encourage intermediaries to take stock, provide facilities and preference over other suppliers.

Examples and cases relating to push-based strategies can be found in Unit 5.

Profile strategy

On some occasions it is necessary to communicate with all stakeholders to convey information about the organization itself rather than its products and services. Issues concerning company performance, its stance on particular policies or just to portray the organization in a positive light to encourage investors and attract the best employees. The task here is to project an appropriate corporate identity in order to build and maintain a solid reputation, hence the term 'Profile strategy'.

Traditionally these activities have been referred to as corporate communications, as they deal, more or less exclusively, with the corporate entity or organization. Corporate communications is the process that translates corporate identity into corporate image and whilst all the tools of the promotional mix have an important role to play, public relations can be the dominant tool. Co-ordinated marketing communications requires that public relations operates within an overall communication framework and this really needs one very senior person to assume responsibility for the organization's total communications.

Identifying different stakeholder groups and determining their attitudes and motivations is an important part of stakeholder analysis. Acting on this information to shape stakeholder perceptions of, and involvement with, the organization is a communications function. This shaping is referred to as a profile strategy.

A profile communications strategy is required to address all matters of structure and internal communications, and the conflicting needs of different stakeholders so as to produce a set of consistent messages, all within the context of a coherent corporate identity programme. You will recall that IMC requires that internal messages to (and from) employees and managers blends with those messages that are sent to (and received from) stakeholders that are external to the organization.

It is possible to identify three central elements to a profile strategy: corporate personality, identity and image (Abratt, 1989).

1. *Corporate personality* – Determined by the internal culture as well as the strategic purpose. Organizational culture reflects the values, beliefs and preferred ways of staff. The degree to which strategy is either formalized and planned or informal and emergent, and whether strategy is well communicated, also plays a major role in shaping the personality of the organization.
2. *Corporate identity* – The way the organization presents itself to its stakeholders. It is the outward projection of who and what the organization is, to its various audiences. To do this it uses identity cues, some of which are planned, and some of which are unplanned and accidental.
3. *Corporate image* – It is the audience's response and images they form of the organization as a result of interpreting the various identity cues. Image results from interpreting the identity cues. Corporate reputation develops through the accumulated images and experiences of an organization and its products.

Organizations, like individuals, project their personalities through their identity. The actual perception of identity results in an image formed and retained by stakeholders. Organizations can and do have multiple images and must develop strategies that attempt to stabilize, and if possible equalize, them.

There may be a gap between actual and desired perception. The scale and significance of such a corporate perception gap may vary for different stakeholders. If a large number of stakeholders appear to view the organization in ways that are very different from how it perceives itself or wishes to be perceived, then communication strategies must address this large gap and attempt to narrow or close it. For example, British Airways is perceived as an expensive airline, and the media strategy based upon TV and its PR work on the relaunch of Concorde are a stark contrast to the price-based positioning used by Ryanair and easyJet who predominantly use newspapers and outdoor media. British Airways needs to correct the misperception, as a large number of their fares are very competitive and they provide a host of value-added services that these competitors have stripped out.

If only a small number of stakeholders perceive a large gap, then a targeted adjustment strategy should aim at those stakeholders while taking care to protect the correct image held by the majority. If a minority of stakeholders see a small gap, a monitoring strategy would be appropriate and resources would be better deployed elsewhere.

If the majority of stakeholders perceived a small difference, a maintenance strategy would be advisable and the good corporate communications continued. The natural extension of this approach is to use it as a base tool in the determination of the communication budget. Funds could be allocated according to the size of the perceived perception gap. These different strategies are depicted in Figure 6.3.

Corporate reputation is about the management of the corporate personality, corporate identity and corporate image. Corporate image is managed through the use of the identity cues. It is important that the variety of these cues is understood.

Case study

Gold raises profile

Gold producers have been seeking new ways to revive flagging interest. The World Gold Council which represents gold producers accounting for some 35 per cent of global output has taken a different approach to the production of advertising for most recent campaigns. Traditionally, products such as gold and other luxury goods would seek to raise their profile using professional models and photographers. Now photographers from National Geographic have been used in order to show that ordinary people have a connection with gold. There is currently an image problem amongst consumers. Global sales have been lower not least as a result of disposable income being spent on electronic gadgets and holidays.

Some other gold producers have taken a more conventional approach in terms of advertising strategy, teaming up with fashion magazines, such as Harpers Bazaar in the US. This provides the South African producer, Anglogold, the opportunity to access the magazine's database of readers, allowing more targeted promotions. The gold campaigns focused on the US as the largest market for gold jewellery in terms of value, India which is the largest by volume, China as it is developing fast, Italy as the largest exporter and design innovation centre and the Middle East where gold is seen as both an investment as well as being attractive to wear.

Billboards and magazines are popular media along with point-of-sale materials and website www.speakgold.com. The advertising platform demonstrates the emotional bonds between the user, mainly female and how it is used in different situations.

Adapted from: An article by Kevin Morrison in the *Financial Times*, 6 January 2005.

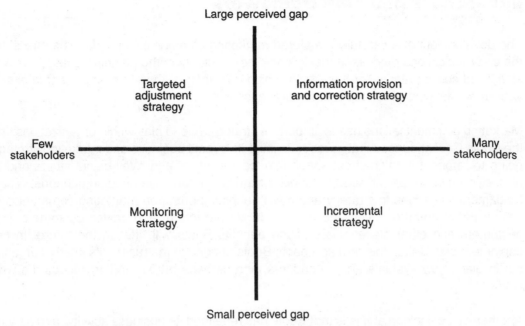

Figure 6.3 Corporate perception grid
Source: Fill (2002)

Case study

Corporate sponsorship raises local profile

The Northern Rock bank has taken a long-term view when developing a charitable trust, the Northern Rock Foundation, into which it contributes 5 per cent of annual pre-tax profits. The Foundation distributes to worthy causes focused in the Bank's Northeast home region. As with other corporate giving schemes, Northern Rock benefit from association with the PR generated from the schemes and projects it supports. These have more recently included development of the Alnwick Garden project and the Sage Gateshead music centre. Many of the project supported are less high profile, but equally significant in developing the Foundation's long-term strategy and recognizes the company's heritage.

Adapted from: An article by Chris Tighe in the *Financial Times*, 30 September 2004.

 ## Activity 6.8

Consider an organization with which you are familiar and try to determine the characteristics of the internal culture.

How do you describe the culture and what would you say describes the personality of the organization?

Communications planning frameworks

The development of a carefully structured marketing communications plan is a critical facet of the communications process. If there is any lack of clarity in the planning phase, this will have significant consequences for the activity which follows. It is, therefore, important to ensure that your understanding of the topic is comprehensive.

Marketing communications has an important strategic role to play within organizations. In 2001, the Boots Co. announced that it was redefining its overall business and marketing strategy, was going to reformat its high-street shops into 'convenience' and 'Well-being' stores and that its alliance with Granada will see the launch of a digital interactive shopping channel. These are fundamental changes to strategy and it will be incumbent upon marketing communications to deliver messages that reflect the new strategy, that inform and advise customers, potential customers and other stakeholders of the benefits Boots will offer in the future. In order to implement and sustain this new approach, Boots needed to restructure its internal organization, put in place new systems and procedures, and perhaps retrain and/or refocus the way staff work.

Another way of looking at this is that Boots has redefined its business activity, and as a result it needed to reposition itself so that customers understood what the Boots brand promises to deliver. The issues here concern marketing strategy, staff and customer perceptions, positioning and branding. All these are important aspects of marketing communications strategy and each is considered in more detail later in this book.

Strategy is not necessarily the same as planning. Strategy might be considered as the purpose and direction of the organization, whereas planning might be considered to be the articulation of the strategic intent. In other words, strategy is about where an organization is headed and planning is about the detail concerning how that strategy is to be accomplished.

Marketing communications strategy is about how an organization can successfully communicate and deliver its marketing strategy, and this inevitably involves a rich complexity of organization, market, human, product and corporate branding issues.

Planning and frameworks

The development of a cohesive and co-ordinated marketing communications plan demands the adoption of a systematic process to ensure that all dimensions of the plan are carefully and thoroughly considered. There is no such thing as the 'ideal' planning format. Each plan must be adapted to meet the specific circumstances which need to be addressed. However, a planning framework can help ensure that all necessary aspects are considered when developing a marketing communications campaign.

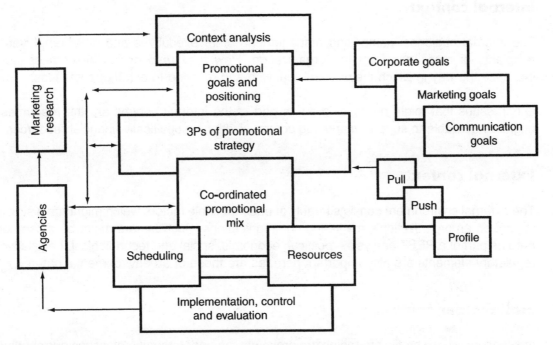

Figure 6.4 The marketing communications planning framework (MCPF)
Source: Fill (2005)

Figure 6.4 sets out the marketing communication planning framework (MCPF). This serves a number of purposes. One is to identify specific aspects of such a plan, the general order in which they occur and to suggest that all the parts are integrated as part of an overall plan. There are linkages between the many parts and these linkages are the 'oil' that makes the plan mobile, that makes it work. A context analysis, looking at different aspects of the organization's situation, will provide the bases for establishing communications objectives. These 'contexts' include business, customer, internal, external and stakeholder. These provide an underpinning which allows further strategic development. The overall context is of course marketing communications with the purpose of the analysis being the production of a coherent and logical strategic marketing communications plan. The context analysis will provide the bases for establishing frameworks for co-ordination of marketing communications activities and it is worth exploring briefly the major aspects of each context.

Business context

The business or market context is important as it is necessary to appreciate the trading/ operating conditions, to know whether the market is growing or declining, to understand the communications tactics and positions of competitors and to understand the segments in which all players are operating.

Customer context

Those issues considered in Unit 1 concerning buyer behaviour are fundamental and of increasing significance in this context. Customers, lapsed customers and potential customers are at the heart of marketing and marketing communications. Purchasing behaviour and the way people understand the world around them is influenced by many different factors.

Internal context

The internal audience, comprising management, other executives and other employees are recipients of messages from the organization. How they respond to these messages will influence the way in which they in turn deal with and respond to external audiences.

Other issues that might be considered as part of the internal context are the resources that might be available to support marketing communications, specifically financial resources.

External context

The external environment consists largely of uncontrollable factors which might have significant impact on an organization's marketing communications. Such factors might be those considered as part of a PEST analysis – political, economic, social and technological. Legislative and regulatory elements are also important here, as are those of an environmental nature.

Stakeholder context

In situations where profile strategies are prevalent, an understanding of issues surrounding the range of stakeholders to be communicated with are important. Stakeholder groups, such as investors, financial institutions, trade associations, government bodies, pressure groups and so on, have different communications needs both in terms of the information they need and how they are to be communicated with.

Determining the marketing communications budget (Syllabus 2.14)

A key task within the framework of marketing communications is the appropriate determination of the levels of expenditure required to fulfil the task established. The amount of money spent on marketing communications differs widely among companies, even within the same industry.

Regular perusal of magazines, such as *Marketing Week*, will give examples of budgets for the support of major brands. Some recent examples include: 'BBH wins £19 million global Smirnoff drinks business', 'Mindshare wins £700 million Unilever media account', 'Publicis Dialog wins £10 million Powergen (direct and digital) account', 'BBH wins £53 million ad account (diary brand) Flora', 'McCann-Erickson Worldwide wins Cadbury Schweppes' £38 million chewing gum and mint account', 'DLKW now overseas almost £40 million of Vauxhall Motors' £56 million advertising budget'.

The primary issue is that of identifying the reasons for this wide variation in expenditure patterns, and of determining an effective approach to the setting of a budgetary level. It should be clear that the determination of the correct level of expenditure must depend on a proper analysis of the context, rather than the use of 'norms', rule of thumb, or 'gut-feel'. According to Simon Broadbent, author of *The Advertising Budget*, the amount to be spent is determined by a process, not a formula. Hence, there is no simple solution. Various methods of budget determination have been suggested and the issue is one of deciding which approach is right for the situation.

In the course of this unit, we will examine some of the most important approaches that have been suggested and consider their application to the real environment. The following list gives most of the ways used to determine the budget:

1. Percentage of previous year's turnover (sales)
2. Percentage of product gross margin
3. Residue of last year's surplus
4. Percentage of anticipated turnover
5. Unit or case/sales ratio method
6. Competitive expenditure/parity
7. Share of voice
8. Media inflation
9. Objective-and-task method
10. Experimentation
11. What we can afford.

Percentage of sales

Probably the most widely used method of budget determination is the calculation of a ratio between past expenditure and sales. The calculation itself is quite straightforward. The previous year's expenditures are calculated as a percentage of total sales, and the resultant figure is used to calculate the budget for the coming year. Thus, if £12 million worth sales was achieved against a communications budget of £300 000, the percentage would be 2.5 per cent. Assuming that the sales forecast for the coming year was £15 million, this would yield a budget of £375 000.

While the process is a quick and easy one, there are flaws in the argument. In the first place, the data used will be considerably out of date by the time that it is implemented. As we do not have a full picture of the current year's sales, we must rely on, at best, the latest 12 months for which we have information on which to base our calculations for next year's activity. Second, the model creates a situation in which the budget only increases against an expectation of higher sales. If sales are expected to decline, then the future communications budget must be reduced to bring it into line with the defined ratio. The inherent danger is that a brand that is under threat – and losing volume – actually has a reduced budget rather than an increased one. Third, the model fails to recognize that marketing communications activity can create sales volume for a brand. The application of the principle, in fact, operates in reverse – with sales being the determinant of expenditure levels.

 Activity 6.9

> Given that your objective is to increase your share of the £550 million pet food market from 10 to 15 per cent, and the leading brands spend approximately £7–9 million on advertising, what marketing communications budget would you recommend, and how would you support your argument?

Percentage of product gross margin

This approach is, essentially, similar to the previous one, except that the gross margin rather than the level of sales is used as the basis for calculating the future level of expenditure. Here, a percentage of either the past or expected gross margin – net sales less the cost of goods – is used.

157

Residue of previous year's surplus

This method is entirely based on prior performance, whereby the excess of income over costs in the previous year is designated as the budget for the following year. Although simple in principle, it clearly demands that a surplus is achieved in order for money to be spent in any future period. It fails to recognize the need for investment in growth brands or, for that matter, the impact of competitive activities.

Percentage of anticipated turnover

This approach is based on the allocation of a fixed percentage of future turnover to the marketing communications budget.

Activity 6.10

After several years of growth, your market has begun to decline at a rate of approximately 5 per cent per annum. Although your share has held up, the volume has begun to decline.

What recommendations would you make, as brand leader, for the setting of next year's marketing communications budget?

Unit or case/sales ratio method

This method, sometimes referred to as the case rate, requires that brand volumes for the next year are estimated and a fixed sum per unit is allocated towards marketing communications expenditure. It is then a simple process of multiplying the expected sales volume (in units or cases) by the fixed allocation to arrive at a total communications budget.

In some instances, comparisons are made between the company's own case rate and those of its competitors in order to explore the relationships between them. Obviously the approach is a simple one, but it begs the question as to how the case rate itself is calculated. In some instances, it may be based on past experience. Usually it is a company or industry norm.

Here again, as with other ratio-based approaches, expenditure patterns reflect past achievement or anticipated sales. As such, the method tends to benefit growth brands and disadvantage those which are declining. It ignores the fact that a brand which is suffering in the marketplace may need increased levels of expenditure in order to arrest the decline, rather than a reduced budget which would be the automatic result of applying the method.

Competitive expenditure

Another frequently used approach is to base a brand's expenditure levels on an assessment of competitors' expenditures. Often a calculation is made of the level of category expenditure and a percentage – usually related to a brand's share of market – is chosen as the basis of calculating the expenditure levels for the brand. In other instances, an attempt is made to achieve parity with a nominated competitor by setting a similar level of expenditure to theirs.

At the very least, this approach has the benefit of ensuring that brand expenditure levels are maintained in line with those of the competition. However, it suffers from the obvious difficulty of being able to make an accurate assessment of the level of competitors' spends. While it is obviously possible to obtain a reasonable fix on advertising spend from published information, the same is not true of sales promotional spend and other categories of marketing communications. Figures for the latter are rarely published. Moreover, the model fails to recognize that the expenditure patterns of a competitor may well be dictated by a totally different set of problems and objectives.

Share of Voice (SoV)

This approach is an extension of the previous one, where management relates the volume share of the product category to expenditure within the category as a whole, and is primarily related to advertising expenditure. Thus, if a brand has a 15 per cent share of the market in which it competes, and total advertising expenditure for the category is £8 million, in order to retain a proportional share of voice a budget of £1.2 million would need to be set. By the same token, the company would have a benchmark against which to establish the levels of expenditure required to drive a brand forward. Hence, it might decide to increase its share of voice to, say, 20 or even 25 per cent in an attempt to gain a greater level of visibility for its brand and a greater share of the overall category. Conversely, it may decide to underspend relative to its competitors and market share. This may be due to profit-taking motives or sheer economies of scale that large brands, in particular, are able to generate through their overall communication effort.

These issues of relative spend are very important as they indicate not only competitive but also strategic communication intention.

Activity 6.11

You are attempting to introduce a new product to the £670 million hot beverage market and are targeting a share of 5 per cent in year one. Describe what factors you would consider to help you determine the budget for marketing communications?

Media inflation

This approach makes the simple assumption that a budget – usually the previous year's – should be increased in line with the growth in media costs to ensure a similar delivery of the message to the target audience. At the lowest level, this approach ensures that the real level of advertising expenditure is maintained. However, it fails to acknowledge any of the other variables which will have an impact on the achievement of marketing objectives.

Objective-and-task method

This method is based on a more realistic examination of the specific objectives which the marketing plan needs to meet, and was established as an attempt to apply a more scientific approach to budget determination. The basis of the approach was a paper commissioned by the American Association of National Advertisers and published in 1961. In the paper 'Defining advertising goals for measuring advertising results' (DAGMAR) the author, Russell Colley, proposed that advertising should be specifically budgeted to accomplish defined goals or objectives.

The DAGMAR approach – also known as the objective-and-task method – requires that specific objectives for the campaign are defined at the outset. These may be expressed in terms of, for example, increasing brand awareness, encouraging sampling and trial, promoting repeat purchase and so on. In each case, a finite numerical target is given and the costs of achieving this target are calculated. The resultant budget is thus based on a series of goals rather than on past or future results and is thus the most realistic in marketing terms.

The method offers the benefit of being able to monitor the campaign achievement against the targets set and provides a more accurate guide to budgetary determination for the future. The limitation on the accuracy of the method is the ability to access sufficient information to ensure that all relevant variables can be considered.

Although the original paper is dealt specifically with the task of establishing advertising budgets, the method is equally applicable to other areas of marketing communications.

Activity 6.12

Why is the objective-and-task method of budget determination increasingly preferred over other approaches?

Experimentation

A guiding principle for budget determination, as with other aspects of marketing, is the need to, on the one hand, protect the company investment; while, on the other, ensuring that sufficient new and innovatory approaches are taken to drive the brand forward. It is for this reason that most major marketing companies use an experimental approach at various times.

Having established the overall marketing communications budget by the normal or most appropriate means, it is possible to create a 'mini-test market' for the purposes of experimenting with a variation. By isolating, say, one region of the country, it is possible to experiment with alternative budget constructions. In many cases, and in the absence of definitive data, it is useful to determine the impact of, for example, an increased level of media expenditure or of a particular sales promotion technique.

The benefit of this approach is that the main sources of business are 'protected', in the sense that they receive the 'normal' support levels. Hence, the position of the brand is not unduly prejudiced. By 'hot housing' a different approach, real experience can be gained and the budgetary process enhanced with the additional knowledge.

The method thus represents an attempt to apply an empirical approach and, therefore, a more scientific method to the process of budget determination. However, it is important to restrict the number of 'experiments' in order to ensure that the data are readable against the norm, and that the individual variables can be properly assessed within a real market environment.

What we can afford

This approach is based on a management assessment of either the brand itself or the overall company position. In effect, management determines the level of profit desired, or the return on investment, and the marketing communications budget is the amount that remains after calculating that level. Of course, the approach fails to recognize the contribution of marketing communications itself, and ignores other environmental factors, such as competitive pressure, which might mitigate against the profit level being achieved.

Although this is a somewhat arbitrary approach to the budgetary process, it should be recognized that the issue of affordability plays an important part in any financial procedure. There will always be competing demands for funds within a company – to support the activities of other brands within the portfolio, to fund areas such as production capability, to finance research and development and so on. It is a fundamental role of management to determine company priorities and to allocate funds accordingly.

Budgets for new products

One area that demands a separate mention is that of developing a marketing communications budget for a new product. Clearly, past data will be unavailable and hence many of the usual budgeting approaches cannot be applied.

At the simplest level, the approach to new products is similar to the objective-and-task method described above. Calculations must be made of the amount of money required to achieve the objectives established for the brand.

 ## Activity 6.13

Why do marketing communications budgets for new product launches have to be given special consideration?

What criteria would you consider using as the basis of budget determination?

It must be recognized that, in most instances, new products require investment in advance of sales performance. Indeed, without the appropriate levels of investment in marketing communications, most new products are unlikely to succeed. A realistic time-frame for achieving the goals set must be established at the outset. It is unrealistic to expect a new product to make a major contribution in the short term.

 ## Activity 6.14

List the methods of budgetary determination described in this unit, and write a few lines explaining each of them.

It is important to restate that there is no hard and fast formula for defining a marketing communications budget. It is important to experiment with a number of the methods described above, and to ensure that appropriate use is made of previous company experience, industry data and experimentation. The imperative for all companies is to ensure that a database of information (both within-company information and information on competitors) is built up, which can be used to enhance the process.

 ## Activity 6.15

You have 20 per cent of the UK spread market (which includes butter and butter substitutes) worth £450 million. Currently you spend around £3 million on advertising, primarily on television and in the colour press. You are planning to enter the European market, and have targeted France and Belgium to spearhead your activity. Discuss what financial recommendations you would make for your launch campaign and what assumptions you would make.

It is important to understand the budgetary implications of marketing communications. On the one hand, candidates will often be required to identify the approach they would adopt towards budget determination within the case study contained in the first part of the exam paper. Indeed, the ability to demonstrate how and why a particular level of expenditure should be allocated will mark out a better candidate. In many similar papers, the Senior Examiner has asked students to identify the key communications issues facing the company set out in the mini-case. Invariably, the communication budget is going to be a central point, and students need to be able to understand the significance and relationship between communication investment and the need for profit, efficiency and competitiveness. Very often aspects of Share of Voice are important as well as competitive parity. In some papers, where total budgets are indicated, candidates are expected to indicate the allocation to the proposed areas of marketing communications and justify their recommendations.

Summary

In this unit, we have seen that there is a need to understand not only what strategy is but how it differs from planning. The significant differences between the use of marketing communications aimed at consumers and organizations have been considered. The MCPF provides a structure upon which it is possible to develop marketing communications activities. Each stage of the framework fulfils an important role; each stage feeds other elements of the structure and the framework needs to be seen as a system of interacting parts. It is important that the objectives are clearly defined and specific tasks for the communications programme are designed to communicate to a defined audience to a defined degree, within a specific time-frame and against a predefined budget.

Further study

More detailed coverage of marketing communications budgeting can be found in the essential texts. You do not have to be an accountant but you do need to appreciate and understand the processes involved.

Typical exam questions

In this section, references are given to specific examination and assignment questions from the June/July 2004 assessments. The questions are set out in Appendix 5. Detailed feedback on these questions from the CIM Senior Examiner and specimen answers can be obtained from the CIM website. Also included are some general examples of question types, briefings on which are included in Appendix 3.

June 2004 Examination Questions 3c and 5b. July 2004 Assignments Question 3.

Question 6.1

Explain the marketing communications planning framework and justify which three key elements that you believe are key to being successful when planning marketing communications activities.

(10 Marks)

Question 6.2

Make brief notes explaining four methods that can be used to determine a marketing communications budget.

(5 Marks)

Hints and tips

The marketing communications trade magazines such as *Campaign* and *Marketing Week* carry information relating to expenditure levels and budgets for different campaigns. These will give you a good feel for how much is necessary depending on the particular situation.

References

Anonymous (2004) 'Flying high', *Marketing Business*, March, p. 11.

Abratt, R. (1989) 'A new approach to the corporate image process', *Journal of Marketing Management*, **5**(1), 63–76.

Fill, C. (2005) *Marketing Communications: Engagement, Strategies and Tactics*, 4th edition, Harlow: Pearson Education.

Morrison, K. (2005) 'Into a new golden age', *Financial Times*, 6 January, p. 10.

Tighe, C. (2004) 'A charity that begins with home loans', *Financial Times*, 30 September, p. 14.

unit 7 media

Finding means through which communications can be channelled is a crucial element of the communications process. Traditional media, such as TV and other broadcast forms, print via newspapers and magazines, have long accounted for the bulk of expenditure by fmcg producers. New technologies have fuelled the growth of new media forms via the Internet and mobile phones, for example. Televisions are now in digital formats allowing interactive communications. Viewers can access a wide range of additional information using their remote controls. Satellite technologies allow access to multichannels from across borders.

Advanced computer technologies facilitate sophisticated database development. This allows marketers to accurately identify and target recipients of direct mail and telemarketing. As discussed in the section on relationship marketing, retailers and other organizations use information about customers to send customized product promotions. Videoconferencing and e-mail allow PR practitioners to pass information on a global scale in seconds.

After completion of this section you will be able to:

o Describe the primary and secondary forms of media used for marketing communications

o Explain the characteristics of both online and offline media forms

o Understand the key concepts involved in media selection

o Describe the principal approaches to evaluation of media effectiveness.

Syllabus references covered: 2.6, 2.7.

Key definition

Media – Are channels of communication that can be used to deliver messages to selected target audiences. These represent any interface or channel which allows communications messages to flow between senders and receivers in both directions.

Media characteristics (Syllabus 2.6)

In order to convey communications messages, whether they be through push, pull or profile approaches, the use of the media will be important, if not vital, if the target audience is to receive the message. Selecting the media is strategically important because of the increasing number of media channels and the break-up of the traditional ITV television audience into many disparate groups. These processes are referred to as audience and media fragmentation. It is a major issue as client-side managers become increasingly pressurized to account for their media spend. The definition of media proposed above suggests that a much wider view of what constitutes media should be taken. 'Exposure' to brands can be ubiquitous. This not only includes what might be termed 'formal media' – that which has been paid for by an organization to communicate specific messages. There are also more passive types of media – product packaging (in home and in store), vending machines (in buildings and on street), seeing others consume products in public places, general media references (not only those resulting from PR activity), delivery vehicles livery. These opportunities should not be ignored when considering co-ordination issues. Company premises also provide media exposure possibilities. The complexities of media decision-making have increased dramatically with the rapid developments in various forms of electronic communications. Whilst these represent exciting new opportunities, the vast majority of communications messages are still delivered via 'traditional' media, TV, newspapers, billboards and direct mail. Campaigns may use a lead medium such as TV for consumer goods but increasingly use a media mix just as they would use a mix of communications tools. Co-ordination is an important aspect of media decisions just as it is for selecting the tools used.

Media can be considered against three separate dimensions:

1. Does it enable the communication of the message?
2. Does it provide cost-effective coverage of the target audience?
3. Is it the appropriate environment in which to place the message?

Table 7.1 presents the main forms of media and their relative strengths and weaknesses.

Table 7.1 Summary of media characteristics

Type of media	Strengths	Weaknesses
Print		
Newspapers	Wide reach	Short lifespan
	High coverage	Advertisements get little exposure
	Low costs	Relatively poor reproduction gives poor impact
	Very flexible	Low attention-getting properties
	Short lead times	
	Speed of consumption controlled by reader	
Magazines	High-quality reproduction which allows high impact	Long lead times
	Specific and specialized target audiences	Visual dimension only
	High readership levels	Slow build-up of impact
	Longevity	Moderate costs
	High levels of information can be delivered	
Television	Flexible format, uses sight, movement and sound	High level of repetition necessary
	High prestige	Short message life
	High reach	High absolute costs
	Mass coverage	Clutter
	Low relative cost so very efficient	Increasing level of fragmentation (potentially)

Radio	Selective audience, e.g. local	Lacks impact
	Low costs (absolute, relative and production)	Audio dimension only
	Flexible	Difficult to get audience attention
	Can involve listeners	Low prestige
Outdoor	High reach	Poor image (but improving)
	High frequency	Long production time
	Low relative costs	Difficult to measure
	Good coverage as a support medium	
	Location orientated	
New media	High level of interaction	Segment specific
	Immediate response possible	Slow development of infrastructure
	Tight targeting	High user set-up costs
	Low absolute and relative costs	Transaction security issues
	Flexible and easy to update	
	Measurable	
Transport	High length of exposure	Poor coverage
	Low costs	Segment specific (travellers)
	Local orientation	Clutter
In-store POP	High attention-getting properties	Segment specific (shoppers)
	Persuasive	Prone to damage and confusion
	Low costs	Clutter
	Flexible	

Source: Fill (2005)

Case study

Weetabix mixes its media up

Weetabix wanted to revitalize the brand and attract a more modern, younger target audience. An 'outside of the box' approach to media use was selected. This involved a multi-layered strategy including, TV, outdoor, radio, print, sponsorship and a viral campaign encouraging online users to forward an amusing creative to others.

Much of the creative execution was aimed at delivering entertaining messages based on current issues to the younger target audiences. Flexibility in media planning facilitated being able to develop communications in line with current and anticipated events.

Source: PHD website – www.phd.co.uk.

 Activity 7.1

Select a brand of product or service and identify the main media that are being used. What do you think the advantages of the different media being used are for the particular brand selected?

Communicating the message – media selection and planning (Syllabus 2.7)

If the nature of the communications message, for example, demands some form of 'live' demonstration of the product or service, then it is likely that the media planner will be driven towards the use of television. If the nature of the conversation with the consumer requires a long explanation of product attributes and benefits, then print media uniquely offers that facility. If the purpose of the campaign is simple product or brand recognition, then posters may fulfil that requirement.

However, media selection and planning essentially revolves around a number of (interrelated) issues.

Reach or coverage

Coverage is the percentage of people within the defined audience who will be exposed to the advertising message, in a particular period of time.

Frequency

Frequency is the number of times people within the defined audience will be exposed to the message, in a particular period of time.

However large the budget, there will never be enough money to maximize both elements, and the planner must determine the balance between the two. Inevitably, some form of trade-off will have to be made between a campaign which achieves the maximum level of coverage, but provides few opportunities for the target audience to see or hear the message, and one which narrows the coverage to enable a greater frequency of exposure.

Although a great deal of work has been done to determine the appropriate balance of coverage and frequency, there are no definitive answers. Even today, much depends on the skills and experience of the media planner in assembling a media schedule which will achieve the objectives that have been set. This will often be seen in the way in which the media campaign is laid down or scheduled (*flighted*). In some instances, in order to achieve the maximum level of impact, media expenditure will be concentrated into a relatively short period.

Often associated with awareness objectives, the *burst* campaign compacts media activity into a series of relatively short time-frames, with relatively long periods of absence from media activity in between.

An alternative approach, mostly associated with reminder campaigns, is to extend the time-scale of the advertising message over a long period. The *DRIP* campaign provides continuity of the message, although at the cost of impact. A compromise between the two is the development of a *pulsing* campaign. Here a comparatively low level of media activity is maintained over a long period of time, with periodic increases in the expenditure pattern, often associated with seasonal or other influences on buyer activity.

 ## Activity 7.2

Under what circumstances would it be more desirable to use pulse advertising rather than spread the available funds evenly over a longer time period?

A third consideration is that of the impact of the message within a given medium. The media environment will be a critical factor in terms of the way the message is received and interpreted by the target audience. In some instances, as noted earlier, the nature of the advertising campaign will, itself, determine the broader issues of media selection – television versus press or radio and so on. However, it is the area of the specific selection of the timing of the appearance of the commercial, the press titles or radio stations selected that will have the greatest level of influence on the advertising message.

No media schedule is ever perfect. The aim must be to maximize the effectiveness of the campaign elements by the careful determination of the format in which the schedule is planned and the specific content of the media in which the advertising will appear.

To ensure that the media campaign continues to deliver against its targets, a proper evaluative process must be implemented. Whether this takes the form of periodic *ad hoc research* activity to investigate specific dimensions of the advertising effectiveness, or continuous market research in the form of a *tracking study* is somewhat less important than the fact that appropriate objective measurements are taken.

Case study

Intensive media approach for Homebase

The media agency PHD selected a flighting strategy of 'intensive frequency' on television when asked by Homebase to improve poor value perceptions and other objectives. With competitors having higher spends, weight and share of voice, TV advertising was needed to drive sales. High frequency was intended to gain dominant share of voice on days when advertising was run. This approach was complemented by sponsorship of the *Better Homes* TV series to support the brand with DIY viewers.

The high intensity strategy enabled Homebase to cut through the communications of their major competitor, B&Q. Awareness levels grew to similar levels of B&Q, doubling over a 3-year period.

Source: PHD website – www.phd.co.uk.

Activity 7.3

Go to the PHD website – www.phd.co.uk. This contains details of a number of case studies of clients they have worked for. You will find these helpful in developing your understanding of media and applications.

Media consumption

In an increasingly complex consumer environment, less time is being spent on activities which may in the past have provided opportunities for marketing communications. Television viewership patterns are changing and newspaper readership is declining. Direct marketing communications including direct mail are on the increase, telemarketing and online activities are also more popular and effective. More homes have the Internet connection and three or four TV sets. This background means that the consumers are exposed to communications messages from a range of different sources and because of that the volume may be becoming more selective about how and whether or not they receive them.

It is now common for media owners to offer a range of different media vehicles. This can help in the drive for co-ordination. It is also interesting to note linkages between platforms within media. Many TV programmes on both terrestrial and satellite channels use web-based and magazine formats which enable viewers continuous involvement with programme content.

Case study

International media consumption

There are, of course, significant differences in the ways in which media is consumed in different markets as a result of media availability. To demonstrate this, the chart below highlights the differences in TV ownership and multichannel penetration in markets across the world.

	Population (M)	TVs per 1000 population	Multi-channel penetration of TV households (%)
Australia	19.7	754	21.5
US	289.5	859	90.0
India	1061.6	85	51.3
Brazil	177.5	372	11.2
France	60.2	668	31.6

Source: PWC/Economist Intelligence Unit in *Financial Times Creative Business*, 22 July 2003.

These figures show significant variations which have implications for the organization of marketing communications activities in these markets. India has around 6000 English and Indian-language news-papers with an estimated 180 million readers. The cable TV sector has grown to 44 million users, the third highest subscriber base in the world.

Restrictions and regulations have to a certain extent limited TV coverage in some markets but in most markets there are a range of similar media available for marketing purposes, particularly print – news-papers and magazines, direct mail, cinema and radio. There are, of course, what might be described international media vehicles in the form of US publications such as *Time, Newsweek* and *Readers Digest* which have international editions. Also newspapers such as the *Financial Times*, have internationally published editions. Large media owners such as News International own TV and print media across the globe.

Creativity

The drive for media attention is leading to a continued search for new or alternative ways to communicate. Newer technologies provide a significant platform in this search but it also includes attempts to find new ways of using traditional media such as billboards and radio as part of co-ordinated campaigns. Different media, of course, allow alternative creative executions. Is movement required to demonstrate product benefits – which might suggest TV or cinema? Are more complex messages to be delivered – newspapers or direct mail?

Marketing flexibility

The communicative effects of all elements of the marketing mix may need to be considered in determining optimal approaches to media selection. Product and packaging design and distribution requirements particularly can be influential in this decision-making process.

Media budgets

How much money is available is perhaps an obvious criteria when it comes to making media choices. Certainly many of the brands we see advertised regularly on TV will require high levels of budget support. However, even when budgets may be restricted this does not necessarily preclude effective communications. Limited media presence may be supported by PR activity which may generate additional media exposure via editorial content. Controversial approaches in message design may stimulate media interest beyond that achieved from paid-for communications.

Co-ordinated approaches to media planning are essential, in order to successfully deliver messages consistently.

Case study

Wella co-ordinate media for Shockwaves

A co-ordinated approach was used by the haircare company Wella to promote its Shockwaves brand. This involved using a mix of radio, magazines, TV, events and online support. A cross media campaign to promote sponsored party nights in clubs around the country featured advertorials, promotions, competitions (online and print), sponsorship and content creation on radio and TV.

Youth brand magazines, *Kiss*, *FHM*, *Heat* and *More!* were used extensively for advertising and editorial content promoting a specially created UK club tour. Competition participants could win attendance at party nights and VIP treatments – including hair styling. Free samples were given out at the clubs.

Cecilla Fleming, Wella's Marketing Group Manager, said Shockwaves were able to deliver synergistic brand messages to their key target audiences via credible media vehicles. Association with the media brands gave added credibility that could not be achieved based solely on advertising.

Adapted from: Case history on www.emapadvertising.com – accessed 24 February 2004.

Efficiency and evaluation (Syllabus 2.5)

Cost per thousand

One of the most used means of evaluating the media costs of reaching a particular target is to calculate a medium's ability to reach every 1000 customers. Not surprisingly perhaps this calculation is known as Cost per thousand (CPT). This is, in fact, a simple calculation achieved by dividing the cost of the communication by the number in the target audience and multiplying by 1000. Cost per thousand allows comparisons between similar media, all newspapers, for example, and different types of media, newspapers and TV. Cost per thousand provides a measure of relative efficiency but does not measure effectiveness.

Television rating points

These provide measures by which TV advertising time is bought. Television ratings (TVRs) are units representing the audience watching any particular TV programme. One TVR represents 1 per cent of the audience and provides a measure of reaching specific audiences. If a programme is being watched by 5 million people and an advertisement 'reaches' only 1 million, that is 20 per cent of the total, then this provides 20 TVRs. Most advertisers would be unhappy with only reaching 20 per cent of their targets but remember this is only the result of one showing of the ad. Most ads are shown a number of times during the course of a campaign, so TVRs would accumulate over time. The Broadcaster's Audience Research Board (BARB) collects TV audience data which is used by advertisers to make TVR calculations and for the media owners to calculate prices.

Gross rating points

These are similar in format to TVRs but are used to measure reach in other media forms. Gross rating points (GRPs) are calculations based on multiplying reach times frequency. If a newspaper ad can reach 50 per cent of the target audience after appearing four times, then the GRPs are 200. The number of times an ad appears is more usually termed 'opportunities to see' (OTS). Media planners can use this measurement to calculate the potential effectiveness of different media plans and help them negotiate prices with media companies.

 Activity 7.4

> Calculate the total GRPs for a media plan that included ads in the *Daily Mirror* which reached 40 per cent of the target audience with 4 OTS, *Heat* magazine with a reach of 60 per cent with 2 OTS and cinema with reach of 25 per cent with 2 OTS.

It should also be recognized that when considering efficiency measures, there will be situations when communications are seen by the same individuals in different types of media. This is known as *Duplication*. Media planners need to take into account the duplication factor in calculating net reach and frequencies. For most campaigns, of course, the objective is to get the communications seen, heard or read by as many people as possible as many times as possible, so duplication is to be encouraged.

The above are all measures of relative efficiency and not effectiveness. The Broadcaster's Audience Research Board information will be used to confirm TV viewing figures which will assist in determining whether TVRs were realistic. Other media research, such as ABC audits provide circulation figures of newspapers and magazines. Of course, the primary measures need to be aimed at determining whether the various communications were successful in achieving overall effectiveness. This would involve looking at the effectiveness of the communications tools used as well as the media that were employed.

Organizations' communications efforts do not take place in isolation. Effectiveness will be affected by competitors' media usage, how much noise is created and other extraneous factors. Further consideration of evaluation is given in Unit 8.

Media buying and briefing

In traditional full service advertising agencies both media planning and buying would have been handled in-house. Much of the former activity still is dealt with by the agency, whereas media buying has been outsourced to specialist buying centres. Such centres are of a significant size and their purchasing power allows attractive rates to be negotiated with media owners. Media planning requires careful attention to detail. Those specialists in this area may play as significant a part in the development of effective communications campaigns as those involved in the more creative aspects of the process. This means that it is important for the briefing process to consider those issues which will allow media planners to be effective. In many cases a similar approach to that discussed in Unit 2 for creative briefing is utilized. At a minimum the brief should include information relating to campaign objectives, target audiences, all associated marketing activity, relevant sales data, previous media history, competitive activity, budgets and timing.

Case study

Tesco offer media solutions

The giant retailer Tesco has launched it's own media services department in order to sell advertising space to the owners of the brands it stocks on it's shelves. This goes significantly beyond brand supported sales promotions or point-of-sale merchandising. The intention is to sell space in car parks, petrol pump handles, shopping baskets and trollies, lorries and the floors of their stores. In addition to this range of ambient-based media, now they are also testing their own TV service in 100 stores to add to the availability of the Clubcard magazines it produces for customers.

This provides an opprtunity for brands to access directly the 16 million shoppers visiting Tesco stores each week. Tesco state that they have twice the number of weekly shoppers than the number who watch Coronation Street. All of this media activity close to the point of sale is targeted to have significant impact on sales. The media service, however, will not be limited to the products and brands it stocks. Car manufacturers will be targeted as well as the traditional fmcg brands. The other significant benefit for Tesco is the additional revenue it can generate from such media sales.

Adapted from: An article by Richard Fletcher in *The Sunday Times*, 28 November 2004.

Media process in relationship building

Various media forms are being utilized in establishing and developing relationships with consumers.

Initial stimulus
'Traditional' media – TV, newspapers, magazines and so on may all provide the initial point of communications stimulus.

Response
As a result of this or some other form of initial stimulus, response may be *passive* in the sense that no response is activated at this stage (although the information may be 'stored' for future reference) or *active*, that is the receiver decides to take action, get further information or make a purchase.

Interactivity

As relationships develop, the media role can change to encompass a wider variety of linked vehicles. This might include the use of online media and call centres.

Ongoing contact and involvement

Knowledge of customers and their purchasing behaviour provides organizations with the essential data they need in order to meet their ongoing requirements. Databases can be utilized for storing and analysis to drive the activities including targeted direct mail and other selective, personalized communications.

Interactive communications (Syllabus 2.6)

Technological advances now allow participants to conduct marketing communication-based 'conversations' at electronic speeds. The essence of this speed attribute is that it allows for interactive-based communications, where enquiries are responded to more or less instantly. So far in this coursebook, little specific attention has been given to the emerging area of interactive communications and the role of the Internet in marketing communications. This is not to belittle the subject.

The Internet is, among other things, a medium for communication. The role for marketing communications is enormous and currently there is a huge amount of experimentation to determine what works and what does not work on the Internet.

As far as this module is concerned you need to be aware of a number of basic dimensions. The fact that the B2B market is bigger than the B2C market in terms of Internet applications is fundamental.

The benefits of the Internet, extranet and intranet applications need to be fully understood; and their strategic role in the way in which organizations can reduce costs, improve communication effectiveness and provide value-added services to consumers, employees and business partners is highly significant.

At the core of a company's Internet activity is their website. Websites are intended to be visited by those browsing the Internet, and once visited the opportunity to interact and form a dialogue becomes more realistic. The commercial attractiveness of a website is based around the opportunities to display product and company information, often in the form of catalogues, as a corporate identity cue and for internal communications; to generate leads; to provide onscreen order forms and customer support at both pre- and post-purchase points; and to collect customer and prospect information for use within a database or as a feedback link for measurement and evaluative purposes. The principal benefits of Internet presence are set out in Table 7.2.

Table 7.2 Benefits of Internet presence

Considerably reduced transaction costs
Opportunities for growth and innovation
Improved competitive position
Encouragement of co-operative behaviour
Stimulates review of business and marketing strategies
Enhances communications with customers
Can improve corporate image and reputation
Information about customers improved
Enhanced measurement and evaluation of customer interaction
Customer service developed

Source: Fill (2002)

The list of benefits is quite extensive and far-ranging. From low barriers to entry for those developing websites and the attraction of considerably lower transaction costs, to improved collaboration and better business relationships and enhanced customer satisfaction, the Internet provides opportunities for considerable development.

The differences between traditional and new media are set out in Table 7.3. The interesting aspect is that the Internet is a medium that provides an opportunity for real dialogue with customers.

Table 7.3 A comparison of new and traditional media

Traditional media	New media
One-to-many	One-to-one and many-to-many
Greater monologue	Greater dialogue
Active provision	Passive provision
Mass marketing	Individualized
General need	Personalized
Branding	Information
Segmentation	Communities

Source: Fill (2002)

Case study

Guardian Unlimited, the online newspaper

Guardian Unlimited (GU) won the media category of the CIM's Marketing Effectiveness Awards in 2002. Launched in 1999, the aim was to provide a complementary brand alongside the newspaper by focusing on product development and innovation. Guardian Unlimited was differentiated from other online newspapers in providing a service that was not just an online version of the newspaper. The GU provides a number of different consumer facing sites including news, sport, travel, money and jobs. It also has B2B sites in education, media and society.

When restructured in 2001, a branding campaign using TV, Internet, radio and press was used. The service is now also available via WAP phones and digital TV. Amongst their major competitors, GU spent just over £300 000 on off-line advertising in 2000/2001, the FT.com spent £1.8 million and the Electronic Telegraph only £4000. Over the same time period, GU had 108 per cent increase in traffic against 41 per cent for FT.com.

Source: Marketing Business – September (2002).

Interactive strategies

The development of interactive brand strategies is less well understood than that for offline brands. Many of the brand and business models developed and launched over the past 4 years have either been removed, replaced or at a minimum adapted mainly due to poor technological and financial performance.

For example, one of the first strategies was to develop websites and online facilities for individual brands but this emphasizes the brand, not the customer. Now fmcg groups, such as Unilever and Procter & Gamble, are looking to cluster products in a more integrated way where the focus is on customer needs. This involves interactive TV and websites based upon providing a facility that customers actually want. Through this, targeting aims to appeal to communities, such as teenagers or young mothers, with each group sharing common information needs.

Therefore, the development of the Internet presence should not be regarded as something that can take place overnight. Experience suggests that organizations develop their Internet facilities according to their needs, preferred business models and knowledge gained through trial and experience. For example, a website can be used as either:

- *A shop window* – To look at the products and service on offer
- *An enquiry facility* – To find out more about the products and services on offer
- *A fully interactive form of engagement* – To buy one or more of the products on offer
- *A fully integrated system* – To embed business systems and procedures with partner organizations.

In this last phase, the transactional activities between organizations are routinized and embedded in the relationship and business processes.

The Interactive Advertising Bureau in the UK reports that online advertising spend in the UK has reached 2 per cent as a proportion of total advertising expenditure in 2003. The total of $151.6 million represents a doubling in less than 2 years. These figures are significant when compared with other more well-established media. It is about double that of cinema and already half the size of radio.

Case study

Viral campaigns add new media dimension

A number of advertisers and their agencies are beginning to recognise that 'viral' e-mail campaigns can allow them to go beyond the boundaries of traditional TV and cinema advertising, potentially reaching far larger audiences much more quickly. Brands including Burger King, Sony and Lynx have all successfully made use of this growing media format. This involves the adaptation of TV ads for use on the internet or in some cases ads are now created specifically for internet distribution in the form of games and interactive clips. This form of media with lower production costs and larger viewing figures is proving popular with not-for-profit organizations and government departments.

Adapted from: An article by Owen Gibson in *Media Guardian*, 17 January 2005.

Websites are the cornerstone of the Internet activity for organizations, regardless of whether they are operating in the B2B or B2C sectors and whether the purpose is merely to provide information or provide fully developed embedded e-commerce (transactional) facilities. The characteristics of a website can be crucial in determining the length of time, activities undertaken and the propensity for a visitor to return to the site at a later time. Should a website visitor experience a satisfactory visit, then both the visitor and the website owner might begin to take on some of the characteristics associated with relationship marketing.

Online facilities have enabled some brands to reach new target audiences, ones which in the offline world would not normally be reached. Abbey National knew that AB categories would not bank with them, so the launch of the Cahoot brand, devoid of any strong family branding and links back to Abbey National, enabled the bank to reach an important new market. Other online banking brands such as Smile (Co-operative Bank) and Egg (Prudential) have been important strategic moves for their owners.

The future for media development seems to hold exciting opportunities. One of the major media services groups, Zenith Media, publish a 'Media Timeline' which looks at media developments from the year 1000 when writing paper was made out of tree bark in Mexico and forecasts anticipated events into the middle of the current century. Amongst the forecasts are that by 2010 most TV ads are interactive, by 2111 bathroom mirrors display e-mail 'ticker' messages (scary!) and reassuringly perhaps, *Coronation Street* will be the highest rated TV programme in the UK in 2025! You may find this interesting to have a look at in full – www.zenithmedia.com.

Case study

Teenage clicks

Record companies are reported to be moving media budgets from TV and press ads into e-marketing and direct mail. Nielsen Media Research say ad spend fell by 4.3 per cent in the year to May 2003 whilst budgets for mobile phone, e-mail and direct mail promotions were all increased. Polydor UK has trebled spend on e-marketing support in less than 3 years and Warner Music also reports significant increase in budgets in these areas. Direct mail is still relatively small in budget terms but important in strategic terms.

Text messaging and e-mail are not surprisingly considered as effective ways of communicating with a young target audience. Traditional TV is less effective as teenagers do not watch this media in the same way than previously, preferring online peer-to-peer recommendations. New interactive media offer short lead times compared to more traditional media – significant in such a fast-moving environment.

Adapted from: An article by Steve Hemsley in the *Financial Times Creative Business*, 15 July 2003.

Summary

This unit has examined the roles that different media play in the communications process. This is a crucial element as ineffective media selection will negate the achievement of communications objectives and, of course, waste valuable resources. There is an increasing variety of media available including many electronic types. Technology plays a significant role in improving what might be considered traditional media forms – better quality printing for print advertisers and direct mail. Telephone technology enables large numbers of calls to be handled simultaneously. Videoconferencing is assisting PR usage.

Further study

The essential texts provide more detail on media usage, planning and selection. The *Excellence in Advertising* text referred to in Unit 3 also addresses media issues.

Typical exam questions

In this section, references are given to specific examination and assignment questions from the June/ July 2004 assessments. The questions are set out in Appendix 5. Detailed feedback on these questions from the CIM Senior Examiner and specimen answers can be obtained from the CIM website. Also included are some general examples of question types, briefings on which are included in Appendix 3. June 2004 Examination Questions 1c and 2b. July 2004 Assignments Question 5.

Question 7.1

Briefly identify and explain four key issues that need to be addressed when introducing new media and associated digital technologies to an organization.

(5 Marks)

Question 7.2

Discuss the advantages and disadvantages of both print and outdoor media.

(10 marks)

Hints and tips

Make an effort to seek out the different media that are being used for different brands. If you see TV ads, find out which other media are being used. The trade press will provide information on the media related to specific campaigns. This should be part of your regular updating.

References

Fill, C. (2005) *Marketing Communications: Engagement, Strategies and Tactics*, 4th edition, Harlow: Pearson Education.

Fletcher, R. (2004) 'Tesco TV takes on the media', *Sunday Times*, 28 November, p. 9.

Gibson, O. (2005) 'The spoof of the pudding', *Media Guardian*, 17 January, pp. 14–15.

Marketing Business, September 2002

www.emapadvertising.com
www.phd.co.uk
www.zenithmedia.com

unit 8 evaluating communications effectiveness

Learning objectives

The complexities involved in marketing communications that have been examined in this coursebook readily indicate that measuring effectiveness will be a difficult task. However, it is crucial in determining where communication budgets are best placed on an ongoing basis. Identifying objectives and finding out whether they have been achieved are crucial elements of any business planning, and marketing communications in particular. The right message to the right targets using the right media at the right time is the real goal of marketing communications. Advertisers have long sought effective ways of determining the effects of their work in any accurate form.

As identified earlier, agencies are under more pressure to produce tangible results from the communications developed, and therefore effectiveness measurement is crucial to their profitability. Market research techniques can be used to measure awareness levels and consumers can be asked what communications they recall. These provide some measure of effectiveness. New technologies provide for potentially more accurate recording via website 'hits', telephone calls made, e-mails sent and received. Just as new forms of communications are being developed, so must measurement techniques be designed to test effectiveness.

After completion of this section you will be able to:

o Understand the importance of evaluation in marketing communications planning

o Demonstrate how different elements of the communications mix can be assessed for effectiveness

o Explain methods used to measure the success of co-ordinated campaigns.

CIM Syllabus references: 2.2 (see also Unit 2), 2.4 (see also Unit 2), 2.5 (see also Unit 2), 2.12, 2.16.

Key definition

Evaluation – Is about finding appropriate ways of measuring effectiveness. There are no 'perfect' measures, but it is important to have some mechanisms for determining the extent to which communications achieved its goals.

Great ad – What was it for? Not a definition but a question that many consumers might ask after having seen a TV ad, particularly if the question is asked some time after the showing, maybe the next day or the next week. Recalling and remembering advertisements and other forms of marketing communications is not high on our list of priorities when we have so many other things to remember that are of more significance and relevance to us. The question is intended to indicate the difficulties communicators have in succeeding in getting their messages remembered and understood.

Evaluating co-ordinated marketing communications (Syllabus 2.5)

Before we examine some of the methods used to measure the effectiveness of specific types of marketing communications, it is important to recognize the significance of evaluation from a holistic perspective. This does not just refer to how well the communications mix or media are co-ordinated. For genuine communications effectiveness to be achieved on a long-term basis, we need to evaluate or audit the component parts of our communications activities and processes. These might include:

o *Analysis* – How thoroughly do we prepare in gaining an understanding of the markets in which we are operating? Context analysis which was covered in Unit 6 will provide a framework for this analysis in identifying those issues which are considered most relevant from a marketing communications perspective. This is not a one-off exercise but an ongoing process which should underpin decisions made about how and when communications might be best employed.

o *Objectives* – These need to be clearly thought through, based on detailed analysis. It is important to relate what communications are setting out to do, to what our overall marketing activities are designed to achieve and further back, to our overall business objectives.

o *Planning* – A logical framework needs to be in place, which sets out how activities are to be co-ordinated. This will involve the analysis and objectives setting phases and subsequently the selection of appropriate strategic options – push, pull and profile. It will also include issues involving scheduling and implementation as well as the design of effective measurement techniques. This is not a linear process but one which evolves over time as experience forms the basis for ongoing analysis to 'feed' fresh inputs into the systems.

o *Budgets* – A crucial question, how much do we need to spend in order to meet our objectives? Or maybe how much can we afford to spend? It is not always necessary to spend vast amounts of money in order for objectives to be achieved. Media fragmentation has facilitated less costly routes, including the use of TV, which may also provide more specific targeting opportunities.

o *Media* – In Unit 7, a number of newer approaches to media selection and planning were outlined. It is important that opportunities to use new (both those which have not been available before and those which a particular firm might not have employed in the past) media are constantly kept under review. Simply because media have been used just because they historically appear to have been successful, they should not prevent a search for more effective platforms as we seek to differentiate.

179

- o *Marketing mix* – Communications alone may not provide genuine effectiveness if other elements of the marketing mix are not being co-ordinated or as identified above, objectives are inconsistent.
- o *Customer service* – This means a number of different things to different organizations. For some, it means what it says and is a genuine attempt to help customers either when they have difficulties or used proactively to support the whole marketing process. Essentially, we need to ensure that when marketing communications are used to encourage customers to make contact with the organization – making enquiries, requesting information, checking account details, making purchases – by telephone, online or in person – the appropriate mechanisms are in place to facilitate the process. Significant budgets may be wasted if advertisements carry messages requesting interested customers to phone free phone lines only for these lines to be jammed or enquirers left in queuing systems listening to poor quality music or repeated messages about how valuable their calls are. Most of us have been there!
- o *Creativity* – This does not just mean being creative in designing clever or award winning ads. Creativity runs through the whole communications process – analysis, planning, strategy selection, tactics, media, scheduling, budgets and so on. It is possible to be creative with numbers, just as it is with words and pictures.

The evaluation of any promotional activity is an important, often neglected, part of managing marketing communications. The outcomes from the evaluation process can provide a rich source of material for the next campaign, and in doing so improve the efficiency and effectiveness of an organization's overall marketing communications. It was identified in Unit 2 that the main communications tools should be considered in terms of their ability to communicate, cost efficiency, credibility and control factors, the '*4Cs Framework*'. Refer back to this to refresh your understanding of the characteristics associated with each communication tool. Ultimately, communications would be measured on a scale which maximizes each of these elements, it would seek to deliver highly credible communications to the whole target audience at minimum cost with maximum control. In reality, this represents an unachievable goal, as there are too many extraneous factors in the communications process for everything to be 'perfect' in this sense. Communicators, therefore, aim at maximizing each aspect taking into account the objectives to be achieved. There will be occasions when decisions are taken to run an advertising campaign at short notice to take advantage of unexpected opportunities such as associations with topical news. This is likely to involve higher media costs because of the short notice and there may be a loss of control on placement for similar reasons. However, communications' effectiveness might be maximized due to the nature of the opportunity that has arisen. For example, the sponsor of a football team that is in the final of a major cup competition shown extensively on national TV might wish to run some press advertising, following this if the team is successful. The media costs would be higher than if the space had been booked several weeks in advance but the communications might not have been so successful without the association of the cup final victory which itself would have received significant media coverage. Credibility would be enhanced when linked to the team's success, particularly amongst the successful team's supporters!

Marketing communications can represent a large investment, so it is important to be sure that the campaign and associated activities are tested to make sure they will do the job required within required timescales and within the available resources. Many organizations do measure the effectiveness of their marketing communications and there are a range of techniques and procedures available to do this. However, because of the size of the investment it makes sense to test different parts of a campaign (e.g. any advertising) before it 'breaks' (released publicly). By testing on a controlled basis, it is possible to see which parts of an ad work well and which need refinement. Therefore, the evaluation process does not happen at the very end of a campaign, it should happen before, during and after a campaign has broken.

Rather than measure the success of individual components of a campaign (which is important), it is the overall impact of a CMC campaign and the degree to which the promotional objectives have been achieved that represents the true measure of the communications.

Good marketing management practice suggests that evaluation of any management activity should always include a consideration of the degree to which the objectives have been satisfied. The primary role of evaluating the performance of a communications strategy is to ensure that the communication's objectives have been met and that the strategy has been effective. The secondary role is to ensure that the strategy has been executed efficiently, that the full potential of the individual promotional tools has been extracted and that resources have been used economically.

Therefore, the measurement of the effectiveness of CMC activities must be based on the degree or level to which the promotional objectives have been satisfied.

Case study

02 – it only works if it all works

The mobile phone service provider needed to develop effective communications in moving from the troubled BT Cellnet brand to 02. Losing market share and money, the brand change and repositioning needed to provide a credible platform on which a longer-term business could be established and developed. The identified role of marketing communications in this process has been substantial both in terms of cost efficiency but the significant forecast of generating over 60 times return on investment at £4.8 billion incremental margin over the long term.

The co-ordinated/integrated strategy has benefited from the efficiencies of a complex visual integration across all media used. There has also been significant value in the level of marketing integration achieved through from the brand idea, product propositions/positioning and into the communications. In addition to consumer communications, the strategy also involved communicating with trade partners and the company's employees via internal communications.

Measurement of the value of the strategic integration came via econometric analysis in quantifying a payback calculation. Factors included in the calculation are:

1. Number of connections attributed directly to the communications
2. Average revenue generated by each connection in any given year
3. Average lifetime values of each new connection (3.5 years depending on consumer type)
4. The 02 margin
5. Cost of media, production and agency fees (£78.3 million).

Upto December 2003 advertising and sponsorship combined, generated £493 million in additional margin for 02 of which 84 per cent was directly attributable to advertising and 16 per cent to the Big Brother TV programme sponsorship. Other evaluation measures include shareholder value, staff morale, market share and trade response – all of which were significantly favourable.

In response to the rebranding at 02, major competitors Vodafone and Orange consistently outspent 02 and the launch budget was significantly less than that of T-Mobile and 3. This resulted in a lowering of 02 share of voice versus the market. The 02 spend on sponsorship of the Big Brother programme at £7.1 million and sponsoring of the England Rugby World Cup team was significantly lower than Vodafone's sponsorship budget of £38 million in 2003/2004.

The 02 communications strategy was effective in all 4C aspects namely communication, cost, credibility and control.

Adapted from: The *IPA Effectiveness Awards* 2004, winning case study by Maunder, Harris, Bamford, Cook and Cox. Accessed via www.warc.com, 24 January 2005.

 Activity 8.1

Go back through the coursebook and make notes on different examples which illustrate all or some of the 4C criteria for evaluation purposes.

Evaluation of advertising (Syllabus 2.16)

Pre-testing

Pre-testing (or copy testing) is about showing unfinished ads to preselected representative groups of the target audience, with a view to ensure that the final creative will meet the advertising objectives. Focus groups are the main qualitative method used.

De Pelsmacker, Geuens and Van den Bergh (2001) describe three different groups of techniques that can be used for pre-testing advertisements. *Internal* – checklists and readability analysis, those measuring, *Communications effects* – physiological tests, recall and direct opinion measurement and those measuring, *Behavioural effects* – designed to measure actual rather than predictive response using trailer tests and split scan procedures.

 Activity 8.2

Get together a small group of friends or other students and study a number of different print advertisements. Discuss and make notes of what the group considers to be positive and negative aspects of each one.

Post-testing

Post-testing is concerned with the evaluation of a campaign once it has been released. These inquiry tests are used to measure the number of inquiries or direct responses stimulated by a single advertisement or campaign, and can take the form of returned coupons and response cards, requests for further literature or actual orders.

Recall tests attempted to assess how memorable particular advertisements are with a target audience. On the other hand, recognition tests are based on the ability of respondents to reprocess information about an advertisement and is the most common of the post-testing procedures for print advertisements.

Sales tests are popular but not necessarily an accurate or useful measure of a campaign's performance. A refined form of sales test is the use of Single-source data. This is derived from the collection of product purchase information from households whose every purchase is monitored through a scanner at supermarket checkouts. These households have agreed to receive controlled sets of ads, made possible through cable television technology. This technique is expensive and although the data is very dependable, it is only appropriate for testing single ads rather than campaigns.

Other tests

Financial tests are important not only to measure and control how much is to be spent, how much has been spent and when money has been spent (invested) but also to determine the relative amount of investment across the tools, across the different media and to ensure that the balance and efficiency of the promotional investment is correct.

A tracking study involves collecting data from buyers on a regular basis (weekly, monthly) in order to assess their perceptions of ads and how these might be affecting their perceptions of the brand.

'Likeability tests' ('how much I liked the advertisement') have emerged as an important and most reliable predictor of sales success. The term refers to the deep set of meanings that individuals attribute to ads.

1. Personally meaningful, relevant, informative, true to life, believable and convincing.
2. Relevant, credible, clear product advantages, product usefulness and importance to 'me'.
3. Stimulates interest or curiosity about the brand; creates warm feelings through enjoyment of the advertisement.

What this indicates is the importance of understanding the way people process information in the first place.

Refer back to Unit 2 for other examples of successful advertising campaigns.

Case study

Procter & Gamble aim to measure performance

It was once (a long time back now) that it was possible to say that 50 per cent of advertising worked, but it was not possible to say which 50 per cent. This quote from Unilever's Chairman Lord Lever, in the relatively early days of advertising, may seem dated but it is only in more recent years that the evaluation of advertising and other forms of communications has become of real significance.

Ironically perhaps, it is Unilever's arch-rival Procter & Gamble that is leading the drive for quantifiable measures of performance, including return on communication investment. Use of econometric and other mathematical modelling led to the redistribution of $400 million of their global advertising budget of $4.3 billion. The use of such approaches to measurement are not in themselves new, but what is the increasing intensity to find quantifiable justification of strategies and tactics employed.

The P&G have more recently announced that they are seeking brand partners to join a proposed Project Apollo to measure advertising effectiveness. The $100 million project will study millions of consumers to determine which are the most effective means of reaching them and which products and brands they prefer. The technology would involve portable tracking devices to guage media consumption and scanners to record purchases.

Adapted from: An article by Gary Silverman in the *Financial Times*, 29 April 2004 and in www.warc.com accessed on 7 December 2004.

Evaluation of sales promotions (Syllabus 2.16)

It is essential, as with any promotional technique, to evaluate the effectiveness of the promotional campaign. Sales promotions, like advertising, is a very expensive activity and therefore it is of primary importance that as a marketer you understand the propensity for the campaign to succeed or fail.

Typical evaluation methods will include:

o *Consumer audits* – This will indicate if there has been a change in consumer behaviour as a result of the sales promotion campaign and will be especially interested in the success of trials and repeat purchase promotions.
o *Sales information* – Should the objective of the sales promotion be to assist the marketing objective of market penetration, then the measure of increase in sales will be a vital performance indicator.
o *Retail audits* – Specialist organizations such as AC Nielson will track changes in stock levels, distribution and market share immediately after the promotional campaign. This will provide an insight into the basis of an increase or decrease in sales.
o *Sales force feedback* – This is a qualitative approach and will be based upon sales force experience of the uptake of the sales promotion opportunities in their region.
o *Voucher/coupon redemption* – It is likely that the vouchers and coupons will be coded in order to ascertain the most successful response rate to sales promotion activities – this will endorse the right selection of media, the right kind of sales promotion activity and potentially the most frequently used distribution outlet.

While evaluating sales promotion is essential, the evaluation of the whole promotional mix programme should be undertaken in order to measure the success or failure of the integrated programme of promotional and communications activities.

Refer back to Unit 2 for examples of successful sales promotions.

Evaluation of public relations (Syllabus 2.16)

Public relations are no exception to the rule when it comes to the necessity for undertaking an evaluation of the successes or failures of particular strategies and the associated objectives.

Haywood (1991) suggested that there are eight commonly used measures of results:

1. *Budget* – An assessment of whether the planned PR activity has been achieved within the budget defined and also within the timescales set.

2. *Awareness* – The measure of awareness can be quite complex and is most likely to be established through a range of marketing research activities to establish the level of brand awareness in the marketplace.

3. *Attitude* – Combined with research on brand awareness can be research on brand attitudes, whether they are positive or negative and whether they have resulted in any change in consumer behaviour.

4. *Media coverage and tone* – First, it will be essential to establish the level of media coverage achieved as a result of planned PR activities. Typical measures might include the number of different media which covered the case, the number of columns taken, key headings and perceived importance of the PR information. Second, the nature and tone in which the PR activities have been covered. Clearly, this is far more qualitative in nature and will perhaps be subject to a twofold approach of looking closely at the perceived nature and tone, and against the measure of attitude towards the organization. For example, what could have been perceived as 'negative' publicity, what is the attitude towards the organization, it is sympathy or empathy? What was it originally and what appears to be the driving force of change?

5. *Positioning* – Measuring the perception of the position of the organization versus that of the competition. The research undertaken to provide an insight into awareness and attitude will also provide the basis for understanding perceived positioning.

6. *Response generation* – This is a very quantitative mechanism and quite easy to generate. It is likely that as with sales promotions, many of the enquiries or leads generated may be subject to some degree of code referencing, or sources of the enquiry will be recorded.

7. *Share price* – For large public companies, this is a particularly good indicator of public confidence in the organization. For example, while Marks & Spencer were subject to a high degree of publicity due to rationalization and streamlining of their operations, their share prices were somewhat reduced, which is representative of the level of shareholder and public confidence in the organization.

8. *Sales* – This is probably the ultimate measure in the successful implementation of a sound and robust PR strategy. However, bearing in mind that PR is often not designed purely with increased sales in mind, this is not always an objective measure of organizational performance. However, it is a known fact that when a negative perspective of the organization is presented, then sales do drop. The PR challenge then, of course, is to retrieve the situation in order to get the sales back on track.

Public Relations is quite an exciting business to be in, and often it does come under the arm of the marketing department. However, in a number of large corporate bodies, PR officers are part of the corporate arm of the organization, whose role is then likely to be underpinned by the provision of appropriate management information by the marketing department.

Refer back to Unit 2 for examples of successful PR campaigns.

Evaluation of direct and interactive marketing communications (Syllabus 2.16)

Evaluation of direct marketing activities relates to measuring the level of response any one campaign might have achieved. The evaluation of success will be based upon the pre-determined objectives of the campaign.

Typical measures for successful implementation of the direct marketing campaign will include:

o   Response rate
o   Conversion rate

185

      o Order value
      o Repeat orders.

This information will be gathered through a range of voucher and campaign response codes that will be able to distinguish the source of the direct mail or promotion. This may establish the most popular direct marketing technique for the organization to pursue in the future.

However, it is also essential that from a budgeting perspective the organization not only measures the effectiveness of the campaign, but also tries to establish the cost per enquiry and cost per order element of the campaign.

The two components combined will enable an evaluation of campaign effectiveness to be achieved in order that future campaigns will become more effective in terms of their actual output.

This form of measurement and evaluation will be typical across the full range of direct marketing tools that have been covered in this unit.

Technology is developing quickly but there is some uncertainty about whether it is possible to measure online advertising effectively. It is possible to measure how many pages have been requested, the time spent on each page and even the type of computers that were used to request the page. AC Nielsen have a 9000-strong consumer panel in the UK. The panel consists of Internet users who have special software loaded on their PCs that records every web page they visit. However, this type of information is largely superficial and fails to provide insight into visitor attitudes, motivation or even tie in with offline behaviour as a result of their online experience.

Click-through rates are one of the more common online measurement approaches but this normally only evaluates behaviour. What is needed is an indicator of the visitor's attitudes.

Response generated

The demand for effectiveness and accountability by clients is leading to the development of techniques aimed at providing the kind of information that will provide the evidence required to measure communications performance. In some cases this is achieved by co-ordinating above-the-line communications with direct response activities.

The Mediacom agency has merged its direct teams with those responsible for branding in order to try and find the right balance of approach. The direct expertise has led to an increasing emphasis on tracking ad performance through response codes and web addresses. This allows how brand activity increases propensity to respond.

Financial services company, Egg, has merged their brand team which looked after TV, with its sales team which deals with direct response print – press ads and direct mail.

Studies by the London Business School and EHS Brann show that direct mail has boosted share of the five major advertising sectors from 12.8 per cent in 2001 to an estimated 13.3 per cent in 2003.

Adapted from: An article by Alistair Ray in the *Financial Times Creative Business*, 29 April 2003.

Evaluation of sponsorship (Syllabus 2.16)

At each stage of the promotional mix, the importance of evaluation has been highlighted. Sponsorship is no exception and, therefore the following methods of evaluation should be undertaken:

- ○ *Media exposure measurement* – How much media coverage did the sponsorship activity actually achieve (a similar process of measurement to PR applies)?
- ○ *Assessment of the sponsorship communication results* – Pre-testing and post-testing of awareness, corporate image perception and improvements in general attitudes and opinions about the sponsor.
- ○ *Feedback from all participants in the sponsorship process* – Obtaining qualitative feedback from all participants as to the success or failure of the sponsorship agreement and ascertaining the position of mutual benefits between the sponsor and the sponsored party.

Activity 8.3

Identify some examples of sponsorships which incorporate a range of different marketing communications methods. Suggest ways in which they may be evaluated.

Refer back to Unit 2 for examples of successful sponsorship activities.

Evaluation of personal sales (Syllabus 2.16)

Evaluating and measuring sales performance will be very much based upon the sales objectives set for the organization. But the objectives set will be SMART, and therefore clearly defined and clearly linked with marketing objectives and overall corporate performance goals.

It is likely that sales performance will be measured against objectives on a regular basis, anything from weekly to quarterly. However, in most organizations, sales performance against actual planned achievement is measured on a monthly basis.

It is also likely that other factors relating to sales performance will be measured, such as:

- ○ *Productivity* – Calls per day, calls per account, total number of orders versus calls
- ○ *Account development* – Total number of new accounts, total number of existing accounts, growth of sales from existing accounts
- ○ *Expenses* – Expenses versus number of calls made, cost per call.

With the evolution of IT, sales measurement techniques are becoming more sophisticated and more effective, and the speed at which information becomes available is of the essence. A drastic reduction in sales performance can mean that other elements of the promotional mix might be subject to increased activity to compensate for the drop in sales. However, the drop in income often inhibits too much marketing expenditure of a contingency nature to be undertaken.

Brand evaluation (Syllabus 2.4, 2.5, 2.12)

There have been a number of studies which have looked at the question of how to measure the overall brand performance. This, of course, does not just relate to marketing communications issues but given the need for enhanced co-ordination of communications activities (and subsequently strategic integration), some consideration of these issues is worthwhile. Branding is quite often taken to mean the communications used to support sales of products and services. This was discussed in Unit 2.

De Chernatony (2001) proposes a multi-dimensional approach to evaluate brand performance. This is based around assessment of internally and externally driven issues. These are classified under headings:

- ○ Brand vision
- ○ Organizational structure
- ○ Brand objectives
- ○ Brand essence
- ○ Implementation and brand resourcing.

In each section, he proposes scoring the answers to a series of questions on a five-point scale to highlight the strengths and weaknesses.

Summary

In this unit, the importance of evaluating marketing communications effectiveness against stated objectives has been considered. This represents a difficult area and one in which there is no 'exact science'. As the pressure by clients on agencies demonstrate performance, because this will determine how much they get paid, the drive for better measurement will increase and pressure will be put on researchers to come up with more reliable techniques. It is worth remembering here also that communications is one element of the marketing mix and that the other elements, namely product, price and place should be subject to evaluation as well. Increasingly, single elements of the communications mix are not used in isolation and that it is the effective co-ordination that determines the overall success.

Further study

The IPA series, Advertising Works, is a collection of case studies published each year of the winners of their Advertising Effectiveness Awards. These contain significant levels of detail on successful advertising-based campaigns. Although the focus is on advertising, increasing examples of co-ordinationare appearing. In fact, in the most recent awards for 2002, the title removed the word advertising in order to seek entries from a wider communications field. This has brought into play the concept of 'media neutrality' which highlights the need to consider other communications disciplines.

Typical exam questions

In this section, references are given to specific examination and assignment questions from the June/ July 2004 assessments. The questions are set out in Appendix 5. Detailed feedback on these questions from the CIM Senior Examiner and specimen answers can be obtained from the CIM website. Also included are some general examples of question types, briefings on which are included in Appendix 4.

June 2004 Examination Question 4a. July 2004 Assignments Question 3 part 4.

Question 8.1

Briefly explain three methods that can be used to evaluate the effectiveness of public relations.

(5 Marks)

Question 8.2

Evaluate the means by which organizations can best evaluate the effectiveness of a marketing communications campaign.

(10 Marks)

Hints and tips

On a more regular basis, the journal *Admap* is a monthly publication that covers many effectiveness and evaluation issues with plenty of examples of measurement techniques and case histories.

References

De Chernatony, L. (2001) *From Brand Vision to Brand Evaluation*, Oxford: Butterworth-Heinemann.

De Pelsmacker, P., Geuens, M. and Van den Bergh, J. (2001) *Marketing Communications*, Harlow: Pearson Education.

Haywood, R. (1991) *All About Public Relations*, 2nd edition, Maidenhead: McGraw-Hill.

Maunder, S., Harris, A., Bamford, J., Cook, L. and Cox, A. (2004) 'It only works if it all works', *IPA Effectiveness Awards*, www.warc.com, accessed 24 January 2005.

Silverman, G. (2004) 'A hard-headed approach to selling a dream', *Financial Times*, 29 April, p. 13.

appendix 1
guidance on examination preparation

Preparing for your examination

You are now nearing the final phase of your studies and it is time to start the hard work of exam preparation.

During your period of study you will have become used to absorbing large amounts of information. You will have tried to understand and apply aspects of knowledge that may have been very new to you, while some of the information provided may have been more familiar. You may even have undertaken many of the activities that are positioned frequently throughout your coursebook, which will have enabled you to apply your learning in practical situations. But whatever the state of your knowledge and understanding, do not allow yourself to fall into the trap of thinking that you know enough, that you understand enough and or even worse, that you can just take it as it comes on the day.

Never underestimate the pressure of the CIM examination.

The whole point of preparing this text for you is to ensure that you never take the examination for granted, and that you do not take an exam unprepared for what might come your way for 3 hours at a time.

One thing is for sure: there is no quick fix, no easy route, no waving a magic wand and finding you know it all.

Whether you have studied alone, in a CIM study centre, or through distance learning, you now need to ensure that this final phase of your learning process is tightly managed, highly structured and objective.

As a candidate in the examination, your role will be to convince the Senior Examiner that you have credibility for this subject. You need to demonstrate to the examiner that you can be trusted to undertake a range of challenges in the context of marketing and that you are able to capitalize on opportunities and manage your way through threats.

You should prove to the Senior Examiner that you are able to apply knowledge, make decisions, respond to situations and solve problems.

Very shortly we are going to look at a range of revision and exam preparation techniques, and at time management issues, and encourage you towards developing and implementing your own revision plan, but before that, let us look at the role of the Senior Examiner.

A bit about the Senior Examiners!

You might be quite shocked to read this, but while it might appear that the examiners are 'relentless question masters' they actually want you to be able to answer the questions and pass the exams! In fact, they would derive no satisfaction or benefits from failing candidates; quite the contrary, they develop the syllabus and exam papers in order that you can learn and then apply that learning effectively so as to pass your examinations. Many of the examiners have said in the past that it is indeed psychologically more difficult to fail students than pass them.

Many of the hints and tips you find within this Appendix have been suggested by the Senior Examiners and authors of the coursebook series. Therefore, you should consider them carefully and resolve to undertake as many of the elements suggested as possible.

The Chartered Institute of Marketing has a range of processes and systems in place within the Examinations Division to ensure that fairness and consistency prevail across the team of examiners, and that the academic and vocational standards that are set and defined are indeed maintained. In doing this, CIM ensures that those who gain the CIM Professional Certificate in Marketing, Professional Diploma in Marketing and the Professional Postgraduate Diploma in Marketing, are worthy of the qualification and perceived as such in the view of employers, actual and potential.

Part of what you will need to do within the examination is be 'examiner friendly' – that means you have to make sure they get what they ask for. This will make life easier for you and for them.

Hints and tips for 'examiner friendly' actions are as follows:

- Show them that you understand the basis of the question, by answering *precisely* the question asked, and not including just about everything you can remember about the subject area.
- Read their needs – How many points is the question asking you to address?
- Respond to the question appropriately. Is the question asking you to take on a role? If so, take on the role and answer the question in respect of the role. For example, you could be positioned as follows:

'You are working as a Marketing Assistant at Nike UK' or 'You are a Marketing Manager for an Engineering Company' or 'As Marketing Manager write a report to the Managing Partner'.

These examples of role-playing requirements are taken from questions in past papers.

- Deliver the answer in the format requested. If the examiner asks for a memo, then provide a memo; likewise, if the examiner asks for a report, then write a report. If you do not do this, in some instances you will fail to gain the necessary marks required to pass.
- Take a business-like approach to your answers. This enhances your credibility. Badly ordered work, untidy work, lack of structure, headings and subheadings can be off-putting. This would be unacceptable in the work situation, likewise it will be unacceptable in the eyes of the Senior Examiners and their marking teams.
- Ensure the examiner has something to mark: give them substance, relevance, definitions, illustrations and demonstration of your knowledge and understanding of the subject area.
- See the examiner as your potential employer or ultimate consumer/customer. The whole purpose and culture of marketing is about meeting customers' needs. Try this approach – it works wonders.
- Provide a strong sense of enthusiasm and professionalism in your answers; support it with relevant up-to-date examples and apply them where appropriate.
- Try to do something that will make your exam paper a little bit different – make it stand out in the crowd.

All of these points might seem quite logical to you, but often in the panic of the examination they 'go out of the window'. Therefore, it is beneficial to remind ourselves of the importance of the examiner. He or she is the 'ultimate customer' – and we all know customers hate to be disappointed.

As we move on, some of these points will be revisited and developed further.

About the examination

In all examinations, with the exception of Marketing Management in Practice at Professional Diploma in Marketing, the paper is divided into two parts.

- o Part A – Mini-case study = 50 marks
- o Part B – Option choice questions (choice of two questions from four) = 50 per cent of the marks (each question attracting 25 per cent).

For the Marketing Management in Practice paper, the same approach is taken. However, all of the questions are directly related to the case study and in this instance the case material is more extensive.

Let us look at the basis of each element.

Part A – Mini-case study

This is based on a mini-case or scenario with one question, possibly subdivided into between two and four points, but totalling 50 per cent of overall marks.

In essence, you, the candidate, are placed in a problem-solving role through the medium of a short scenario. On occasions, the scenario may consist of an article from a journal in relation to a well-known organization.

Alternatively, it will be based upon a fictional company, and the examiner will have prepared it in order that the right balance of knowledge, understanding, application and skills is used.

Approaches to the mini-case study

When undertaking the mini-case study there are a number of key areas you should consider.

Structure/content
The mini-case that you will be presented with will vary slightly from paper to paper and, of course, from one examination to the other. Normally, the scenario presented will be 600–800-words long, and will centre on a particular organization and its problems or may even relate to a specific industry. However, please note, for Marketing Management in Practice, the case study is more significant as all the questions are based upon the case materials.

The length of the mini-case study means that usually only a brief outline is provided of the situation, the organization and its marketing problems, and you must therefore learn to cope with analysing information and preparing your answer on the basis of a very limited amount of detail.

Time management

There are many differing views on time management and the approaches you can take to manage your time within the examination. You must find an approach to suit your way of working, but always remember, whatever you do, you must ensure that you allow enough time to complete the examination. Unfinished exams mean lost marks.

A typical example of managing time is as follows:

Your paper is designed to assess you over a 3-hour period. With 50 per cent of the marks being allocated to the mini-case, it means that you should dedicate somewhere around 100 minutes of your time to both read and write up the answer on this mini-case, leaving a further 80 minutes for the remaining questions. Some students, however, will prefer to allocate nearly half of their time (90 minutes) on the mini-case, so that they can read and fully absorb the case, and answer the questions in the context of it. This is also acceptable as long as you ensure that you work extremely 'SMART' for the remaining time in order to finish the examination.

Do not forget that while there is only one question within the mini-case, it can have a number of components. You must answer all the components in that question, which is where the balance of time comes into play.

Knowledge/skills tested

Throughout all the CIM papers, your knowledge, skills and ability to apply those skills will be tested. However, the mini-cases are used particularly to test application, that is your ability to take your knowledge and apply it in a structured way to a given scenario. The examiners will be looking at your decision-making ability, your analytical and communication skills and, depending on the level, your ability as a manager to solve particular marketing problems.

When the examiner is marking your paper, he or she will be looking to see how you differentiate yourself, looking at your own individual 'unique selling points'. The examiner will also want to see if you can personally apply the knowledge or whether you are only able to repeat the textbook materials.

Format of answers

On many occasions, and within all examinations, you will most likely be given a particular communication method to use. If this is the case, you must ensure that you adhere to the requirements of the examiner. This is all part of meeting customer needs.

The likely communication tools you will be expected to use are as follows:

- o Memorandum
- o Memorandum/report
- o Report
- o Briefing notes
- o Presentation
- o Press release
- o Advertisement
- o Plan.

Make sure that you familiarize yourself with these particular communication tools and practice using them to ensure that, on the day, you will be able to respond confidently to the communication requests of the examiner.

By the same token, while communication methods are important, so is meeting the specific requirements of the question. This means you must understand what is meant by the precise instruction given. *Note the following terms carefully*:

- ○ *Identify* – Select key issues, point out key learning points, establish clearly what the examiner expects you to identify.
- ○ *Illustrate* – The examiner expects you to provide examples, scenarios and key concepts that illustrate your learning.
- ○ *Compare and contrast* – Look at the range of similarities between the two situations, contexts or even organizations. Then compare them, that is ascertain and list how activities, features and so on agree or disagree. Contrasting means highlighting the differences between the two.
- ○ *Discuss* – Questions that have 'discuss' in them offer a tremendous opportunity for you to debate, argue, justify your approach or understanding of the subject area – *caution* it is not an opportunity to waffle.
- ○ *Briefly explain* – This means being succinct, structured and concise in your explanation, within the answer. Make your points clear, transparent and relevant.
- ○ *State* – Present in a clear, brief format.
- ○ *Interpret* – Expound the meaning of, make clear and explicit what it is you see and understand within the data provided.
- ○ *Outline* – Provide the examiner with the main concepts and features being asked for and avoid minor technical details. Structure will be critical here, or else you could find it difficult to contain your answer.
- ○ *Relate* – Show how different aspects of the syllabus connect together.
- ○ *Evaluate* – Review and reflect upon an area of the syllabus, a particular practice, an article and so on, and consider its overall worth in respect of its use as a tool or a model and its overall effectiveness in the role it plays.

Source: Worsam, Mike (1989) *How to Pass Marketing*, Croner.

Your approach to mini-cases

There is no one right way to approach and tackle a mini-case study, indeed it will be down to each individual to use their own creativity in tackling the tasks presented. You will have to use your initiative and discretion about how best to approach the mini-case. Having said this, however, there are some basic steps you can take.

- ○ Ensure that you read through the case study at least twice before making any judgements, starting to analyse the information provided, or indeed writing the answers.
- ○ On the third occasion read through the mini-case and, using a highlighter, start marking the essential and relevant information critical to the content and context. Then turn your attention to the question again, this time reading slowly and carefully to assess what it is you are expected to do. Note any instructions that the examiner gives you, and then start to plan how you might answer the question. Whatever the question, ensure the answer has a structure: a beginning, a structured central part and, finally, always a conclusion.
- ○ Keep the context of the question continually in mind: that is, the specifics of the case and the role which you might be performing.
- ○ Because there is limited material available, you will sometimes need to make assumptions. Don't be afraid to do this, it will show initiative on your part. Assumptions are an important part of dealing with case studies and can help you to be quite creative with your answer. However, do explain the basis of your assumptions within your answer so that the examiner understands the nature of them, and why you have arrived at your particular outcome. *Always ensure that your assumptions are realistic.*

    o Only now you are approaching the stage where it is time to start writing your answer to the question, tackling the problems, making decisions and recommendations on the case scenario set before you. As mentioned previously, your points will often be best set out in a report or memo-type format, particularly if the examiner does not specify a communication method.

    o Ensure that your writing is succinct, avoids waffle and responds directly to the questions asked.

Part B – Options choice questions

Each of Part B is comprised of four traditional questions, each worth 25 per cent. You will be expected to choose two of those questions, to make up the remaining 50 per cent of available marks. (Again please note that the structure is the same for Marketing Management in Practice, but that all questions are applied to the case study.)

Realistically, the same principles apply for these questions as in the case study. Communication formats, reading through the questions, structure, role-play, context and so on – everything is the same.

Part B will cover a number of broader issues from within the syllabus and will be taken from any element of it. The examiner makes the choice, and no prior direction is given to students or tutors on what that might be.

As regards time management in this area, if you use about 100 minutes for the mini-case you should have around 80 minutes left. This provides you with around 40 minutes to plan and write a question, to write, review and revise your answers. Keep practising – use a cooker timer, alarm clock or mobile phone alarm as your timer and work hard at answering questions within the time-frame given.

Specimen examination papers and answers

To help you prepare and understand the nature of the paper, go to www.cim.co.uk/learningzone to access Specimen Answers and Senior Examiner's advice for these exam questions. During your study, the author of your coursebook may have, on occasions, asked you to refer to these papers and answer the questions. You should undertake these exercises and utilize every opportunity to practise meeting examination requirements.

The specimen answers are vital learning tools. They are not always perfect, as they are answers written by students and annotated by the Senior Examiners, but they will give you a good indication of the approaches you could take, and the examiners' annotations suggest how these answers might be improved. Please use them.

The CIM learning zone website provides you with links to many useful case studies which would help you to put your learning into context when you are revising.

Key elements of preparation

One Senior Examiner suggests the three elements involved in preparing for your examination can be summarized thus:

1. Learning
2. Memory
3. Revision.

Let us look at each point in turn.

Learning

Quite often, students find it difficult to learn properly. You can passively read books, look at some of the materials, perhaps revise a little, and regurgitate it all in the examination. In the main, however, this is rather an unsatisfactory method of learning. It is meaningless, shallow and ultimately of little use in practice.

For learning to be truly effective it must be active and applied. You must involve yourself in the learning process by thinking about what you have read, testing it against your experience by reflecting on how you use particular aspects of marketing, and how you could perhaps improve your own performance by implementing particular aspects of your learning into your everyday life. You should adopt the old adage of 'learning by doing'. If you do, you will find that passive learning has no place in your study life.

Below are some suggestions that have been prepared to assist you with the learning pathway throughout your revision.

- Always make your own notes, in words you understand, and ensure that you combine all the sources of information and activities within them.
- Always try to relate your learning back to your own organization.
- Make sure you define key terms concisely, wherever possible.
- Do not try to memorize your ideas, but work on the basis of understanding and, most important, applying them.
- Think about the relevant and topical questions that might be set – use the questions and answers in your coursebooks to identify typical questions that might be asked in the future.
- Attempt all the questions within each of your coursebooks since these are vital tests of your active learning and understanding.

Memory

If you are prepared to undertake an active learning programme then your knowledge will be considerably enhanced, as understanding and application of knowledge does tend to stay in your 'long-term' memory. It is likely that passive learning will only stay in your 'short-term' memory.

Do not try to memorize in parrot fashion; it is not helpful and, even more important, examiners are experienced in identifying various memorizing techniques and therefore will spot them as such.

Having said this, it is quite useful to memorize various acronyms such as SWOT, PEST, PESTEL, STEEPLE, or indeed various models such as Ansoff, GE Matrix, Shell Directional

Policy Matrix and so on, as in some of the questions you may be required to use illustrations of these to assist your answer.

Revision

The third and final stage to consider is 'revision', which is what we will concentrate on in detail below. Here, just a few key tips are offered.

Revision should be an ongoing process rather than a panic measure that you decide to undertake just before the examination. You should be preparing notes *throughout* your course, with the view to using them as part of your revision process. Therefore, ensure that your notes are sufficiently comprehensive that you can reuse them successfully.

For each concept you learn about, you should identify, through your reading and your own personal experience, at least two or three examples that you could use; this then gives you some scope to broaden your perspective during the examination. It will, of course, help you gain some points for initiative with the examiners.

Knowledge is not something you will gain overnight – as we saw earlier, it is not a quick fix; it involves a process of learning that enables you to lay solid foundations upon which to build your long-term understanding and application. This will benefit you significantly in the future, not just in the examination.

In essence, you should ensure that you do the following in the period before the real intensive revision process begins.

- o Keep your study file well organized, updated, and full of newspaper and journal cuttings that may help you formulate examples in your mind for use during the examination.
- o Practice defining key terms and acronyms from memory.
- o Prepare topic outlines and essay answer plans.
- o When you start your intensive revision, ensure it is planned and structured in the way described below. And then finally, read your concentrated notes the night before the examination.

Revision planning

You are now on a critical path – although hopefully not too critical at this time – with somewhere in the region of between 4 and 6 weeks to go to the examination. The following hints and tips will help you plan out your revision study.

- o You will, as already explained, need to be very organized. Therefore, before doing anything else, put your files, examples, reading material and so on, in good order, so that you are able to work with them in the future and, of course, make sense of them.
- o Ensure that you have a quiet area within which to work. It is very easy to get distracted when preparing for an examination.
- o Take out your file along with your syllabus, and make a list of key topic areas that you have studied and which you now need to revise. You could use the basis of this book to do that, by taking each unit a step at a time.
- o Plan the use of your time carefully. Ideally you should start your revision at least 6 weeks prior to the exam, therefore work out how many spare hours you could give to the revision process and then start to allocate time in your diary, and do not double-book with anything else.

○ Give up your social life for a short period of time. As the saying goes 'no pain – no gain'.

○ Looking at each of the subject areas in turn, identify which are your strengths and which are your weaknesses. Which areas have you grasped and understood, and which are the areas that you have really struggled with? Split your page into two and make a list on each side. For example:

Planning and control	
Strengths	**Weaknesses**
Audit – PEST, SWOT, Models	Ratio analysis
Portfolio analysis	Market sensing
	Productivity analysis
	Trend extrapolation
	Forecasting

○ Breakdown your list again and divide the points of weakness, giving priority in the first instance to your weakest areas and even prioritizing them by giving each of them a number. This will enable you to master the more difficult areas. Up to 60 per cent of your remaining revision time should be given over to that, as you may find you have to undertake a range of additional reading and also perhaps seeking tutor support, if you are studying at a CIM Accredited Study Centre.

○ The rest of the time should be spent reinforcing your knowledge and understanding of the stronger areas, spending time testing yourself on how much you really know.

○ Should you be taking two examinations or more at any one time, then the breakdown and managing of your time will be critical.

○ Taking a subject at a time, work through your notes and start breaking them down into subsections of learning, and ultimately into key learning points, items that you can refer to time and time again, that are meaningful and that your mind will absorb. You yourself will know how best you remember the key points. Some people try to develop acronyms, flowcharts or matrices, mind maps, fishbone diagrams and so on, or various connection diagrams that help them recall certain aspects of models. You could also develop processes that enable you to remember approaches to various options. (But do remember what we said earlier about regurgitating stuff, parrot fashion.)

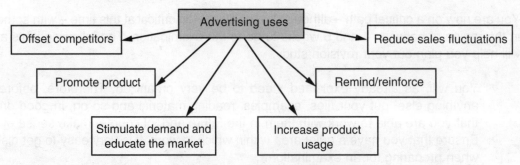

Figure A1.1 Use of a diagram to summarize key components of a concept
Source: Adapted from Dibb, Simkin, Pride and Ferrell, *Marketing Concepts and Strategies*, 4th edition, Houghton Mifflin, 2001

Figure A1.1 is just a brief example of how you could use a 'bomb-burst' diagram (which, in this case, highlights the uses of advertising) as a very helpful approach to memorizing key elements of learning.

o Eventually you should reduce your key learning to bullet points. For example, imagine you were looking at the concept of Time Management – you could eventually reduce your key learning to a bullet list containing the following points in relation to 'Effective Prioritization'.

- Organize
- Take time
- Delegate
- Review.

o Each of these headings would then remind you of the elements you need to discuss associated with the subject area.

o Avoid getting involved in reading too many textbooks at this stage, as you may start to find that you are getting confused overall.

o Look at examination questions in previous papers, and start to observe closely the various roles and tasks they expect you to undertake, and importantly, the context in which they are set.

o *Use the specimen exam papers and specimen answers* to support your learning and see how you could actually improve upon them.

o Without exception, find an associated examination question for the areas that you have studied and revised, and undertake it (more than once, if necessary).

o Without referring to notes or books, try to draft an answer plan with the key concepts, knowledge, models and information that are needed to successfully complete the answer. Then refer to the specimen answer to see how close you are to the actual outline presented. Planning your answer, and ensuring that key components are included and that the question has a meaningful structure, is one of the most beneficial activities that you can undertake.

o Now write the answer out in full, time constrained and written by hand, not with the use of IT. (At this stage, you are still expected to be the scribe for the examination and present handwritten work. Many of us find this increasingly difficult as we spend more and more time using our computers to present information. Do your best to be neat. Spidery handwriting is often off-putting to the examiner.)

o When writing answers as part of your revision process, also be sure to practice the following essential examinations techniques:

- *Identify and use the communication method* – Requested by the examiner.
- *Always have three key parts to the answer* – An introduction, a middle section that develops your answer in full and a conclusion. Where appropriate, ensure that you have an introduction, a main section, a summary/conclusion and, if requested or helpful, recommendations.
- *Always answer the question in the context or role set.*
- *Always comply with the nature and terms of the question.*
- *Leave white space* – Do not overcrowd your page; leave space between para-graphs, and make sure your sentences do not merge into one blur. (Don't worry, there is always plenty of paper available to use in the examination.)
- *Count* – How many actions the question asks you to undertake and double-check at the end that you have met the full range of demands of the question.
- *Use examples* – To demonstrate your knowledge and understanding of the parti-cular syllabus area. These can be from journals, the Internet, the press, or your own experience.
- *Display your vigour and enthusiasm for marketing* – Remember to think of the Senior Examiner as your customer, or future employer, and do your best to deliver what is wanted to satisfy their needs. Impress them and show them how you are a 'cut above the rest'.

o Review all your practice answers critically, with the above points in mind.

199

Practical actions

The critical path is becoming even more critical now as the examination looms. The following are vital points:

o Have you registered with CIM?
o Do you know where you are taking your examination? CIM should let you know approximately 1 month in advance.
o Do you know where your examination centre is? If not, find out, take a drive, time it – whatever you do don't be late!
o Make sure you have all the tools of the examination ready. A dictionary, calculator, pens, pencils, ruler and so on. Try not to use multiple shades of pens, but at the same time make your work look professional. *Avoid using red and green as these are the colours that will be used for marking.*

Summary

Above all, you must remember that you personally have invested a tremendous amount of time, effort and money in studying for this programme and it is therefore imperative that you consider the suggestions given here, as they will help to maximize your return on your investment.

Many of the hints and tips offered here are generic and will work across most of the CIM courses. We have tried to select those that will help you most in taking a sensible, planned approach to your study and revision.

The key to your success is being prepared to put in the time and effort required, planning your revision, and equally important is planning and answering your questions in a way that will ensure that you pass your examination on the day.

The advice offered here aims to guide you from a practical perspective. Guidance on syllabus content and developments associated with your learning will become clear to you as you work through this coursebook. The authors of each coursebook have given subject-specific guidance on the approach to the examination and on how to ensure that you meet the content requirements of the kind of question you will face. These considerations are in addition to the structuring issues we have been discussing throughout this Appendix.

Each of the authors and Senior Examiners will guide you on their preferred approach to questions and answers as they go. Therefore, where you are presented with an opportunity to be involved in some activity or undertake an examination question either during or at the end of your study units, do take it. It not only prepares you for the examination, but also helps you learn in the applied way we discussed above.

Here, then, is a last reminder:

o Ensure you make the most of your learning process throughout.
o Keep structured and orderly notes from which to revise.
o Plan your revision, don't let it just happen.
o Provide examples to enhance your answers.
o Practise your writing skills in order that you present your work well and your writing is readable.
o Take as many opportunities as possible to test your knowledge and measure your progress.
o Plan and structure your answers.
o Always do as the question asks you, especially with regard to context and communication method.
o *Do not leave it until the last minute!*

The writers would like to take this opportunity to wish you every success in your endeavours to study, to revise and to pass your examinations.

Karen Beamish
Academic Development Advisor

appendix 2
assignment-based assessment

Introduction – the basis to the assignments and the integrative project

Within the CIM qualifications at both Professional Certificate and Professional Diploma in Marketing, there are several assessment options available. These are detailed in the outline of modules below. The purpose of an assignment is to provide another format to complete each module for students who want to apply the syllabus concepts from a module to their own or a selected organization. For either qualification there are three modules providing assessment via an assignment and one module assessed via an integrative work-based project. The module assessed via the integrative project is the summative module for each qualification.

	Entry modules	Research & analysis	Planning	Implementation	Management of Marketing
Post Graduate Professional Diploma	Entry module – Post Graduate Professional Diploma	Analysis & Evaluation	Strategic Marketing Decisions	Managing Marketing Performance	Strategic Marketing in Practice
Professional Diploma	Entry module – Professional Diploma	Marketing Research & Information	Marketing Planning	Marketing Communications	Marketing Management in Practice
Professional Certificate		Marketing Environment	Marketing Fundamentals	Customer Communications	Marketing in Practice
Introductory Certificate		Supporting marketing processes (research & analysis, planning and implementation)			

Outline of CIM 'standard' syllabus, (The Chartered Institute of Marketing, September 2003)

The use of assignments does not mean that this route is easier than an examination. Both formats are carefully evaluated to ensure that a grade B in the assessment/integrative project route is the same as a grade B in the examination. However, the use of assignments does allow a student to complete the assessment for a module over a longer period of time than a 3-hour examination. This will inevitably mean work being undertaken over the time span of a module. For those used to cramming for exams, writing an assignment over several weeks which comprises a total of four separate questions will be a very different approach.

Each module within the qualification contains a different assignment written specifically for the module. These are designed to test understanding and provide the opportunity for you to demonstrate your abilities through the application of theory to practice. The format and structure of each module's assignment is identical, although the questions asked will differ and the exact type of assignment varies. The questions within an assignment will relate directly to the syllabus for that particular module, thereby giving the opportunity to demonstrate understanding and application.

The assignment structure

The assignment for each module is broken down into a range of questions. These consist of a core question, and a selection of optional questions. The core question will always relate to the main aspects of each module's syllabus. Coupled with this are a range of four optional questions which will each draw from a different part of the syllabus. Students are requested to select two optional questions from the four available. In addition, a reflective statement requires a student to evaluate their learning from the module. When put together these form the assessment for the entire module. The overall pass mark for the module is the same as through an examination route, which is set at 50 per cent. In addition, the grade band structure is also identical to that of an examination.

Core question

This is the longest and therefore the most important section of your assignment. Covering the major components of the syllabus, the core question is designed to provide a challenging assignment which both tests the theoretical element and also permits application to a selected organization or situation. Please observe the word limit for the core and optional elements and abide by the assignment rubric. Additional information should be in the form of appendices. However, the appendices should be kept to a minimum. Advice here is that there should be no longer than five pages of additional pertinent information.

Optional questions

There are a total of four questions provided for Professional Certificate and Professional Diploma in Marketing syllabus from which a student is asked to select two. Each answer is expected to provide a challenge although the actual task required varies. As mentioned above, please observe the word limits outlined in the rubric, as it is important to follow the guidelines outlined by CIM.

These are designed to test areas of the syllabus not covered by the core question. As such it is possible to base all of your questions on the same organization although there is significant benefit in using more than one organization as a basis for your assignment. Some of the questions specifically require a different organization to be selected from the one used for the core question. This occurs only where the questions are requiring similar areas to be investigated and will be specified clearly on the question itself.

Within the assignment there are several types of questions that may be asked, including:

○ *A report* – The question requires a formal report to be completed, detailing an answer to the specific question set. This will often be reporting on a specific issue to an individual.

○ *A briefing paper or notes* – Preparing a briefing paper or a series of notes which may be used for a presentation.

○ *A presentation* – You may be required to either prepare the presentation only or to deliver the presentation in addition to its preparation. The audience for the presentation should be considered carefully and ICT used where possible.

○ *A discussion paper* – The question requires an academic discussion paper to be prepared. You should show a range of sources and concepts within the paper. You may also be required to present the discussion paper as part of a question.

○ *A project plan or action plan* – Some questions ask for planning techniques to be demonstrated. As such, the plan must be for the timescale given and costs shown where applicable. The use of ICT is recommended here in order to create the plan diagrammatically.

○ *Planning a research project* – Whilst market research may be required, questions have often asked for simply a research plan in a given situation. This would normally include timescales, the type(s) of research to be gathered, sampling, planned data collection and analysis.

○ *Conducting research* – Following on from a research plan, a question can require the student(s) to undertake a research-gathering exercise. A research question can be either an individual or a group activity depending upon the question. This will usually result in a report of the findings of the exercise plus any recommendations arising from your findings.

○ *Gathering of information and reporting* – Within many questions, information will need gathering. The request for information can form part or all of a question. This may be a background to the organization, the activities contained in the question or external market and environmental information. It is advisable to detail the types of information utilized, their sources and report on any findings. Such a question will often ask for recommendations for the organization – these should be drawn from the data and not simply personal opinion.

○ *An advisory document* – A question here will require students to evaluate a situation and present advice and recommendations drawn from findings and theory. Again, any advice should be backed up with evidence and not a personal perspective only.

○ *An exercise either planning and/or delivering the exercise* – At both Professional Certificate and Professional Diploma, exercises are offered as optional questions. These provide students with the opportunity to devise an exercise and may also require the delivery of this exercise. Such an activity should be evidenced where possible.

○ *A role-play with associated documentation* – Several questions have asked students to undertake role-plays in exercises such as team-building. These are usually videoed and documentation demonstrating the objectives of the exercise provided.

Each of these questions relate directly towards specific issues to be investigated, evaluated and answered. In addition, some of the questions asked present situations to be considered. These provide opportunities for specific answers relating directly to the question asked.

In order to aid students completing the assignment, each question is provided with an outline of marking guidance. This relates to the different categories by which each question is marked. The marker of your assignment will be provided with a detailed marking scheme constructed around the same marking guidance provided to students.

For both the core and optional questions, it is important to use referencing where sources have been utilized. This has been a weakness in the past and continues to be an issue. There have been cases of plagiarism identified during marking and moderation, together with a distinct lack of references and bibliography. It is highly recommended that a bibliography be included with each question and sources are cited within the text itself. The type of referencing method used is not important, only that sources are referred to.

Integrative project structure

The integrative project is designed to provide an in-company approach to assessment rather than having specified assignments. Utilized within the summative module element of each level's syllabus, this offers a student the chance to produce a piece of work which tackles a specific issue. The integrative project can only be completed after undertaking other modules as it will rely on information in each of these as guidance. The integrative project is approximately 5000 words in length. The integrative project is marked by CIM assessors and not your own tutors.

Assignments – Marketing Communications

A new module at Professional Diploma in Marketing, the elements within this module are concerned with branding, marketing communications, channel management and customer relationship management. The module draws together elements of the previous Marketing Customer Interface module at Advanced Certificate and Integrated Marketing Communications at Postgraduate Diploma to create a cohesive whole examining issues of buyer behaviour and the role of communications in the decision-making and relationship management process. Comprising four elements, the module covers the key aspects responsible for communications within marketing.

Element 1 – Understanding customer dynamics

This element concerns itself with buyer behaviour, covering the decision-making process and the role of communications within marketing. In addition, corporate responsibility and ethics are also included and their impact on communications. This leads to a range of potential question areas covering decision-making, buyer behaviour plus other aspects.

Your organization operates a graduate recruitment programme, drawing in up to 15 new graduates each year as part of a growth plan. Many of these graduates come from non-business areas, although this is not believed to hamper their overall performance. However, these graduates often have a steeper learning curve in the early part of their training as they learn about business skills and concepts.

As part of the induction process for a new graduate trainee in your section of the organization, who has a chemistry degree, you have been asked to spend a session with him discussing the area of decision-making and in particular, buyer behaviour. In addition, the organization wants to be viewed as socially responsible and therefore this should be incorporated into the session. The session can take any format you wish, although it needs to be suitable for the participants.

An answer to this question needs to cover the aspects within element one, including the concept of buyer behaviour and decision-making. The situation is not given and therefore it is possible to select either or both B2C and B2B buyer behaviour. The best route to follow would be to provide a perspective of both types, together with the decision-making process in each.

In addition, the format is not specified. Here, a range of alternatives is possible from a formal presentation through to a discussion document. The graduate is from a chemistry background and therefore will expect scientific evidence and theory to substantiate any point made. An answer, therefore, should include the following:

- A background and situation for the organization is selected as a basis for an answer to the question. The format of the session should be evaluated, and a rationale provided for the selection.
- A background to the organization is required, together with information on the types of buyers involved with the organization.
- An answer needs to include concepts of buyer behaviour, illustrated with examples. This will be related to the process of marketing communications and the decision-making process in relation to buyer behaviour and information.
- As per earlier advice, it is sensible to utilize both consumer and organizational buyer behaviour. This provides the opportunity to undertake an evaluation of both types of behaviour in the situation of the organization.
- The element covers ethics and corporate responsibility. As such, its role in any process of marketing communications and buyer behaviour will require highlighting.
- As the format is free choice, evidence will be required of the session even if it is to be a discussion. The most sensible solution for all parties would be a discussion document, identifying the key concepts in buyer behaviour and relating this to the organization selected.

Element 2 – Co-ordinated marketing communications

The second element of the module goes further into the communications process. Examining the roles marketing communication plays through the DRIP process, communication strategies and the actual communication mechanisms involved, this element covers 50 per cent of the module. As such, it lends itself to being a core question and offers a number of possibilities as a basis for questions to be asked.

You have been invited to participate in the annual 'out of the balloon' joint institute challenge. This comprises four participants; one each from the Chartered Institute of Marketing, the Chartered Institute for Purchasing and Supply, the Association of Chartered and Certified Accountants and the Chartered Institute of Personnel and Development. The session is 'refereed' by the Chartered Management Institute. The purpose is to persuade the audience of the value of your job role rather than the others, with the loser in each round being 'thrown out' of the balloon. The losing members then each donates £250 to a charity of the winner's choosing.

Over the past few years, the rivalry has been friendly but competition intense. To be the first out of the balloon has been the embarrassing result of the Chartered Institute of Marketing speaker for the past 3 years, with few CIM members attending last year's competition due to their low expectation. You have been given the poison chalice and the opportunity to redeem your institute. As part of your process of survival, you have a 15-minute presentation to make on the role and importance of marketing communications.

This is a challenging situation. Not only can you manage to humiliate yourself but also your professional institute at the same time. The format calls for a presentation and this should be followed. In addition, the nature of the audience must be considered – there will be a range of professions listening, many of whom may not feel affection for marketing. The first stage in an answer might be to consider how to get more CIM members to attend in order to balance the voting!

o The format of the presentation should be through PowerPoint. However, the nature of the audience means that there will be a range of levels of knowledge listening to the presentation.
o The presentation needs to identify the role of marketing communications within marketing, together with the DRIP factors in marketing communication.
o Aspects of push, pull and profile strategies would help a presentation, together with above-, through- and below-the-line communications. Key accounts and KAM would also provide a link to other professions.
o The presentation would also cover the different types of communications media with their characteristics plus measurement methods of effectiveness. Budgets should not be ignored and international/cultural dimensions need to be incorporated into the presentation.
o A copy of the presentation plus notes should be provided on disk and in paper format.

Element 3 – Marketing channels

Building on introductory thinking regarding marketing channels from Professional Certificate in Marketing, this element takes the thinking further. It covers B2C, B2B and trade channels and the role of the promotional mix within each of these. Drawing in issues of channel relationships, conflict and ICT-based relationships there are several questions which present themselves. These will usually be based around the channel issues and may form a range of perspectives.

> *Your organization wishes to evaluate the opportunities of using an Internet-based marketing communications route to manage their commercial purchasing or sales channels. In order to provide an understanding of the issues in using an Internet-based marketing communications channel you have been asked to prepare a report which considers the implications of developing a new marketing communications channel.*

This question draws in a wide selection of areas upon which the answer can be based. The organization can be of any type and use any form of marketing channel. The move of introducing an Internet-based marketing communications channel could be used for purchasing or sales, drawing in a consideration of channel management. There needs to be a background to the organization contained in the answer, together with an evaluation of the potential opportunity plus any drawback which exists. Combining theory with practical investigation here would cover all the components of the element. The answer needs to include:

o A background to the organization and a rationale for its selection. This also needs to include details of the current marketing channels used plus any history of using the Internet for marketing communications and managing marketing channels.
o An explanation of the role of marketing communications and the different channels available. Issues of using marketing channel management and using marketing communications within channels are needed here. This would cover channel conflict and control plus how marketing communications can enhance the effect of marketing channels.
o Consideration of the use of Internet-based communications to enhance and manage the channel is required. In addition, issues resulting from this also need including. These may include the suitability of the digital medium, technology and effectiveness.
o The format requested is a report and therefore the answer should be produced in a report format. However, references used need to be included as a bibliography.

Element 4 – Relationship management

The final element within the Marketing Communications module covers marketing relationships in transaction and relationship marketing. It also includes agency relationships as part of the element plus regulatory and other arrangements. Questions within this element will draw in aspects from other elements and other modules. However, any question asked will usually concentrate on the relationship aspect of marketing communications, as demonstrated in the example question below:

You have been asked to produce a briefing paper about managing the relationships of either agencies or stakeholders within your organization through marketing communications. This should cover the purpose, role and use of marketing communications as part of relationship management.

This question draws in the core aspects of the element, together with areas of other modules when considering relationships of all types. Two options are offered here; agencies or stakeholders and an answer will have to select one of these. In addition, the question asks for a briefing paper and this format should be followed, rather than a report. An answer will usually contain:

○ A background to the organization selected and a rationale for selection of either agencies or stakeholders.

○ A background to relationship marketing, with a comparison of how this differs to traditional marketing. In addition, a description of relationship marketing and how relationships can be managed through marketing communications will be required as part of the answer.

○ For an answer examining stakeholder relationships, this needs to evaluate how marketing communications can improve the management of these relationships. A range of stakeholders should be evaluated and the best format for communicating with these and managing the relationship needs to be identified.

○ An answer regarding agencies would centre upon the relationship between an agency and its clients. This could include how marketing communications helps an agency manage its activities or how agencies meet client needs through marketing communications and relationship management.

○ The assignment needs to be prepared as a briefing paper, not a report.

Assignment regulations

There have been a number of changes to the assignment structure compared with previous years, timed with the introduction of the new syllabi. These have been designed to provide consistency in approach for a student whether they are completing the assessment for a module by examination, assignment or integrative project. The more significant changes include:

○ *For the current academic year tutors at CIM centres will mark assignments* – These are then moderated by CIM assessors. An integrative project is marked by CIM assessors only.

○ *No resubmission of assignments, as per an examination* – In previous years a range of assignments were being submitted. Where a student does not achieve the 50 per cent pass mark, they were requested to re-take the assessment for the module through examination or assignment/integrative project.

○ *Whichever assessment route is selected is fixed rather than having the option to change at the last minute* – Past history has shown that students sometimes begin on an assignment route, change to an examination at the last minute due to not meeting the deadline and then score badly in the examination. The paths to an assignment or examination are different and therefore it is unadvisable to switch, which is the reason for the change of rule.

○ *In the 2002–2003 academic year word limits for questions and assignments were introduced* – This was introduced due to assignments being submitted which were of a wide variety of lengths. These ranged from under 2000 words to over 25 000 words.

Where a student is completing four modules by assignment this would equal over 100 000 words – the equivalent of a medium-sized textbook or novel. As such, it became impossible for two assignments to be considered together. Therefore the word limit guidance was introduced in order to provide equality for all students undertaking the assessment by assignment.

○ *Two sets of assignments per year as with the examination route* – With this change, students are required to complete the assignment aimed at the nearest examination session. Previously students had between 3 and 9 months to complete an assignment depending upon whether it was given out in September for a June deadline or in March for the June deadline. Therefore a decision was made to follow the examination route with the intention of giving all students equal time to complete an assignment.

These summarize the key changes which have occurred due to the introduction of new syllabi with the assignment/integrative project route in order that there is parity of assessment at all levels and using all formats. Some of these changes have been significant, others minor. However, all the changes have been considered thoughtfully and with the best intentions for the students in mind.

Use of case studies

For anyone who is not working or has difficulty in access to information on their or another organization, there are a number of case studies available which allow the completion of a module using a case-based approach rather than basing it upon an organization identified by the student. These case studies are provided on a request-only basis through your accredited CIM centre and should only be used as a last resort. Using a case study as the basis for your assignment will not mean an easier approach to the assignment. However, they do provide an opportunity to undertake assignments when no other alternative exists. Each case study comes with a certain amount of information which can be used specifically for the completion of a question. Additional information may need to be assumed or researched in order to create a comprehensive assignment.

Submission of assignments/integrative project

The following information will aid not only yourself and your tutor who marks your work but also the CIM assessor who will be moderating your work and the integrative project. In addition, the flow diagram represents the process of an assignment/integrative project from start to final mark.

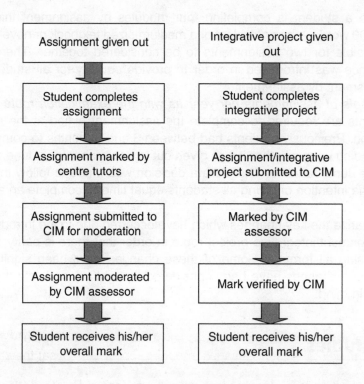

When completing and submitting assignments or the integrative project, refer to the following for guidance:

o Read through each question before starting out. Particularly with the core question there will be a considerable amount of work to undertake. Choose your optional questions wisely.
o Answer the question set and use the mark guidance given regarding the marking scheme.
o Reference each question within the assignment and use a bibliography.
o Complete all documentation thoroughly. This is designed to aid both the CIM and yourself.
o Ensure that the assignment is bound as per instructions given. Currently, assignments are requested not to be submitted in plastic wallets or folders as work can become detached or lost. Following the submission instructions provided aids both the CIM administrators and the CIM assessor who will be marking (integrative project) or moderating (assignments) your work.
o Complete the candidate declaration sheet showing that you have undertaken this work yourself. *Please note that if you wish the information contained in your assignment to remain confidential you must state this on the front of the assignment.* Whilst CIM assessors will not use any information pertaining to your or another organization, CIM may wish to use the answer to a question as an example.

An assignment will be marked by a tutor at your CIM centre followed by moderation by a CIM assessor. The integrative project will be marked by a CIM assessor as per an examination with moderation by the CIM. To ensure objectivity by CIM assessors there exists a marking meeting prior to any marking in order that standardization can occur. The senior assessor for each subject also undertakes further verification of both examinations and assessments to ensure parity between each type of assessment.

Chris Fill, Senior Examiner, February 2004
Based on the appendix written by David Lane,
Former Senior Moderator (Advanced Certificate), February 2003

appendix 3
answers and debriefings

Unit 1

Debriefing Activity 1.1

This will give you a general feel for the range of communications received and their effects. Most of these we ignore or take little notice of. This activity will hopefully encourage you to take a more critical look at these messages and try to understand what they are about.

Debriefing Activity 1.2

This could involve a whole host of different examples from Michael Jordan to Michael Jackson. The former is an example of where clear linkages were established and the latter where controversy overcame the benefits.

Debriefing Activity 1.3

Make and keep your notes. These kind of examples will provide useful reminders for exam revision.

Debriefing Activity 1.4

Most television car ads stress something (technological) that is new to the brand and provide an informational point of differentiation. Direct response ads for wine make a point about the quality, variety and source of their products.

Debriefing Activity 1.5

Compare these to your answer for the third activity.

Debriefing Activity 1.6

To determine change you may need to look at past ads for a brand.

Debriefing Activity 1.7

New variants, comparative communications and distinctive directive copy (new facilities which provide new benefits and 'have you tried new').

To reinforce beliefs, use copy that reassures the audience, shows people (slice of life) just like the target audience and maintains the same positioning statement.

Debriefing Activity 1.8

To a large extent, this will depend on the item and the contextual conditions present during the decision. However, price, product performance and comparisons with other immediate products are of most use.

Debriefing Activity 1.9

In order to prevent the onset of cognitive dissonance, marketing communications need to be used after purchase to reward customers and to prepare them for a repeat purchase. It can also be used to stimulate word-of-mouth communications.

Debriefing Activity 1.10

Support, reassurance and a reason to buy.

Debriefing Activity 1.11

As per individual preferences.

Debriefing Activity 1.12

Look for direct delivery which will reduce time risk, price to reduce financial risk and performance risk reduced by comparisons and illustrations of the product in use by happy users.

Debriefing Activity 1.13

This will result in a range of different examples. If these are in print form, keep them in a file, they will be useful for revision and provide examples that you may be able to use in your assignment or examination.

Debriefing Activity 1.14

Hopefully, this was a stimulating activity! The results will provide more examples of different approaches and encourage you to take a more critical perspective on the concept of likeability.

Debriefing Activity 1.15

Set out the role of advertising as you understand it and present the benefits. Then comment on the marketing concept that seeks to satisfy customer needs, not imaginary needs. Customers may buy a product once but will not buy it again if it fails to satisfy their needs. Advertising communicates the marketing strategy and consumers are intelligent information processors, not passive, unthinking people who are manipulated by predatory organizations.

Debriefing Question 1.1

Satisfactory answers to this question should explain the key characteristics of each element and in turn provide simple examples drawn from the mini-case. A table can be used in this circumstance if sufficient information is provided, because no comparison or evaluation is required.

Debriefing Question 1.2

Satisfactory answers to this question should explain the six types of perceived risk and then show how marketing communication tools and messages can reduce risk. For example, sales promotions (free mud flaps) to reduce functional and time risk or guarantees to reduce financial and performance risk.

Answers should attempt to evaluate the extent to which risk can be effectively reduced and the examples must be drawn on the scenario (cars).

Debriefing Question 1.3

Satisfactory answers to this question should start by defining what is meant by the term promotional message, then define the various stages of the purchase cycle and then attempt to bring the two elements together. Therefore, messages that develop awareness are required first, and this will normally involve advertising and/or public relations in the consumer sector. In addition, it may be important to develop a position in order to differentiate the brand. Then work through the various stages using the different tools, messages, media and perhaps the DRIP framework.

Debriefing Question 1.4

Satisfactory answers to this question should start by demonstrating understanding of the attitude construct (learn–feel–do) and then set out what source credibility means.

The key here is to evaluate the statement and draw out that source credibility might help build trust and positive attitudes need to be maintained in order to sustain commitment.

Unit 2

Debriefing Activity 2.1

This report highlights a number of key issues for marketers and communicators. Their impact will vary according to the type of businesses you consider. You might want to enter into CIM's debate on these issues.

Debriefing Activity 2.2

The examples that you have found should reflect good use of advertising, sales promotion, public relations, personal selling and direct marketing.

These examples can be found in journals such as *Marketing, Marketing Week* and *PR Week*. The goals are likely to be many and various but one of advertising's goals might be to raise awareness, direct marketing to create leads for the sales force or to make a sale. Public relations goals may be to create interest and sales promotions to create immediate sales.

Debriefing Activity 2.3

The object of this exercise is to see the way different market sectors utilize marketing communications. An fmcg will often use lots of mass advertising and sales promotion whereas a service relies not only on advertising but also public relations, personal selling (the service encounter) and, very often, greater use of interactive technologies.

Debriefing Activity 2.4

There is no central answer to this question as it depends upon the examples chosen. However, if you choose two different sectors (e.g. travel and banking) you may be able to see some clear differences. One of the reasons for the differences is that the task of marketing communications may be to reposition a brand, introduce a new brand or simply increase awareness. Another reason may be that buyer's behaviour in the two sectors is very different or that buyers may need to be shown how to use one of the products.

Debriefing Activity 2.5

Again there are plenty of examples to be found.

Differentiate – Brand (re)positioning such as:

- o *Remind/Reassure* – Virgin trains following various trains accidents
- o *Inform* – New products and new variant introductions
- o *Persuade* – Direct marketing and call to action advertising programmes.

Debriefing Activity 2.6

Objectives not only provide definition and direction for the advertising campaign, but they also put it into the context of the marketing strategy and plan in respect of implementation.

Setting of objectives ensures that there is value to the advertising programme, that is measurable, achievable, realistic and timebound.

It is essential that the objectives also relate to other elements of the promotional mix so that the advertising is relevant and complementary to the promotional mix strategy.

Debriefing Activity 2.7

While advertising on its own can work, to optimize effectiveness it is essential that either the advertising, associated sales promotions and direct marketing, provide the opportunity for customers to respond or to take action to either try or adopt the product. Due to the technical nature of some products, it might be that while advertising provides the awareness, personal selling, aided by direct marketing, might actually provide the information required to solve the problem of purchase, inducing early adoption of the product and associated services.

Debriefing Activity 2.8

LIST OF PRODUCTS/SALES PROMOTIONS

Debriefing Activity 2.9

Typical sales promotional activities from manufacturer to consumer includes elements relating to a pull strategy, pulling the products up through the supply chain for adoption and purchase:

- o *Encouraging trial* – Samples, gifts, trial drives of vehicles – allow customers to decide for themselves
- o *Disseminating information* – Information packs on a door-to-door basis, perhaps closely linked with a direct marketing campaign (again utilizing the integrated marketing communications approach)
- o *Trading up* – Encouraging customers to trade-up from their existing models – a typical activity of car manufacturers and white goods manufacturers.

Debriefing Activity 2.10

Public Relations complements the promotional mix in a number of ways – these are just some ways to point you in the right direction:

- o Creates a broader awareness of the brand and the organization
- o Increases coverage to principal events, and draws further attention to the corporate brand and profile
- o It represents the organization fully in both negative and positive response to events
- o It provides the basis for securing greater awareness of product developments, products launched
- o It is a form of advertising
- o As a function it might run sales promotion campaigns
- o It covers a broader potential audience than, perhaps, advertising and therefore creates awareness in new markets.

Debriefing Activity 2.11

The promotional mix should take an integrated approach to ensuring successful achievements of the marketing objectives and implementation of the strategy. Therefore, advertising, sales promotions and direct marketing present the opportunity for an awareness-raising, incentive-boosting, informative communications campaign.

As previously suggested, advertising creates the awareness, sales promotion creates the incentive and the direct mail (direct marketing) provides the channel for communication in relation to the promotion, possibly including a voucher.

The three of these promotional mix mechanisms are very compatible promotional tools.

Debriefing Question 2.1

Satisfactory answers to this question should set out the characteristics of each promotional tool against each of the 4C criteria and then provide an element of comparison.

Debriefing Question 2.2

Satisfactory answers to this question should start by establishing briefly what direct marketing is and then establish the research and audit, objectives, stages, target audience, approach, creative/media selection, resourcing, implementing and evaluation cycle.

Unit 3

Debriefing Activity 3.1

This should give you a perspective on the different approaches to agency structures. It is a changing area. Keep your eyes on relevant trade media for set-up and structure examples.

Debriefing Activity 3.2

Full service agencies provide a full suite of skills including:

- Creative skills
- Artwork
- Media buying
- Public relations
- Direct marketing
- Market research.

Under one roof, or the umbrella of the organization. Therefore in respect of standards, full service provision, integration and co-ordination, it is possibly more beneficial to select a full service agency.

A limited service agency, while they might be experienced in specific elements of advertising, do not offer the full suite of skills in-house, and therefore have to rely on outsourcing the remainder of the work. In this situation, the brief is passed on and the quality assurance issues of standardization might be diluted by introducing a third party to the client.

Debriefing Activity 3.3

This will give you a good overview of the processes involved.

Debriefing Activity 3.4

Largely a question of benefits of local knowledge and costs.

Debriefing Activity 3.5

Coca-Cola would be advised to integrate their various communications activities as strongly as possible.

Research has shown (Crimmins and Horn, 1998) that sponsorship that is integrated with advertising before, during and after the sponsored event is much more effective than without the co-ordinated advertising activity.

Debriefing Activity 3.6

The interesting part of your answer depends on those elements of the identity that you perceive as important. It may be the quality and consistency of the product/service component or are there any ethical issues that you have considered, recent news stories, what is it that dominates your thinking about these organizations?

Debriefing Activity 3.7

Saturation of domestic and regional markets, drive for economies of scale and to reduce costs, pressure to reward shareholders.

Debriefing Activity 3.8

Look for differences in presentation, copy and overall positioning. What may be apparent is the similarities rather than the differences between brands in the same market.

Debriefing Activity 3.9

- o Agency specification and resources
- o Customer and market information
- o Culture
- o Media and technological facilities (including stability and costs).

Debriefing Activity 3.10

As per the selected product.

Debriefing Activity 3.11

The principles are the same regardless of the overall context. However, differences in terms of media, message and evaluation will need to be accommodated.

Debriefing Activity 3.12

The answer depends partly upon the strategy each manufacturer has adopted or has in place. However, it is highly likely (advisable) that should existing messages be culturally acceptable (understood) in each of the new markets, adaptation to local market needs (language, dialect, media, colours, symbols) will be required.

Debriefing Activity 3.13

- ○ Language
- ○ Culture and tradition
- ○ Legal and regulatory requirements
- ○ Buying habits and motivational factors
- ○ Standards of living
- ○ Media availability and usage
- ○ The competitive environment.

Company policy on standardization and adaptation needs to be decided upon. Market and Marketing Research needs to be undertaken in order to minimize the potential difficulties.

Debriefing Activity 3.14

Your answer should consider a variety of issues: media, colours, religious reaction, cultural sensitivity, names, the message, degree of body/skin exposure and language.

Debriefing Activity 3.15

This is really about reducing costs, reaching wider geographic audiences, cultural convergence, message standardization and the threats posed by a few media owners controlling editorial perspectives and possible support for a few (rich) brands at the expense of smaller brands unable to gain (afford) access to the media.

Debriefing Activity 3.16

This will give you a wealth of information about industry practices and perspectives in different areas of communications.

Debriefing Question 3.1

Satisfactory answers to this question should set out the operational processes and, in particular, detail the various briefing and contact meetings necessary to manage the campaign. Very good answers will set out the different stages associated with a campaign right through continuous and overall campaign evaluation.

Debriefing Question 3.2

Satisfactory answers to this question should attend to the structure in terms of changing media ownership, audience and media fragmentation, regulation and controls and the impact of both technology, finance and PEST factors.

Unit 4

Debriefing Activity 4.1

This list might include retailers that you commonly use, such as a bank, leisure clubs, car dealer/repairer. Does it include branded goods suppliers?

Debriefing Activity 4.2

You will very likely be surprised at the extent of relationships that you are currently involved in the workplace. However, the challenge will be to manage them successfully in the true context of relationship marketing.

Debriefing Activity 4.3

This site contains a lot of information on different communication issues and concepts which you will find helpful to study.

Debriefing Activity 4.4

The discussion will feature an appraisal of the use of a variety of above- and below-the-line communications methods.

Debriefing Activity 4.5

Organizational markets – Require high levels of relationship management due to the intensity and time dimensions of the process of purchase. The market is essentially less fickle and more rational, which provides the basis of establishing closer links.

Closer links mean working towards gaining preferred supplier status. Achieving this will ultimately mean long-term supplier/buyer relationships and effectively putting a relationship on a strong footing.

Essentially, relationship marketing is about collaborative relationships, working together, optimizing opportunities and maximizing potential. (Taken from within the text – this should form the basis of your answer.)

Debriefing Activity 4.6

Differentiate:

Inform them of their contribution to the brand and how they are different from competitors.

Remind/Reassure:

Thank and congratulate them on their performance, send messages that remind them of their contribution to the brand performance.

Inform:

Make them aware of market conditions, brand improvements and track performance.

Persuade:

Encourage through reward, legitimation and expertise.

Debriefing Activity 4.7

The value of key account management is based on the concept of interrelated key account management – where there is almost a partnership concept between the supplier and the buyer exhibiting some of the following points:

- o Both organizations acknowledge importance to each other
- o Preferred supplier status could be achieved
- o Exit from the relationship is more difficult
- o High level of information exchange – some, information sensitive
- o Wider range of joint and innovative activity between the supplier and the buyer
- o Larger number of multifunctional contacts
- o Streamlined processes
- o Both sides are prepared to invest in the relationship
- o High volume of sales achieved
- o Better understanding of the customer
- o Developing social relationships
- o Development of trust
- o Cost savings
- o Proactive rather than reactive
- o Joint strategic planning and focus on the future
- o Opportunity to grow business.

Debriefing Question 4.1

Satisfactory answers to this question should define what KAM means and then detail the various stages of the KAM process (e.g. as per McDonald or Wilson). A short descriptive answer is all that is necessary but just listing the elements with no elaboration is not sufficient.

Debriefing Question 4.2

Satisfactory answers to this question should first establish the centrality and meaning of the terms 'trust' and 'commitment' and then show how each of the relevant tools and messages might assist. For example, the significance of personal selling should not be overlooked in this capacity and the role of public relations in establishing and maintaining reputation.

Unit 5

Debriefing Activity 5.1

The tasks are focused on providing service outputs for retailers:

- o Assure product availability
- o Provide customer service
- o Extend credit and financial support
- o Offer product assortment and convenience
- o Provide technical service and support
- o Break bulk.

Debriefing Activity 5.2

These notes need to show that there are two main reasons:

1. To improve exchange efficiencies
2. To improve performance.

This is achieved through:

- o Reducing (or sharing) risk
- o Selling and buying
- o Assist transportation – speed and safety
- o Facilitating storage
- o Providing finance and working capital
- o Generating market information.

Debriefing Activity 5.3

Consumers do not actively seek to form relationships with their suppliers.

The variety and nature of the products and services exchanged are different.

Channel intermediaries do not consume products but add value themselves.

Debriefing Activity 5.4

An example would be the holiday organization TUI. They own:

Tour operators – for example Portland Direct and Thomson

Travel agents – for example Lunn Poly and Callers Pegasus

Airlines – for example Britannia Airways and Corsair

Hotel companies – for example Iberotel and Atlantica

Incoming agencies – for example TUI Portugal

Specialist travel – for example TQ3 Travel Solutions

Management companies.

Debriefing Activity 5.5

If this activity is undertaken across two or more sectors you will be able to see the contrast. For example, channels in fmcg tend to be long and indirect compared to business market channels, short and more direct.

In the consumer markets, note the variety of direct, wholesaler, retailer only and electronic channels.

Debriefing Activity 5.6

Disputes over deliveries, product quality, territories and geographic exclusivity rights, payments, stocking competitor's products, discounting, new product development, commissions and product customization, to name a few.

Debriefing Activity 5.7

Your examples will reflect the variety and intensity of conflict. Some instances will become public knowledge and others will be contained, perhaps within your company or organization.

Debriefing Activity 5.8

Communications between channel members is important to:

- o Provide product and technical information
- o Provide customer service and support
- o Demonstrate trust and commitment
- o Enable the various channel flows to operate
- o Provide a point of differentiation
- o Persuade dealers to take stock.

Debriefing Activity 5.9

Information in serial flows is repeated to different audiences. Information may become distorted (unintentionally) and may be symbolic of hierarchy and customer value.

Simultaneous flows allow for information to be disseminated equally and without deviance.

Debriefing Question 5.1

Satisfactory answers to this question should focus on the three main forms of conflict and then recommend ways in which marketing communications might assist. For example, domain-based conflict can be reduced by all parties sharing information more openly and this can be implemented through personal selling, greater use of extranets, contact meetings, collaborative advertising, corporate reputation, public relations and so on.

Debriefing Question 5.2

Satisfactory responses to this question should be in context (cosmetics manufacturer) and should be based on a good understanding of what trust and commitment mean and what a retailer might need in terms of information and support. The answer needs to consider the issues and make a judgement about whether factors other than marketing communications might impact more on a retailer's trust and commitment in a supplier.

Unit 6

Debriefing Activity 6.1

Differentiate – To position.

Remind and reassure – To support, encourage and keep established customers.

Inform – To educate, make aware and develop understanding.

Persuade – To encourage people to a behave in a particular way (e.g. buy, call for a brochure or visit a website).

Debriefing Activity 6.2

Copy that reads 'do you remember how good it tastes (feels, looks, etc.)' is an immediate example. British Gas are currently (February 02) running a campaign telling us that over 2 million people have returned to them after trying a competitor's brand. The best examples, however, are those that are repeated again and again (high frequency) so that we (rote) learn to associate a need with a brand. This is particularly prevalent with financial services organizations (e.g. Lombard North).

Debriefing Activity 6.3

The execution and the copy are the most obvious differences. Due to the differences in levels of involvement, the fmcg brand will need high levels of above-the-line exposure and reasonably high levels of frequency. The copy will be brief and often designed to deliver high impact. The consumer durable on the other hand will use below-the-line approaches, provide more technical information, and rely on personal selling and the Internet.

Debriefing Activity 6.4

This question is asking specifically about the differences between the nature of B2C and B2B markets and then asking you to interpret the implications for marketing communications.

So, generally speaking, mass markets for B2C = mass communications, and smaller markets for B2B = individual and tailored communications.

In B2C situations, it is invariably an individual that makes the buying decisions, whereas in B2B contexts it is a team of people who contribute to the DMU. Marketing communications, therefore, need to be more highly targeted in B2B situations than in B2C.

Work through the list of differences in Table 6.1.

Debriefing Activity 6.5

The role of the DMU is to make purchase decisions on behalf of an organization with a view to using shareholder funds efficiently and effectively. The DMU seeks to bring together the different interests so that a balanced and informed decision can be reached.

Marketing communications messages need to be targeted at the different DMU members to deliver messages that reflect their individual role and interests in the purchase decision. The Finance Director will be interested in ROI and value for money; the user will be interested in performance and reliability whilst deciders will be interested in consistency and speed; and purchasing managers want their criteria to be met and product performance guarantees clarified.

Debriefing Activity 6.6

To answer this you need to:

- ○ Draw or sketch the MCPF.
- ○ Complete the Context Analysis by making assumptions about this fictitious organization. Create a problem in terms of the way customers perceive you to be expensive whereas your prices are the lowest in the top quartile.
- ○ From your objectives these should state that the marketing communication objective is to change the way customers perceive your brand put in SMART terms.
- ○ Decide on your strategy and then draw the appropriate strategic eclipse.
- ○ Formulate the promotional mix and then, using the Objective-and-Task approach, try to do a rough costing, the aim being to stay within the budget.
- ○ The evaluation phase needs to be accounted for how will this be done? (Answer = against the objectives!)

Debriefing Activity 6.7

The co-operative dealers will be involved with high frequency communications, prefer informal content and indirect methods of communication.

The other type of dealers might benefit from low frequency communications, prefer messages that are more formal in content and which are delivered through direct methods.

See pp. 369–373 in the essential text for a more detailed understanding.

Debriefing Activity 6.8

You do not need to go into great depths of cultural analysis but it may be useful to compare organizations operating in the same market (e.g. Microsoft and IBM, British Airways and Virgin

Atlantic) and isolate some of the key characteristics. Bureaucratic or flexible, fast or slow, traditional or modern, caring or dictatorial, risk taker or cautious.

Debriefing Activity 6.9

Making the assumptions that yours is a leading brand and that the ad spend is £8 million. Using the principle that ad spend should be a given percentage of sales, then 10 per cent = £8 million, 15 per cent = £12 million.

Workings: 10 per cent of £550 million sales = £55 million and £8 million = ad spend. Then, 8/55 = 14.5 per cent

15 per cent of £550 million sales = £82.5 million and so, 14.5 per cent/82.5 million = 11.9 million say £12 million.

Debriefing Activity 6.10

Following the principle of anticipated sales, the most obvious course of action is to set the communications budget at 5 per cent less than it was this year.

A more enlightened management team might suggest maintaining current spend levels in a declining market and in doing so prevent any threat from the market's number two brand and thus consolidate your market leadership position.

Debriefing Activity 6.11

Of course, a 5 per cent share in year one is extremely ambitious and to a large extent unrealistic. However, despite this constraint, the main determinants of the budget would be the communication tasks and the current spend levels of competitors already established in the market. It is very likely (see Share of Voice) that a new brand will need to spend 4 to 5 per cent over the required share of market. This means that to achieve MS = 5 per cent, a 9 per cent SOV will be required. Assuming a total market ad spend of £47 million, then, 9 per cent = £4.23 million.

Debriefing Activity 6.12

This approach is preferred as it is based on the real costs of achieving the set goals of the campaign. It is market-focused and makes no assumptions.

Debriefing Activity 6.13

New product launches are always difficult because of the need to be successful and recover the investment put into the project. Therefore, rather than being cautious, brand managers tend to be more bullish and try to secure a greater share of an organization's overall spend in order to get the brand off to a steady start. In some markets (fmcg), heavy initial investment in above-the-line work is considered to be the conventional approach.

The criteria to be used range from the level of the organization's overall resources, the level of competitors' spend and the communications tasks that need to be accomplished.

Debriefing Activity 6.14

Refer to the text for the full list.

Debriefing Activity 6.15

The answer is that the spend levels in the UK probably have no significance with regard to overseas market entry. Any financial recommendations would have to be based on knowledge of the respective markets, competitors, spend levels and desired level of activity.

Debriefing Question 6.1

Satisfactory answers to this question should demonstrate understanding and knowledge of each element of the marketing communications planning framework. Three elements should then be selected and a brief justification provided to support the argument that they are key to the overall process.

Debriefing Question 6.2

Satisfactory answers to this question should be confined to note format and they should itemize and explain four budgetary methods. Answers which just list four methods will be awarded minimal marks.

Unit 7

Debriefing Activity 7.1

Refer to the table in the text and compare your answers.

Debriefing Activity 7.2

Pulsing is more appropriate for fashion items and fads where consumer interest is limited to a short period of time. Sales and special offers will need to be exposed for a short rather than longer period of time.

Debriefing Activity 7.3

These cases will give you good examples for inclusion in relevant exam questions. They also cover a range of different sectors. It will also give you some idea on what a media agency does.

Debriefing Activity 7.4

A total of GRP would be 330. *Daily Mirror* 40 per cent × 4 OTS = 160, *Heat* 60 per cent × 2 OTS = 120 and cinema 25 per cent × 2 OTS = 50.

Debriefing Question 7.1

Satisfactory answers to this question need to briefly explain four of the following: informing key stakeholders, providing training facilities where necessary, understanding about culture, fear of change and technology, internal and external support, provision of timely and accurate information, training, marketing orientation and lead from the top.

Debriefing Question 7.2

Satisfactory answers to this question should list a minimum of four different advantages and disadvantages for each media and discuss their relative weighting and overall effectiveness. This type of question is best answered in the context in which the question is set.

Unit 8

Debriefing Activity 8.1

This exercise will provide a useful revision and consolidate your understanding of applications in key areas.

Debriefing Activity 8.2

In a group context, you will have a range of views, attitudes and perceptions which will provide you with more examples for use in the examinations.

Debriefing Activity 8.3

This will involve evaluating the individual communications methods used but you should consider the co-ordinated benefits from using the 4Cs Framework.

Debriefing Question 8.1

Satisfactory answers to this question should provide brief explanations about three methods available to evaluate public relations. An easy 5 marks.

Debriefing Question 8.2

Satisfactory answers to this question should refer to sales-based (ROI, market share, sales volume, sales value) approaches and communication-based methods (awareness, knowledge, attitude, preference) and then conclude by referring to the campaign objectives. Top marks will be awarded to answers which attempt to evaluate the merit of the two different approaches.

appendix 4

marketing communication assignments and examinations

In Appendix 2, general guidelines to assignment approaches were outlined, including samples for each element of the syllabus. This section provides details of the assignments and examinations that were actually set for assessment in the first period of the 2003–2004 cycle. The CIM student website will provide access to suggested approaches and the Senior Examiner report. The commentaries provided here and the characteristics of stronger and weaker answers provide additional support which you will find helpful in understanding the requirements of this aspect of assessment.

Assignments

This section commences with the instructions for the Marketing Communication assignments, which are issued by CIM, to a CIM centre and then despatched to the candidates wishing to undertake the assessment via coursework. After each question, there is a critique of what is required and a discussion of strengths and weaknesses found in the work from candidates who undertook these assignments.

MARKETING COMMUNICATION ASSIGNMENTS

There are **THREE** separate elements to complete the assignment, as detailed below:

○ The **Core Section** is compulsory and worth 50 per cent of your total mark. It should be approximately **3500** words in length.
○ The **Elective Section** has four options from which you must complete **TWO**. EACH of these options is worth 25 per cent of your total mark and should be approximately 1500 words in length.

Please note: As these assignments have been designed to test the application of knowledge, it will be insufficient to rely on theory alone for your answers. All work should be professionally produced, with arguments presented that are compelling and well reasoned. Any sources of information, definitions, methodologies and applications should be stated.

It is suggested that the answers for all the sections should be based on an organization of your choice, preferably your own, and that you should use the same organization throughout. This will present a more holistic account and involve you in less research.

If you are not in a position to use your own organization, you may use an alternative organization with which you are familiar, but your choice should be made following discussion with your tutor to ensure the best use of your study time.

You should submit your assignment by securing pages in the top left-hand corner with a treasury tag – do not use staples as these can come apart. No folders or wallets will be accepted.

The above word counts are guides only and you will not be penalized if you do exceed this recommendation. However, the professionalism of the presentation of your assignment, which includes producing concise and appropriate work, will be taken into consideration.

Core Section – 50 per cent weighting

Question No. 1 – (50 per cent weighting) The Communication mix

Using either your employing organization/SBU or an organization/SBU with which you are familiar, you are to evaluate aspects of the organization's marketing communications. You are required to write a report which:

- o Evaluates the key buyer behaviour characteristics of an identified target audience.
- o Describes the choice of tools and media used by the organization to convey messages to the target audience.
- o Evaluates the configuration of the marketing communications mix used to reach the target audience in the light of the key buying characteristics.
- o Explains how the organization does (or might) use WoM communications to best effect.
- o Recommends ways in which the marketing communications might be improved.

Within the question you should consider the linkages between buyer behaviour and marketing communications. In particular, emphasis should be given to the mix of tools and messages used.

Note: This is an individual assignment; as such the report must be completed individually and not as part of a group. Recommended word count 3500 words, excluding relevant appendices.

Syllabus references – 1.1, 1.2, 1.3, 2.4, 2.5, 2.6, 4.2, 4.3

Assessment criteria
- o Identification of the key buyer behaviour characteristics and demonstration of their influence on marketing communications activities.
- o Depth of consideration of the mix of tools and media used and ability to relate to other marketing activities.
- o Explanation of the WoM concept and ability to relate to the organization's context.
- o Justification and logic regarding the recommendations.
- o Relevance of answer to the questions.
- o Use of concepts and frameworks to support arguments, points and recommendations.
- o Presentation, format and tone of the report.

Question 1 – Commentary

This question required candidates to write a formal report based on a number of areas. Therefore, candidates should have included title page and contents pages, covering the areas required. There should have been summary as well as a conclusion and an appropriate academic list of references (not necessarily a bibliography) and appendices (which are not included in the word count).

The context for this assignment was an organization with which the student had some familiarity. Therefore, candidates should have been able to use their own work experience to answer the question. Although students could use any organization to undertake this work, they were advised that answers should reflect the degree to which organizations attempt to co-ordinate their mixes. To that extent, detailed information about individual tools was not required, it was the aggregate impact that required.

This assignment was designed to test the student's knowledge of the promotional tools and media used to communicate with a particular target audience. The linkage with buyer behaviour was important and students were advised that these questions are interlinked so their answers should have tried to reflect joined up marketing communications. Many students failed to evaluate this linkage and so revealed a less than adequate understanding of audience-centred marketing communications.

The specialist part of this task concerned WoM communications. Students were required to understand why word of mouth is used rather than just stating that it is used. This requires some understanding of the concepts underpinning word of mouth and opinion leadership.

Students were also required to consider the context of the organization and the target audience in order to justify (or reject) the current format of the tools and media mixes.

Answers to this question were encouraging. However, students struggled to find their way through the vast amount of material on buyer behaviour and often ended up rewriting Kotler's chapter on the subject. It had been hoped that a focus would have been given to attitudes and to involvement and to the decision-making processes. Links into the promotional mix produced variable responses with the media mix often ignored.

The WoM question was answered well by some but generally this proved troublesome to most students. Had they read the core text they would have been able to tackle this question more easily. The outcome was often an explanation about opinion leaders and opinion formers and the processes of adoption and diffusion. Some students believe that the linear model of communication was originated by Kotler (wrong Schramm or Shannon and Weaver) and that it is the same as the multi- or two-step model of communication. The AIDA model was also used by some but this is a low level framework designed for personal selling. It is generally discredited in terms of marketing communications and should not be used. Better to use one of the later hierarchical models or, better still, the attitude framework.

A solid conclusion should have been included, which summarized the points made and high-lighted the key regarding the organization's use of the promotional mix.

Characteristics of stronger answers

Good answers focused on key aspects of buyer behaviour, for example attitudes, involvement, perceived risk, decision-making processes.

Better answers considered the linkage between behaviour and marketing communications.

Included conceptual materials and interpreted the organization's marketing communications in the light of the theories and frameworks.

Good academic referencing illustrating journal reading.

Good structure of the report and diagrams illustrating points made.

Good answers made recommendations that were thoughtful and which lead logically from the preceding material.

Characteristics of weaker answers

Poor answers tried to relate everything the student knew about buyer behaviour.

Used only one book as a reference throughout.

Did not cite their sources nor did they provide a 'List of References'.

Poorer students often neglected the media within their answers.

Wrote a description or explanation of what an organization did, and did not include any theoretical or conceptual material.

Did not answer the question.

Poor structure and presentation.

Elective section – 25 per cent weighting for each of TWO options

Question No. 2 – Option – (25 per cent weighting) Channel member relationships

Your manager has asked you to prepare a report outlining the effectiveness of the relationship between your organization (or one with which you are familiar) and another in the marketing channel in which it operates.

The aim of this report is to evaluate the form and nature of communications used by the two organizations to communicate with each other and to determine areas in which the channel relationship might be improved.

Using suitable examples, your report should consider relevant issues from both parties perspective, drawing on appropriate relationship marketing concepts and highlighting the nature and characteristics of actual or potential channel conflict.

Note: This is an individual assignment; as such the report must be completed individually and not as part of a group. Recommended word count 2000 words, excluding relevant appendices.

Syllabus references – 2.1, 3.1, 3.2, 3.3, 3.4, 3.5, 4.3

Assessment criteria
- Evaluation of the communications tools and media used by both parties.
- Application of key marketing relationship concepts.
- Identification of the sources of (potential) conflict.

- ○ Recommendations concerning areas for improving the relationship.
- ○ Relevance of answer to the questions.
- ○ Use of concepts and frameworks to support arguments, points and recommendations.
- ○ Presentation, format and tone of the report.

Question 2 – Commentary

This assignment required students to consider two organizations in a marketing channel relationship. Students could choose to consider two organizations using public information or, with strict guidance, use hypothetical organizations.

The ancillary element to the question was the issue of conflict which may arise should relationship processes and procedures be insufficient or breakdown. The requirement to make recommendations to improve the relationship should have enabled better students to be extended and earn higher marks.

Students who attempted this question generally managed the tools and media aspects satisfactorily. However, the depth achieved with marketing relationship concepts was sometimes disappointing. Issues concerning trust, commitment and customer satisfaction were often ignored at the expense of loyalty and retention.

It is generally accepted that channel conflict occurs because of one of three main issues: competing or incompatible goals, tensions due to issues about domains and differing perceptions of reality. Very rarely was this framework (or similar) used to structure answers to this part of the question. Invariably students determined their own interpretations for possible conflict, which although creative and imaginative, suggested that little reading was undertaken in the area.

A report format should have been used with the normal structuring and quality of presentation.

Characteristics of stronger answers

General understanding of the variety of methods used to communicate with the partner organization.

Included conceptual materials and interpreted the organization's channel communications in the light of relationship marketing theories and concepts.

Attempted to evaluate the effectiveness of the communications.

Good academic referencing illustrating journal reading.

Good structure of the report and diagrams illustrating points made.

Good answers made recommendations that were thoughtful and which lead logically from the preceding material.

Characteristics of weaker answers

Poor understanding of the reasons for conflict.

Did not utilize relationship marketing concepts and in particular did not refer to trust and commitment.

Used only one book as a reference throughout.

Did not cite their sources nor did they provide a 'List of References'.

Did not answer the question.

Poor structure and presentation.

Question No. 3 – Option – (25 per cent weighting) Role of marketing communications

Your manager has asked you to evaluate and report on the marketing communications used by your organization. It is considering the adoption of a more customer-focused business strategy. Prepare a report which:

- o Briefly appraises the role that marketing communications is required to currently fulfil at your organization (or for a brand in your organization).
- o Briefly explains the degree to which its marketing communications are already customer focused.
- o Evaluates the degree to which the organization recognizes the importance of its corporate and ethical responsibilities.
- o Considers the degree to which the organization reflects this responsibility through its marketing communications.
- o Recommends how the organization might use marketing communications to improve the way it conveys messages about corporate and ethical matters.

Note: This is an individual assignment; as such the report must be completed individually and not as part of a group. Recommended word count 2000 words, excluding relevant appendices.

Syllabus references – 1.5, 2.1, 2.2, 2.4, 2.8, 4.3

Assessment criteria
- o Depth of appraisal relating to the relevant DRIP roles.
- o Evaluation of the organization being customer-focused.
- o Consideration of the pertinent arguments concerning corporate and ethical responsibilities.
- o Depth of understanding regarding the use of marketing communications to convey issues regarding corporate and ethical matters.
- o Quality of practical solutions offered to improve related marketing communications.
- o Relevance of answer to the questions.
- o Use of concepts and frameworks to support arguments, points and recommendations.
- o Presentation, format and tone of report.

Question 3 – Commentary
Students were required to consider the role of communications and the ideal approach would have been to consider the DRIP framework. This question was not about the individual aspects of the promotional mix.

The other major aspect of this task was to explore issues concerning corporate responsibility and the role marketing communications can, or should, play in conveying suitable messages. Therefore, students should have approached this by first considering the ethical and moral issues facing the organization and then moving on to explore the role marketing communications adopts in relation to communicating relevant issues to target audiences.

This was not the most popular question but those who attempted it achieved good marks. In particular, the first two sub-questions were approached satisfactorily, most using the DRIP framework. However, many candidates thought that all aspects of the framework can be or

233

should be applied to all campaigns or promotional activities within an organization. This is patently not the case and students need to be advised accordingly.

The main weakness with answers to this question concerned the treatment of ethical and corporate responsibility. It is accepted that not all such issues can be covered where there is a word limit but some of the responses were very vague and failed to even mention main-line issues. Some students did not refer to the background legislation and social movement about ethical issues, did not mention any of the current examples exhibited in the media nor did they base their comments on any thoughtful base of good practice. This is one topic guaranteed to be tested again.

Characteristics of stronger answers
General understanding of the DRIP concept.

Use of conceptual materials and an evaluation of the degree to which the organization's communications are customer-focused.

Attempted to consider the ethical issues associated with the communications.

Good academic referencing illustrating journal reading.

Good structure of the report and diagrams illustrating points made.

Good answers made recommendations that were thoughtful and which lead logically from the preceding material.

Characteristics of weaker answers
Did not understand the DRIP framework.

Lacked any reference to ethical issues or corporate responsibility.

Poor or no recommendations.

Used only one book as a reference throughout.

Did not cite their sources nor did they provide a 'List of References'.

Did not answer the question.

Poor structure and presentation.

Question No. 4 – Option – (25 per cent weighting) Public relations

The increasing use of public relations has helped reduce the amount spent on above-the-line activities and increased the effectiveness of marketing communications messages. Using a variety of brands or organizations of your choice, examine the ways in which public relations is practised, paying particular attention to the following:

- ○ The characteristics of public relations, including the nature and use of press releases.
- ○ The techniques and methods used to establish source credibility and the role of opinion formers.
- ○ An evaluation of the means by which public relations activities can be measured.
- ○ Use of practical examples to illustrate points.

This question should focus of the practical methods used by organizations and should be evaluative in style.

Note: This is an individual assignment; as such the question must be completed individually and not as part of a group. Recommended word count 2000 words, excluding relevant appendices.

Syllabus references – 1.1, 1.3, 2.2, 2.4, 2.9, 2.16

Assessment criteria
- o Use of suitable criteria to consider the characteristics of public relations.
- o Explanation of source credibility and use of examples to illustrate application and understanding.
- o Understanding of the techniques associated with media relations and press releases.
- o Depth of evaluation of measurement techniques.
- o Relevance of answer to the questions.
- o Use of practical examples to support arguments, points and recommendations.
- o Presentation, tone and format of report.

Question 4 – Commentary
This assignment was designed to test the student's understanding of public relations and especially media-based activities.

Students were free to choose any brands or organizations in order to illustrate their answer. They were not restricted to their employing organization. Students needed to consider the role and characteristics of public relations, the technical aspects associated with the design creation and dissemination of press releases.

The main ancillary issue concerned the measurement and evaluation of public relations activities. These should have included an evaluation of current techniques and an appraisal of their efficacy, although very few actually included this last aspect in their answers.

It had been expected that this was going to be a popular question and many did attempt it. Responses were generally competent although the question on source credibility did evoke a fair amount of waffle and confusion about their role and what (or who) an opinion former might be. Future students are advised to clarify their understanding of the differences between Opinion Leaders and Opinion Formers and to have examples prepared to illustrate their understanding.

The evaluation aspect seems to have been managed well and the salient points were high-lighted. Although requested to use examples, this type of question tended to provoke a formal or textbook response and the use of examples was sometimes ignored. Students should be encouraged to stick to answering the question at all times.

Characteristics of stronger answers
Good general understanding about the scope and role of public relations.

Attempted to consider the characteristics and use of press releases.

Understanding of the measurement techniques.

Good academic referencing illustrating journal reading.

Good structure of the report and diagrams illustrating points made.

Good answers made recommendations that were thoughtful and which lead logically from the preceding material.

Characteristics of weaker answers
Did not understand the role of press releases.

Failed to establish understanding of source credibility.

Poor linkages between source credibility and public relations.

Failure to incorporate software and digital evaluation techniques.

Used only one book as a reference throughout.

Did not cite their sources nor did they provide a 'List of References'.

Did not answer the question.

Poor structure and presentation.

Question No. 5 – Option – (25 per cent weighting) Interactive marketing communications

You are a newly qualified Marketing Executive working for an organization operating in a consumer goods market of your choice. You have been asked by your department manager to prepare information about the influence of the Internet on marketing communications. In particular you are to compare the use of traditional (offline) marketing communications with that of the Internet (Online)-based marketing communications. Prepare a report which addresses the following requirements:

o Evaluate the differences/similarities between online and offline marketing communications.
o Consider the impact of online communications on brand development.
o Consider how marketing communications can address security concerns potential buyers have for not buying online.
o Recommend ways in which organizations might be improve their online communications.
o Use examples to illustrate the points you make.

Note: This is an individual assignment; as such the question must be completed individually and not as part of a group. Recommended word count 2000 words, excluding relevant appendices.

Syllabus references – 1.3, 2.6, 2.8, 2.12, 3.5, 4.3

Assessment criteria
o Depth of evaluation of both online and offline marketing communications.
o Understanding of the possible types of impact on brand development.
o Explanation about the nature of online security issues.
o Breadth of suggestions regarding the means by which marketing communications can be used to reduce these perceived risks.
o Use and application of examples.
o Relevance of answer to the questions.

- o Use of concepts and frameworks to support arguments, points and recommendations.
- o Presentation, format and tone of documentation.

Question 5 – Commentary

This question was designed to assess a student's understanding of the impact of offline and online communications. The setting was deliberately B2C in order to consider brand development implications and encourage discussion about the combined impact of offline and online marketing communications.

Students should have considered aspects of security (and privacy) associated with online purchase behaviour. This should then have stimulated thought about the role marketing communications can play in reducing perceived risk, from both an online and offline perspective.

This was the most popular question and the one which generated the widest range of marks. One of the common errors was a failure to evaluate the differences/similarities. Most students made lists of the various characteristics but some did not evaluate them or draw out the similarities. The brand development issue produced some interesting ideas but all too often they were not rooted within the consumer goods market.

Questions which require the differences or a comparison to be made are best dealt with by using a common framework or list of elements against which the differences can be exposed. Many students lacked these simple skills and wrote rather rambling, uncoordinated and poorly structured answers. Some of those that did use a table failed to draw out the salient points, presumably leaving the examiner to make the deductions. This approach will not work.

Issues concerning risk and security were well managed and those that used the Settle and Alreck framework did better than most.

Characteristics of stronger answers

Good general description of the characteristics of both online and offline communications.

Attempted to make an evaluation of the differences.

Tried to incorporate an understanding of perceived risk.

Good academic referencing illustrating journal reading.

Good structure of the report and diagrams illustrating points made.

Good answers made recommendations that were thoughtful and which lead logically from the preceding material.

Characteristics of weaker answers

Did not draw out the differences between online and offline communications.

Failed to understand the role of perceived risk in the question.

Provided a superficial understanding or brand development and marketing communications.

Used only one book as a reference throughout.

Did not cite their sources nor did they provide a 'List of References'.

Did not answer the question.

Poor structure and presentation.

Some general points

This paper is set at Level 3, or final year undergraduate study. There are, therefore, some important requirements if assignments are to be judged to have reached the required standards.

Many of the assignments submitted were excessively descriptive and often failed to provide evidence of evaluative or discursive skills. Students often described what their organization does in terms of the particular aspect of marketing communications. This is not acceptable and students in future are advised to provide an evaluation or to discuss, or to compare and contrast, whenever the question requires them. Furthermore, where examples are requested, examples should be provided. These can be very important indicators or a student's understanding of a topic. Good students will provide an example and then demonstrate, explicitly, how the example supports the point they are trying to make.

Students are required (not expected) to use models, frameworks and theories to support their work. They should use these materials as evidence of their knowledge and understanding. Candidates should then interpret an organization's promotional activities in the light of the models and frameworks that they know about. This is not a request, it is a requirement.

In addition, the work of others should always be clearly referenced and a list of references should be supplied at the end of the report (or answer). Students should use Harvard (APA) referencing style at all times. Students who do not cite their sources of information are guilty of plagiarism or cheating. The technical term is kidnapping but whatever be the term, students or employees should know not to steal the intellectual property of others and to try and pass it off as their own.

The future

The structure adopted for this paper will be continued. The nature of the questions, the way they are presented and contextualized will also be replicated. Assignment papers will be set so that a substantial proportion of the syllabus will be covered. This means that students will need to read widely and develop their knowledge before attempting to write their assignments.

Answers need to be rooted in the context of each question and where the words *evaluation*, *discussion* or *appraisal* appear in a question, students must understand that this is what is required.

In future the more explicit use of frameworks and theoretical ideas in the transfer to working practice will be expected. Referencing is also expected and will be a requirement in order that assignments are marked.

Conclusion

The clues are in the CIM briefing schedules. When undertaking the assignment, look at the assessment criteria and *ensure* that you cover all the elements! It is disappointing to see the lack of academic references, or perhaps the use of just one or two books in the assignment work. This does not indicate good reading in the area.

Tutors will be able to provide you with suggestions of further reading where required, so take advantage of this.

Remember, these assignments are not just marked by the tutor, but they are sent to CIM and they are moderated, so ensure that if your work is confidential, this is marked clearly and boldly on the front.

This sort of assignment work is a very good method of ensuring that deep learning has taken place and this has to be illustrated within the work presented for grading. These assignments are not marked as exam papers as they have not been prepared in a restrictive environment, therefore, assessors are looking for different qualities, as indicated in this section.

Good luck and enjoy writing your assignments.

Examination papers for marketing communications

This section considers the examination assessment method and considers the December 2003 paper to illustrate key points.

Introduction

The examination papers for the Professional diploma in marketing modules are structured around a Part A core and a Part B elective question structure. All students must attempt the core (compulsory) question which is worth 50 per cent of the total marks and they must then attempt two from the other four elective questions in Part B. These are each worth 25 per cent of the marks.

The core question will invariably test students across all four elements of the syllabus, in some way or other. Each of the questions in Section B will test students across a minimum of two elements. In this way students are encouraged to see the subject in an integrative way rather than treat each topic as an independent entity, removed form all aspects of the other topics. This also helps to develop joined-up thinking skills.

Students should answer the examination questions using particular techniques. These techniques are not rocket science but if practiced and developed will inevitably lead to high performance and high marks.

Answer the question that is actually asked, not one that you thought was asked when you skim read the question just once. Read the question three times before you begin to write your answer.

(a)   Tell the examiner what you know simply and clearly using clear written communications.

(b)   Each question requires that you answer by:

   (i)   Explaining the particular knowledge (definitions, theories, concepts and frameworks) that is relevant to the question.
   (ii)   Applying these concepts to the scenario presented in the question.
   (iii)   Discussing, evaluating or appraising as requested, in parts of your answer, and writing in the required format (e.g. notes, report, etc.)
   (iv)   If required, use examples and relate them back to the question.

(v)   Structuring your answer using an Introduction, Middle and Conclusion.

(vi)   Allocate time strictly on the basis of the marks available to each question or sub-question.

(c)   You should not use bullet points unless you refer to two or three key points and expand upon them.

(d)   You should not make tables unless you develop particular points from them.

You do not need to use references in your examination paper. However, if you know who the author of the DRIP framework is, for example, then you should state who it is as follows (Fill, 2002). Nothing else is required. Similarly you should not use a large number of diagrams unless they are an integral part of the question/answer. The use of one or two to illustrate a point of knowledge is acceptable.

Students often fail because they simply explain all they know about a topic without relating their understanding to the scenario or the particular topic asked in the question. This dumping process will not lead to success. Please do not fall for this silly oversight. Practice regularly and ask your tutor or a friend to read your work.

The following questions are taken from the actual December 2003 paper.

Section A

Because I'm worth it

L'Oréal is one of the world's leading cosmetics and fragrances companies operating in more than 130 countries around the world. The company is structured around four distinct customer markets, luxury goods, consumer goods, professional and pharmacies (drugstores). In each of these sectors L'Oréal has a limited range of brands, a policy which enables the organization to generate economies of scale in production, advertising and packaging. However, whilst there are benefits from these shared resources, each brand retains its own individual style and consumer appeal. The international flavour of the company is demonstrated by brands that not only promote a French way of life (as with **Lancôme** and **L'Oréal Paris**), but also reflect Italian style (**Giorgio Armani** fragrances and cosmetics) and American vitality (**Maybelline New York, Redken 5th Avenue NYC** and **Matrix**). Such diversity might help ensure that L'Oréal appeals to a large number of different consumer segments.

Lancôme is a brand from the luxury goods division, one which seeks to maintain very high levels of quality with regard to the product, packaging, merchandising and all associated communications. One of the brand's principles is to provide personal relationships with their customers. Selective distribution is through department stores and fine perfumeries and this helps to ensure that official beauty consultants are able to help customers maximise their relationship with the brand.

The **L'Oréal Paris** and **Garnier** brands are both part of the Consumer Products division whose aim is to offer consumers innovative, high technology beauty products at competitive prices. This is a global strategy yet it is intentionally combined with a local understanding of the needs of women and men of all ages. Synonymous with the *'Because you're worth it'* strapline, this division remains the premium mass-market offering, allowing consumers accessible luxury through high performance products. Distribution is through mass-market retail outlets such as supermarkets and leading independent and chain store chemists.

The L'Oréal Professional Products Division is dedicated to providing the world's hairdressing industry not only with the most technologically advanced haircare and styling products but also in helping to develop hairdressers' businesses through technical education, management seminars and fashion shows. Many professional haircare products are developed for use solely in salon, whilst others can also be sold through salons, to clients for home care use.

The final division, Active Cosmétique develops dermo-cosmetic healthcare brands for sale through pharmacies and drugstores. These skincare products, which are subject to extensive pharmaceutical research, are only available through pharmacists and dermatologists.

Therefore, L'Oréal market a range of brands internationally, through different distribution channels to reach mass-market customers, hair salons, department stores, drugstores. These are summarised in Table 1.1.

Table 1.1 Summary of L'Oréal's Markets and Distribution Outlets

Division	Market	Distribution channel outlets	Promotional message
Luxury	Affluent/ Prestige	Department stores	Sophistication and exclusivity
Consumer	Mass market	Supermarkets and high street chemists	Image and value
Professional	Hair stylists	Hair salons	Technical supremacy
Drugstore	Pharmacists	Drugstores and pharmacies	Efficacy

The traditional industry approach to consumer cosmetic advertising is based upon a formula that involves prestigious locations, glamorous models and exaggerated messages that promise life enhancement based on unique product attributes. The media used are normally rich, high-quality glossy magazines although television is used for some leading brands.

Brand promotion at L'Oréal is partly based upon the use of various supermodels such as Andie MacDowell, Milla Joovich, and Judith Gidreche and celebrities such as Catherine Deneuve and Jennifer Aniston, who became the face of the brand. However, marketing communications messages used to support these brands varies considerably. At one extreme, some brands (e.g. **Lancôme's** anti-aging cream targeted at the over 55s) are supported by advertising messages which are stylish, luxurious and supported with minimal packaging and substantial product-based information delivered across the counter by experts.

At another extreme, consumer division brands such as **L'Oréal Paris** and **Garnier** attempt to convey brand images based upon spokespersons, beauty, price and attractive packaging. At yet another extreme, messages targeted at the Professional (and exclusive) hair stylists, such as Charles Worthington, are detailed and supported with a range of ancillary technical information.

Some luxury and consumer cosmetic brands have tried to overcome an increasingly cluttered market by trying to stimulate both awareness and trial through online communications. For example, **L'Oréal Paris** developed a virtual make-over site 'Easy Make Up' allowing customers to upload digital photos of themselves onto the site and to then experiment onscreen with different colours and techniques.

Question 1	Marks

As a member of a marketing audit team working on the **L'Oréal** account you have been requested by the Audit Project Manager to prepare a short report in answer to the following questions.

1a Evaluate the overall content and approach of the marketing communication messages used to support brands in both the Professional and Consumer Products Divisions.   **10**

1b Evaluate the extent to which L'Oréal use source credibility to enhance their marketing communications.   **10**

1c Explain how marketing communications can be influenced by an organization's international marketing strategy.   **15**

1d Recommend and justify ways in which L'Oréal might use marketing communications to influence relationships with their intermediaries (hair salons)?   **15**

This question complements syllabus elements: 1.3, 1.4, 2.8, 2.15, 3.1, 3.3, 4.3.

Three of these four questions are directly related to L'Oréal and need to be answered in that context. The remaining question does not specify L'Oréal but because of the information available on international communication issues it makes sense to argue in context.

Question 1a requires an evaluation of the consumer, and trade channel messages. Many candidates tried to refer to the overall communications but the question was specifically targeted at messages. The essential difference concerns the emotional versus the rational approach. This should then be supported by an evaluation of the use of types of messages in terms of information, benefits, lifestyle and tone of voice such as professional/aspirational. Good answers made an explicit statement referring to the audience characteristics.

Question 1b required a statement regarding the meaning of source credibility and reference to the essential aspects of trust and expertise. Examples could easily be drawn from the four divisions.

Question 1c was the first of two more heavily weighted questions. Therefore, more time should have been devoted to answering these two questions than the first two.

This question was not answered very well and it was a minority that considered the standardization/localization debate and then referred to L'Oréal for examples. Issues about agency availability, funding and resource availability and for the more able students, reference to Polycentric or Geocentric approaches would have been appropriate. The majority of students went straight for the use of PEST analysis and although some marks were awarded this approach fails to answer the question. The question refers to the strategy and its impact on marketing communications, not environmental factors.

Question 1d, the final compulsory question, looks specifically at trade channel communications. Many candidates referred to personal selling, trade advertising and direct marketing which was satisfactory. However, more advanced answers looked at the frequency of communication, the development of trust and commitment through education, advice, support and the deliberate approach to reduce or avoid conflict.

Overall the first question was answered reasonably well. However, a large number of students spent a lot time writing around the question and not always relating their answers to the case scenario.

Section B

Question 2	Marks
As a newly appointed Marketing Manager at an organization that produces a brand of energy drinks, your Marketing Director has asked you to prepare notes for her use at a forthcoming meeting with their current advertising agency. She is concerned that there is too much promotional activity targeted at brand development and too little at encouraging product purchase.	
Prepare your notes in answer to the following questions:	
2a Using appropriate criteria, compare and contrast the effectiveness of the following two promotional tools: direct marketing and advertising.	10
2b Explain how the promotional mix might be best evaluated in order to maximize its effectiveness in achieving the stated objectives.	10
2c Recommend ways in which word-of-mouth communications might be encouraged as part of the promotional effort.	5

This question complements syllabus elements: 1.1, 2.2, 2.8, 2.16

Question 2a was a popular question and was answered quite well. However, many students failed to compare and contrast the two tools, simply preparing lists and tables of their characteristics. This was not sufficient and students should be aware that this is not acceptable However, their knowledge of the tools was generally satisfactory. The best way to answer this question was to use a common framework to aid comparison. The most flexible framework and one used by most students is the 4Cs framework, namely cost, communication effectiveness, control and credibility.

Answers to 2b were reasonable although the depth attained was not always very good. Rather than evaluate the promotional mix as a total unit, some students answered in terms of how each individual tool might be evaluated. This was not intended and although these responses were marked sympathetically this time, candidates should take care to make sure whether the mix or a tool is the focus of the question. If the question asks for an evaluation of an individual tool then the question will state this. Good answers were structured around the Sales and Communication objectives. For example, campaigns evaluated against sales goals refer to: trial, sales volume, sales value, market share, ROI and shelf space. Campaigns evaluated against communication goals refer to: awareness, perception, attitude, likeability and comprehension. Good quality answers were always presented in the context of the energy drinks scenario.

Question 2c enabled students to show their command of WoM communications and of opinion formers and opinion leaders. Although only 5 marks were available some students misunderstood the differences between leaders and formers. The main issue concerned the nature and role of WoM. The majority of answers were lightweight and only a few knew about the role of motivation and involvement as key drivers of WoM. The energy drink context allowed for viral marketing to be introduced as well as reference to the use of opinion leaders and opinion formers, whispering campaigns and of course sampling, events, media leakage and PR. Students who knew of Dichter's (1966) framework of product, self, message and other interest reasons did exceedingly well.

Question 3	Marks

The national airline, in a country of your choice, wishes to continue targeting full fare business and leisure travellers, who prefer the full range of services offered by such airlines. However, low price competitors continue to grow as new travellers enter the market.

The Marketing Communications Manager for the national airline has asked you to research and prepare a report in order to help reverse their current disappointing operating performance.

Your report should answer the following questions:

3a	Discuss the advantages and disadvantages of both outdoor and print media.	10
3b	Explain how four different sales promotions techniques work.	5
3c	Make recommendations concerning the adoption of a relationship marketing approach, based upon a comparison with transaction marketing.	10

This question complements syllabus elements: 2.1, 2.2, 2.4, 2.6, 2.12, 4.1, 4.2, 4.3

Question 3a led many students in preparing lists and tables. Responses were generally acceptable but greater depth would allow for maximum marks to be awarded. For future reference a minimum of four advantages and four disadvantages is expected when nothing is specified in the question.

Question 3b was worth just 5 marks. Most who attempted it were able to offer four different techniques, however, the answers to how they work were often based on how they operate rather than explain the incentive in terms of the behaviour and attitude change that might have been brought about. A selection of promotions were used from: Coupons, Competitions and Sweepstakes, Premiums, Product Deals, Price Deals/Discounts, Sampling, Allowances, Points collection, Brochures and Sales Literature. Those candidates that related their answers to the airline context of the question did better than most.

Question 3c was answered by those who attempted it fairly comfortably. However, the depth of answer was not always as it should be. A comparison of the two approaches was required and several elements needed to be presented in order to show that the student had sufficient knowledge. Students are expected to know these differences and be able to discuss them. The recommendations were an important part of the question and hence required an answer based around means of creating trust and commitment. The question gave ample opportunity to relate answers to the national airline but few students did this.

Question 4	Marks

Checkmate Burgers is a franchise-based company that is considering entry into your country. Working as a Marketing Adviser you have been asked to provide information to help them shape their marketing communication activities *prior* to entry.

Prepare notes for a presentation in which you will advise them about the following issues.

4a	Evaluate the key issues facing the marketing communications industry in your country.	5
4b	Describe the principal regulatory arrangements that are used to control and manage marketing communications in your country.	10
4c	Make recommendations to Checkmate Burgers, about the importance of ethical behaviour and the need for corporate responsibility when developing their brand in your country.	10

This question complements syllabus elements: 1.5, 2.1, 4.2, 4.3, 4.4

Question 4a represented an easy 5 marks. By identifying a few key issues related to the marketing communications industry all that was then required was a brief comment about the severity or degree to which the issue was a problem, in order to pick up 5 marks. There are a wealth of issues to be explored from: Structure and Ownership, levels of concentration – very large and very small units (UK), growth and decline, media availability and costs, measurement facilities, regulations and control – the voluntary and legal balance, the increasing strength of the voice that consumers are developing, tightening budgets and ethical and social issues are just some that could have been developed.

Question 4b was answered poorly and this question will used regularly. It is important that students understand the way in which the marketing communications industry is structured and regulated. All students should go to into this exam fully armed with industry knowledge and examples. Most countries have a balance between legal and voluntary controls but few students seemed to understand this point nor where they able to develop their limited knowledge into an examination of the various panels, associations and methods that are employed.

Question 4c follows on naturally from the previous question. Issues regarding ethical and corporate behaviour are an important part of the syllabus. However, students only displayed a superficial knowledge of this topic and consequently were not able to offer a deep or considered opinion in their answers. The hint is that this area should always be prepared in advance of the examination. There are numerous examples of infringements in these areas and a good answer would have offered a statement about the nature of ethical, and responsible corporate behaviour would have made associations between quality of relationship with brand development, the fragility of brand strength and potential brand damage and would have made a minimum of three recommendations.

Question 5	Marks

The HIGH FIVE company seeks an agency to help relaunch their range of electronic consumer products such as hi-fis, televisions, DVDs and videos. The advertising agency for whom you work has just been invited to pitch for HIGH FIVE's international account following a successful credentials visit.

As the potential Account Planner for this client you are required to prepare the following for inclusion in an information pack that will be given to the client at the pitch.

You are required to:

		Marks
5a	Explain the sources of information and processes that HIGH FIVE could use to help find and appoint a new agency?	5
5b	Evaluate the key factors that HIGH FIVE should consider when appointing a new agency.	10
5c	Describe four methods the agency might recommend to evaluate the effectiveness of an advertising campaign.	10

This question complements syllabus elements: 1.2, 1.3, 2.1, 2.4, 2.5, 2.8, 4.5, 4.6

Knowledge about the way the industry works is as important as knowledge about its structure and regulation. Students must always be prepared to discuss issues concerning the processes relating to the appointment and development of relationships between client and agencies. This is a pivotal topic in this syllabus.

Question 5a was answered well, although some candidates did not answer the part of the question about processes. The Information element of the question should have been addressed through: AAR, clients, Agencies, Trade Press, Websites, Directories, Experience and WoM.

The process element should have been answered by reference to: general visits, credentials visits, pitching and contracts.

Question 5b brought out a range of factors and generally they were reasonable. Really good answers were keyed back into the electronic consumer products scenario. A minimum of four points from the following need to be mentioned and considered: Background, Experience, Contracts, Colleagues, Clients, Costs, Competitors, Creative Ideas and Proposals, Track Record, Awards Won, Empathy, Satisfied Clients and 3rd Party endorsements.

Question 5c, the last question in this section, brought out a range of answers. I believe many were the result of guesswork. Answers that related to Sales, Communication Targets and Goals, Brand Strength (Equity), Ability to reach Target Audience, Retention rates reflected good understanding. Indeed, the more able candidates were able to move away from purely sales/market-based responses and referred to campaign objectives, communication-related goals and to the quality of the relationship between client and agency.

The future

The structure used to frame this first examination paper will be continued. The nature of the questions, the way they are presented and contextualized will also continue. Papers will be set so that a substantial proportion of the syllabus will be covered. This means that students need to widen their range of knowledge and not concentrate on just a few prime areas. Students must appreciate the issues concerned with marketing relationships, agency – client relationships as well as the operational characteristics associated with the promotional tools and media.

In this paper some students referred to IMC. This is a strategic (and highly contentious) area and is not of direct concern to this syllabus. Students should, therefore, not be concerned with this nor associated with strategic issues. Students will be asked questions regarding B2B marketing communications, issues related to relationship marketing and will be expected to know about how the promotional tools and media work across different sectors and help the development of relationships.

Answers need to be rooted in the context of each question and where the words *evaluation*, *discussion* or *appraisal* appear in a question, students must understand that this is what is required. In terms of key syllabus topics, students should have knowledge of the following:

- o Audience and buyer behaviour and how this links with marketing communications.
- o All the promotional tools and media (including online and interactive media) in terms of their characteristics and how they work.
- o Relationship Marketing and associated concepts and their impact on marketing communications.
- o Client/Agency relationships, operations and campaign development processes and procedures.
- o The marketing communications industry: structure, issues and regulation.

This list is not intended to be definitive but a strong knowledge of these topics should go a long way not only to help students understand contemporary operational marketing communications but to also help them comfortably pass this assessment.

appendix 5
past examination papers and examiners' reports

The Chartered
Institute of Marketing

Professional Diploma
in Marketing

Marketing Communications

43: **Marketing Communications**

Time: 09.30-12.30

Date: 10th June, 2004

3 Hours Duration

This examination is in two sections.

PART A – Is compulsory and worth 50% of total marks.

PART B – Has **FOUR** questions; select **TWO**. Each answer will be worth 25% of the total marks.

DO NOT repeat the question in your answer, but show clearly the number of the question attempted on the appropriate pages of the answer book.

Rough workings should be included in the answer book and ruled through after use.

© The Chartered Institute of Marketing

Professional Diploma in Marketing

43:   Marketing Communications

PART A

Car Recovery Services

In the UK car recovery and breakdown market the Royal Automobile Club (RAC) is regarded as the challenger brand with the Automobile Association (AA) as the undisputed market leader. In addition, Direct Line Rescue (DLR) has entered the market recently and taken a 10% market share.

The perceived benefits of motor organisation membership have changed over the last ten years. The provision of reassurance and driver support have become more important while there has been a decline in the importance of financial and economic factors. Motorists now tend to more concerned about getting home quickly with or without their car than they are about the economic arguments between using motorist organisation membership and ad hoc services. In addition, customers in this market are no longer simply users of the vehicle breakdown services but expect a broad range of products and services, which the motoring organisations aim to satisfy in different ways.

Attitudes towards membership have changed for a number of reasons. Demographic factors are significant because the percentage of young and female drivers has increased at the expense of middle-aged male drivers. Motorists are now less willing to perform roadside repairs while cars are becoming more complex. The reliability of cars has increased but they are more challenging for drivers when they do go wrong. This is simply because of the nature of contemporary engine components (sealed units) and the need for specialist equipment to diagnose computer related faults.

Traditionally, marketing communications messages in this market have been based on advertising and the development of brand values. Messages have been very product-focused, typified by messages featuring speed of recovery, 'get you home' services, helpfulness of staff and a range of ancillary products such as car finance and legal and advisory services. During the 1990s, the promotional emphasis of the main motoring organisations changed from one that emphasised economic and tangible attributes to one that gave higher prominence to driver safety and reassurance. In addition to changes in the core messages used by the RAC and AA, greater emphasis has been placed on the other promotional tools, partly in response to the market entry and aggression of DLR.

In response to competitive pressures, profit margins declining on recovery services and private membership rising only slightly, the RAC has moved into Direct Response TV (DRTV) to support their ancillary services. One such campaign attempted to convey the idea that the RAC can help people afford their dream car, regardless of what it is, and secure the finance from a trusted brand to help them buy it. The adverts encouraged viewers to call a free phone number to apply for a loan and get an instant decision. Every successful loan applicant received free RAC Breakdown cover.

In addition, the RAC have developed their 36-page RAC Magazine as a means of communicating with their different markets. Of the several million copies mailed out three times a year everyone receives the standard 20 pages of content but in addition, there is also a 16-page insert that takes account of a person's LifeStage and their length of membership.

DLR is a very strong brand and lends itself to strong imagery and straightforward messages. It has been DLR's intention to develop a much closer relationship with their customers and they too have strategies that are designed to offer more than just vehicle breakdown services.

A recent campaign was designed to target customers of the RAC and AA and to reinforce their Rescue brand, which has nearly 1 million customers. Through their direct marketing agency they developed a series of mail packs, each containing a letter, envelope and insert, targeting different messages to existing AA and RAC members. These messages instructed recipients to "Stop Paying Too Much" by switching to Direct Line. Direct Line's own car insurance customers received a third pack which said that "First we save u money, then we save u". This was intended to highlight the breakdown cover offer from £35 and to reassure people about the high level of service whilst prompting them to respond through bold calls to action and guaranteed low prices.

Source: This mini case has been prepared from a variety of sources. Some of the material has been changed for assessment purposes and does not reflect the current management practices.

PART A

Question 1.

As a member of the direct marketing agency which recently won the DLR account you are required to prepare answers to the following questions.

a. Explain the characteristics of rational and emotional based messages and provide examples based on the Car Recovery market.

(10 marks)

b. Examine the ways in which marketing communications can be used to change motorists' attitudes towards vehicle recovery services.

(15 marks)

c. Evaluate the extent to which customer magazines can help develop relationships with customers.

(10 marks)

d. Recommend the key processes and procedures necessary to develop and implement an effective direct mail campaign.

(15 marks)
(50 marks in total)

PART B – Answer TWO Questions Only

Question 2.

The organisation you work for manufactures robotic equipment, which is used by other organisations as part of their production and assembly facilities. Having recently attended a conference on the impact of technology on marketing communications, you wish to share some ideas with colleagues, for improving the effectiveness of your organisation's marketing communications.

In preparation for this meeting, prepare notes on the following topics.

a.   Evaluate the business-to-business (b2b) marketing communication mix and explain the main roles that promotional activities need to undertake.

(10 marks)

b.   Explain how the use of new media and associated digital technologies can assist the use of personal selling activities in the b2b sector.

(10 marks)

c.   Recommend ways in which Key Account Management might assist the development of relationships in the organisation.

(5 marks)
(25 marks in total)

Question 3.

A leading soft drinks brand is considering broadening its communications strategy by expanding its below-the-line activities. As an Account Planner working at the advertising agency currently assigned to the brand, you have been asked to consider possible implications arising from this change in the communications strategy and to comment on the following questions:

a.   Discuss the nature and characteristics of above- and below-the-line communications.

(5 marks)

b.   Explain how a relationship marketing programme for the brand might benefit from the inclusion of direct marketing.

(10 marks)

c.   Evaluate the potential impact of such a shift in promotional expenditure on the brand's established values.

(10 marks)
(25 marks in total)

Question 4.

The use and role of public relations in the promotional mix is often understated and misunderstood. You work in the marketing department for a City Council which is seeking to build a major tourist attraction but the project has suffered from a sequence of delays and disagreements between the various stakeholders associated with the project. This has led to substantial negative press comments and hostility from parts of the local community. Prepare briefing notes for an interview your Marketing Manager is going to give to local journalists concerning this issue. Your notes must concentrate on addressing the following issues.

a.   Using appropriate criteria, compare and contrast the effectiveness of the following two promotional tools: public relations and advertising.

(10 marks)

b.   Explain how messages delivered through public relations might be regarded as more credible by the local community.

(5 marks)

c.   Recommend ways in which marketing communications might be used to help improve relationships and reduce levels of conflict among the different stakeholders.

(10 marks)
(25 marks in total)

Question 5.

You are the Account Handler at an advertising agency that has been working on the creative account for a major fast-moving consumer goods (FMCG) account for several years. The client has indicated that they are proposing a change from a localised to global communications strategy. Your manager has asked you to evaluate and report on the issues facing your client as it considers changing its international promotional strategy with respect to a region of the world (your choice of region).

In particular you are to prepare a report which examines the following topics:

a.   Evaluate the advantages and disadvantages of such a change from the client's perspective.

(10 marks)

b.   Consider the possible impact this change may have on your agency.

(5 marks)

c.   Examine the structure of the marketing communications industry in a country/region of your choice and consider some of the current issues.

(10 marks)
(25 marks in total)

The Chartered
Institute of Marketing

Professional Diploma in Marketing

Marketing Communications

43:   **Marketing Communications**

SENIOR EXAMINER'S REPORT FOR JUNE 2004 EXAMINATION PAPER

© The Chartered Institute of Marketing

SENIOR EXAMINER'S REPORT FOR
JUNE 2004 EXAMINATION PAPER

MODULE NAME: Marketing Communications

AWARD NAME: Professional Diploma

DATE: 21 July 2004

1. Introduction

This report aims to provide feedback regarding student performance in the June Marketing Communications examination. The comments expressed here relate to the overall quality of the answers and are not specific to any centre, region or type of student.

This report reviews student answers to each of the questions, explores some of the key points arising, highlights some of the strengths and weaknesses in the answers provided to each question, provides information about future papers and indicates where learning effort should be concentrated.

Generally the results are positive with some lessons learned following the December 2003 examination. There were many centres achieving very high pass rates and they are all to be congratulated. A large number of students achieved individually outstanding performances with marks of 80+ being achieved by some. These students are to be congratulated as well.

2. Content and Knowledge

As reported in January students need to be better prepared to answer questions about relationships and to understand how marketing communications can be used to assist the development of buyer-seller relationships. The syllabus is large but if students understand the basic concepts in each of the two main areas they will, in my experience, begin to understand the linkages, which will be reflected in deeper, more satisfactory answers. At present there is an imbalance, reflected in the answer papers where, as a generalisation, students know more about communications and related concepts and issues than they do about relationships. For example, few students know about the reasons for conflict, many understand the characteristics of advertising. Both are important parts of the overall syllabus

Many students understand the principles underpinning attitudes and they were able to explain the main constructs. However, some were unable to translate this theoretical knowledge into the practice of marketing communications. Once again too many students wanted to show off how much they knew about push, pull and profile strategies and were not able to explain in depth concepts such as source credibility or local / globalised marketing communication strategies.

Tutors are advised not to labour the strategic perspective, but to use it for perspective purposes only. Students must know about the characteristics of the principal promotional tools and media and a little about how they work (from an attitudinal and behavioural perspective). For example, many answers to the question about how direct mail works were very superficial and lacked any conviction.

I was surprised that so many students were unable to provide depth in their answers with regard to the marketing communications industry. This is a fundamental aspect of the topic and students must appreciate the industry structure and be able to explain some, not all, of the key issues the industry is facing in their country. I suspect the reason for the poor answers is because these issues are not addressed in class. If a greater focus was given to this aspect students might better appreciate the bigger picture. Again students appeared to know very little about the causes or nature of interorganisational conflict although some were able to relate to concepts such as trust, commitment and customer satisfaction.

Answers to the mini-case questions were generally sound and of a better quality than those to Section B. A significant number of students tried to relate their answers to the DLR context in comparison to the answers offered in Section B. Here the context of the question was often ignored, which cost candidates a lot of marks.

As a general comment, candidates' knowledge was not as deep as it needs to be and reflects a lack of directed and appropriate reading.

3. General Strengths and Weaknesses of Candidates

Subject Areas of Relative Strength	Subject Areas in Need of Attention
Characteristics of the promotional tools Characteristics of the media Agency appointment Transaction/Relationship marketing	Marketing Communications industry Word of Mouth communications Source Credibility Relationships - trust, commitment and customer satisfaction Messages – form, structure & presentation Channel based communications Understanding about how the promotional tools work. Ethics and corporate responsibility

Table 1.1: *General Interpretation of Students' Ability Across the Areas Tested in the June 2004 Examination*

Table 1.1 sets out some of the points to be derived from answers presented at the June examination. Please remember that this is a general interpretation, is relative to the number of students who attempted each question and is intended to highlight areas where knowledge appears to be restricted yet recognises that some students (and centres) generated some very good answers.

4. Examination Methods and Technique

The level of content knowledge is improving but too many students failed to capitalise on this advantage by applying their knowledge to the context provided in the question. This lack of contextualisation is something that tutors can easily work on in class, if only by using past examination papers. To repeat my comment in January, I recommend that in future groups of students use this paper to practice applying their knowledge and developing their examination technique. They can do this in their own time, or collectively in workshops. However, once they are able to see the difference their new skill will be of immense help to them, not only in this module but in the others they are sitting as well.

As usual some students wrote too much material that was irrelevant to the question. For example, some candidates spent valuable time either writing all the materials and theory as a two page introduction to their answer or spent too much time writing copious answers for just 5 marks. Having said that, a large number of students were unable to write a sufficient number of words to their answers. This is worrying and indicates either a lack of knowledge and /or an absence of practice. The importance of writing focused answers and using time management properly is very important and needs to be brought to their attention.

It is very important for students to understand the need to structure their answers clearly and to present their responses in a clear and professional manner. There were some excellent examples of appropriate structure but a number of valuable marks were lost (not gained) through spider like, poorly structured and rambling answers. Students are to be advised to number their various sections and paragraphs within their reports and this will help their structure. Students should also be advised about how to allocate their time in proportion to the number of marks available for each sub-part of a question.

The use of bullet points and lists is not encouraged unless candidates extract several points and expand upon them. This bare knowledge approach will not enable students to pass. I would rather students discussed a few points at length and depth rather than provide a full list with no embellishment.

In principle, each question contains a sub-question that requires discussion, evaluation or comparison. Too many candidates did not gain marks because they ignored this aspect of the question and merely described or explained. Some just dumped as much theory as they could think of, and most of the time it was information that was irrelevant to the question. At this level students must demonstrate their capacity to discuss and compare issues. Where requested students must develop an evaluative approach to their answers. They should challenge the collective wisdom and learn to apply their knowledge in the context presented in the questions. Not only would more students have passed had they not been so descriptive in their answers but had they written more and not been so brief they would have scored more heavily.

It would be helpful if tutors spent time encouraging students to understand the depth of knowledge required at this level. The questions will be demanding and require students to apply their knowledge based on a sound understanding of conceptual theories and frameworks.

5. Strengths and Weaknesses by Question

Question 1

Answers to question 1a were generally sound with most students able to explain the key differences. Question 1a was answered reasonably well, which was a relief as the question develops the same theme as that used in 1a for the December 2003 paper. Therefore, most students scored good marks and got off to a good start. However, a large number of students were able to explain the concepts but too many did not contextualise their answers.

Answers to question 1b were again satisfactory with large numbers of students able to identify the cognitive, affective and conative construct. However, the question focused on the ways in which marketing communications could be used to change attitudes and it is here that too many candidates resorted to the promotional mix rather than an attribute approach.

The question about customer magazines was probably a surprise for most candidates. However, technical accuracy in the answers was not expected but a general awareness of the connections between the medium, relationship development and direct marketing was a reasonable expectation.

The final question within Section A challenged students with regard to their knowledge about planning within direct mail programmes. Some students reflected specialised knowledge and did well but too many students seemed to panic and failed to think about the question and the key aspects associated with direct mail activities. Targeting, database and list management issues together with the design of the direct mail piece will obviously be central issues within a planning framework but too many fell back just on the MCPF.

Overall the theoretical content of answers was satisfactory but too many failed to relate their knowledge to the mini-case study.

Question 2

This was a very popular question and parts 2a and 2b were answered satisfactorily. Answers to 2c were of a lower standard. The questions 2a and 2b did not explicitly require contextualisation to the stem of the question. However, those answers that did attempt this were usually superior.

Most students who attempted this question were able to identify the key elements of the B2B promotional mix, namely personal selling and direct marketing. Most used the DRIP framework to answer the second part of the question. Some students had difficulty with the word *role* but a large majority failed to be evaluative and this resulted in lost marks.

Answers to 2b were reasonable although the depth attained was not always very good. Some candidates did not understand what a sales person needs in terms of technology in order to do their job. More encouragingly, a few more able students connected the use of technology with the need to build and sustain relationships, but sadly this was a minority. It was surprising that so few knew about Sales Force Automation (SFA) and the relationship building activities.

Question 2c was not answered very well and so it was fortunate that only 5 marks were attached to it. Most candidates used the KAM frameworks as the core of their answer, which was fine except that they often neglected to develop the relationship aspect of their response.

Question 3

A large number of candidates who attempted this question seemed uncomfortable adjusting to the role of the agency and therefore had trouble answering the question in context. Marks awarded therefore tended to be lower when compared with some of the other questions.

Question 3a should have been a quick fire, easy 5 marks and for most students this proved the case.

Question 3b proved to be more challenging and as one of the examining team commented, "students often had difficulty in marrying the two concepts together to produce a cohesive answer". Candidates tended to know about DM and RM but only those who pulled the two elements together gained the higher marks.

The final question was answered poorly. Students did not understand the probable implications for the brand's values by switching to a below-the-line strategy. There was certainly a dearth of evaluative content. More time should be spent discussing with students the role of above and below the line communications, the balance between creating brand values and inducing behavioural responses.

Question 4

This question was the second least popular question based on the number of candidates attempting it. This is surprising in view of the fundamental nature of 4a, one which all students should have been well prepared and capable of answering. Many correctly used the 4Cs framework to structure their answer and in general these responses were fine. However, the most common mistake was that students failed to compare and contrast and as a result failed to get anything other than a bare pass.

4b represented a challenge for those unaware of the issues associated with source credibility and the role of public relations. Many provided theoretical answers, others tried a purely practical approach while few attempted to bring these two aspects together.

Answers to question 4c were most notable for the absence of information related to the nature and types of conflict that exist. As a result, answering this question becomes extremely difficult with the inevitable result that answers become vague. Answers needed to address the three elements in the question and then consolidate essential aspects from them all. In future, candidates should be advised to understand the nature of conflict, the impact on relationships and then be able to comment on the role marketing communications might play throughout the various relationship phases, including times when conflict breaks out.

Question 5

This question was the least popular and those that attempted it often had problems relating to the appropriate context.

Question 5a was fairly straightforward and required a list of advantages and disadvantages, which then had to be evaluated. It was this last aspect that many candidates failed to do.

Question 5b was not answered very well. Candidates did not appreciate the possible impact of lost business, declining fees, need for new skills, reporting structures, operating processes and new policies.

Question 5c was again answered poorly and in view of the comments made in my last report this was disappointing. All candidates should know about the structure of the marketing communications industry in their country and should have a feel for some of the key issues.

6. The Future

The structure used to frame this paper will be continued. The nature of the questions, the way they are presented and contextualised will also continue. Papers will be set so that a substantial proportion of the syllabus will be covered. This means that students need to widen their range of knowledge and not concentrate on just a few prime areas. Students must appreciate the issues concerned with marketing relationships, agency – client relationships as well as the operational characteristics associated with the promotional tools and media.

Students will be asked questions regarding marketing channel relationships and the ways in which marketing communications can be used to assist the development and maintenance of such relationships. Conflict, trust and commitment will be examined again. In addition, aspects concerning ethics and corporate responsibility as they relate to marketing communications will almost certainly be examined. Similarly, questions about the marketing communications industry and associated issues will also reappear.

Students must practice answering these questions concentrating not just on structure and content but also on the need to *evaluate* and not just describe content. However, to repeat a comment made previously in this report, students must contextualise their answers and relate theory to practice, the essence of this qualification.

Thank you for your time taken to read through this, for your support of all our students and for your continued interest and teaching of marketing communications.

appendix 6

curriculum information and reading list

Aim

The Marketing Communications unit provides the skills and knowledge that enable marketers to manage marketing communications and brand support activities within organizations. It provides students with an understanding of the concepts and practice of promotional activity at an operational level. Although reference is made to relevant strategic issues in order to provide a relevant context for learning, the focus is primarily on creating applied co-ordinated promotional activities, campaign development and the management of relationships with a variety of stakeholders, particularly customers and members of marketing channels.

Related statements of practice

Cc.1   Create and build competitive brands.
Cc.2   Manage competitive brands.
Dc.1   Create effective communications plans.
Dc.2   Manage communications activities.
Gc.2   Manage and monitor support to channel members.
Hc.1   Establish and monitor activities and information for delivering effective customer relationships.
Hc.2   Manage and monitor provision of effective customer service.

Learning outcomes

Students will be able to:

8.43.1   Explain the role of marketing communications and advise how personal influences might be used to develop promotional effectiveness.
8.43.2   Explain how the tools of the promotional mix can be co-ordinated in order to communicate effectively with customers and a range of stakeholders.
8.43.3   Devise a basic media plan based on specific campaign requirements using both offline and online media.
8.43.4   Develop marketing communication and brand support activities based on an understanding of the salient characteristics of the target audience.

8.43.5 Explain the main elements, activities and linkages associated with the formulation and implementation of a marketing communications plan.

8.43.6 Recommend a suitable marketing communications budget.

8.43.7 Explain the importance of developing long-term relationships with customers, channel members, agencies and other stakeholders and transfer such knowledge to the development of marketing communication activities.

8.43.8 Suggest suitable methods to influence the relationships an organization has with its customers, any marketing channel partners and other stakeholders, using marketing communications.

8.43.9 Use the vocabulary of the marketing communications industry and be able to communicate effectively with other marketing practitioners.

Knowledge and skill requirements

Element 1: Understanding customer dynamics (20 per cent)

1.1 Explain how individuals can influence the effectiveness of marketing communications through word-of-mouth communications, as opinion leaders, as opinion formers or in multi-step models.

1.2 Describe the main concepts associated with buyer information processing and explain how marketing communications might be used to change or reinforce attitudes, alter perceptions and develop knowledge and understanding about a brand.

1.3 Describe the main concepts associated with the purchase decision making process, including source credibility, involvement, perceived risk, and how they influence marketing communications.

1.4 Assess the principal differences between consumer and organizational markets and consider how they impact on marketing communications.

1.5 Summarise the importance for organizations of ethics and corporate responsibility, and their impact on brand reputation.

Element 2: Co-ordinated marketing communications (50 per cent)

2.1 Define and explain the roles of marketing communications to differentiate, remind or reassure, inform and persuade (DRIP).

2.2 Evaluate the effectiveness of each of the promotional tools using appropriate criteria such as cost, communication effectiveness, credibility and control.

2.3 Explain the meaning of the terms above-, through- and below-the-line.

2.4 Explain the role of each of the promotional tools within a co-ordinated marketing communications mix.

2.5 Evaluate the effectiveness of co-ordinated campaigns.

2.6 Identify primary and secondary media (online and offline) and contrast their main characteristics.

2.7 Explain key media concepts (reach, frequency, duplication, GRPs, flighting), and describe the principal approaches used to measure media effectiveness.

2.8 Compare information- and emotional-based advertising messages and explain the concept of likeability.

2.9 Outline the key characteristics associated with push, pull and profile strategies.

2.10 Describe the main characteristics of key accounts and explain the stages and issues associated with KAM.

2.11 Describe how CMC can be used to develop key account relationships.

2.12 Explain how marketing communications can be used to launch new products, support brands, maintain market share, develop retention levels encourage customer loyalty, and support internal marketing within the organization.

2.13 Draw and describe the main parts of a marketing communications planning framework and explain the principal linkages between the various elements.

2.14 Explain the main methods used to determine a marketing communications budget.

2.15 Discuss the main issues concerning the use of marketing communications in an international and global context, such as media availability, culture, religion, education and literacy.

2.16 Evaluate the effectiveness of marketing communications activities, tools, media and campaigns.

Element 3: Marketing channels (15 per cent)

3.1 Identify and explain how the promotional mix can be suitably configured for use in a range of marketing channels and B2B situations.

3.2 Explain, in terms of the impact on marketing communications within a relationship context, the structural concepts: interdependence, independence, disintermediation and reintermediation.

3.3 Explain the role of trust, commitment and satisfaction when developing marketing communication activities for use in the marketing channel and B2B contexts.

3.4 Identify the causes of conflict in trade channels and explain how marketing communications can be used to resolve such disagreements.

3.5 Explain how Internet- and digital-based technologies can been used to enhance marketing communications and relationships within channels and between B2B partners.

Element 4: Relationship management (15 per cent)

4.1 Compare the principles of transaction and relationship marketing.

4.2 Explain the characteristics of relationship marketing including the features, types, levels, development and implementation steps and communication issues.

4.3 Describe how marketing communications can be used to develop relationships with a range of stakeholders, based on an understanding of source credibility, trust and commitment.

4.4 Explain in broad terms the nature, structure, ownership and any key issues facing the marketing communications industry in any single country or region.

4.5 Describe how agencies manage their operations in order to meet their clients' needs: pitching, briefing, structure, review, the role of account planners and managers, relationship management.

4.6 Explain how advertising agencies and marketing communication agencies use resources to meet the needs of clients with international and global requirements.

4.7 Describe in broad terms the regulatory and voluntary arrangements that are used to manage relationships between the public, customers, clients and agencies.

Related key skills

Key skill	Relevance to unit knowledge and skills
Communication	Present and justify a plan
	Produce effective marketing communications
	Assess the impact of a campaign
Application of number	Forecast likely response rates
	Set and justify a budget
	Measure communications effectiveness
Information technology	Use IT tools for forecasting, modelling options, budgetting and measuring performance for a communications campaign
Working with others	
Improving own learning and performance	Review current capabilities
	Identify opportunities and set realistic targets for development and learning
	Plan how these targets will be met (methods, timescales, resources)
	Use a variety of methods for learning
	Seek feedback, monitor performance and modify approach
	Assess effectiveness of learning and development approach
Problem-solving	Formulate a communication solution within defined constraints

Assessment

CIM will offer two forms of assessment for this unit from which study centres may choose: written examination and an assignment. CIM may also recognize, or make joint awards for, units at an equivalent level undertaken with other professional marketing bodies and educational institutions.

Marketing Communications

Recommended support materials

Core Texts

De Pelsmacker, P., Geuens, M. and Van den Bergh, J. (2004) *Marketing Communications: A European Perspective*, 2nd edition, Harlow: Pearson.

Fill, C. (2005) *Marketing Communications*, 4th edition, Harlow: Pearson.

Workbooks

BPP (2005) *Marketing Communications Study Text*, London: BPP Publishing.

Hughes, G. and Fill, C (2005) *Marketing Communications*, Oxford: BH/Elsevier.

Supplementary Readings

Brierley, S. (2001) *The Advertising handbook*, 2nd edition, London: Routledge.

Chaffey, D., Mayer, R., Johnston, K. and Ellis-Chadwick, F. (2002) *Internet Marketing: Strategy, Implementation and Practice*, 2nd edition, Harlow: Prentice Hall.

Christopher, M., Payne, A. and Ballentyne, D. (2002) *Relationship Marketing: Creating Stakeholder Value*, 3rd edition, Oxford: Butterworth-Heinemann.

Coughlon, A., Anderson, E., Stern, L. and EL-Ansary, A. (2001) *Marketing Channels*, 6th international edition, Harlow: Pearson.

Hackley, C. (2005) *Advertising and Promotion: Communicating Brands*, London: Sage.

Pickton, D. and Broderick, A. (2004) *Integrated Marketing Communications*, 2nd edition, Harlow: Prentice Hall.

Shimp, T. (2003) *Advertising, Promotion and Supplemental Aspects of Integrated Marketing Communications*, 6th edition, US: South Western College Publishing.

Smith, P. and Taylor, T. (2004) *Marketing Communications: An Integrated Approach*, 4th edition, London: Kogan Page.

Tapp, A. (2004) *Principles of Direct and Database Marketing*, 3rd edition, Harlow: Prentice Hall.

BPP (2005) *Marketing Communications Practice and Revision Kit*, BPP Publishing.

BH (2005) *CIM Revision Cards: Marketing Communications*, Oxford: BH/Elsevier.

Marketing journals

Students can keep abreast of developments in the academic field of marketing by reference to the main marketing journals, a selection of which are listed in the Appendix to this document.

Press

Students will be expected to have access to current examples of marketing campaigns and so should be sure to keep up to date with the appropriate marketing and quality daily press. A selection of marketing press titles is given in the Appendix to this document.

Websites

A list of websites that tutors and students may find useful is shown in the Appendix at the end of this document.

Overview and rationale

Over the past few years, there has been increased interest in the nature and form of the relationships organizations develop with a range of stakeholders. Of these, customers are regarded as central in many market sectors. The development of long-lasting, profitable relationships is now regarded as a requirement within organizations and often it is marketing people who are at the forefront of this activity.

In addition, one of the pivotal roles of marketing communications is to deliver the marketing plan to target audiences. Indeed a great part of marketing activity in organizations is consumed on communications-related activities. Communications also play a determining role in the development of successful marketing relationships. This unit brings these two elements together and provides an exciting opportunity for students to learn about and develop new skills and be able to make a significant contribution to organizations in marketing communications operations and associated activities, both internally and externally with agencies and other outsourced providers.

Approach

The aim is to provide students with the necessary conceptual frameworks and tools for determining and managing marketing communications in order to help form suitable relationships. In order to achieve this, the unit will consider knowledge and develop understanding in the areas of customer information processing and purchase decision-making, the management of the promotional mix and develop projects and activities associated with the management of relationships with a range of stakeholders.

The overall focus is upon the operational, medium-term management of marketing communication issues. It does not dwell on the strategic aspects of the subject, although it is recognized that certain strategic topics will be encountered if only to put events into context. It is also recognized that the development of relationship marketing is a long-term strategic issue.

Students will be expected to relate their knowledge and understanding to practical examples. To do this successfully, students will need to understand certain concepts and theoretical frameworks and use examples to illustrate their understanding. To be successful at this level, students will need to explain, describe and illustrate their knowledge through practical examples, rather than through evaluation, critical appraisal and discussion. They should be encouraged to develop simple communications plans – a skill that will be developed further in the Marketing Management in Practice unit.

Syllabus content

This syllabus draws on a number of strands. The essence has been drawn from the IMC unit in the outgoing Postgraduate Diploma syllabus. However, this new syllabus deliberately avoids the word 'integrated' for a number of reasons. The first is that the term 'integrated' is synonymous with strategy and this unit sits just below that level. A new word 'co-ordinated' is introduced in order to focus attention on the promotional mix and the co-ordination of communications in developing relationships. The word also provides a point of differentiation and to help provide clarity. A further reason is that the strategic issues concerning IMC are considered throughout Professional Postgraduate Diploma.

The syllabus has four elements in order to segregate the core topics embedded in the unit. Students are expected to illustrate their understanding and knowledge of this syllabus through the application of examples.

Element 1: Understanding customer dynamics (20 per cent)

This element introduces buyer behaviour in order that students develop their marketing communications skills and knowledge on a customer-focused foundation. These concepts and frameworks are concerned with how people process information and how they make purchase decisions. Marketing communications need to reflect this knowledge if they are to be successful. The emphasis in this element is upon students being able to explain and demonstrate how these theories and frameworks are applied in practice, not on learning the theories themselves in isolation.

Element 2: Co-ordinated marketing communications (50 per cent)

In terms of weighting, this is the most important element of this unit. Here the syllabus concentrates on the tools and media used to communicate co-ordinated messages with target audiences.

Students will develop their understanding at Professional Certificate about the characteristics of the promotional tools and consider them as part of a co-ordinated promotional mix designed to support a brand and other business activities. International marketing communications issues are introduced, as are budgeting techniques and evaluation methods concerning campaigns, tools and media.

Although key terms associated with marketing communications strategy, namely push, pull and profile strategies, are mentioned, these are only considered briefly in order to provide knowledge of the overall scope of activities.

Knowledge of the components of a marketing communications planning framework and the way the parts are linked together is developed. This is intended to provide structure and context for understanding the various parts of this subject and for developing plans for co-ordinated communications campaigns.

Again it is the use of practical examples to demonstrate understanding that is required.

Element 3: Marketing channels (15 per cent)

For a long time, marketing communications education has focused on B2C and B2B end-user customers and have tended to marginalize members of marketing channels. This unit helps to correct this imbalance and introduces aspects of trade channel marketing communications. The mix of tools is obviously important but here the importance of relationships is considered and how marketing communications can play a crucial role in helping managers achieve channel objectives.

Element 4: Marketing relationships (15 per cent)

This final element looks at relationship marketing concepts and at how trust and commitment through marketing communications can be developed. Inevitably, there is a level of overlap with other elements in the syllabus, but that is useful since it should show the interaction between communications and relationship development.

This element is also important because it introduces the agency dimension and the relationships that develop between client and agency. By learning about how agencies are structured, operated and influenced by managers and the industry itself, students are in a far better position to manage their employers' agency relationships more effectively.

Delivery approach

Ideally, this unit is delivered after students have completed the Marketing Planning unit where they cover planning processes and techniques.

The syllabus is quite extensive and requires a balance of theory and practical application through consideration of real-life examples. Exam answers and assignments need to demonstrate an excellent understanding of theory used effectively in the context of marketing communications and the relationships organizations have with a range of stakeholders.

It is unlikely that it will be effective to deliver this unit on a lecture-only basis. The more appropriate role for the unit leader is as a facilitator helping, guiding and encouraging students to develop their own knowledge and skills through self-study. To help make this work, students should secure a copy of the recommended textbook, supplemented by workbooks and other texts, and use these to develop their base knowledge. They should be encouraged to read more widely from marketing journals, marketing press and the quality newspapers.

Sessions should be used for presentations and small group work looking at cases and, perhaps, answers to short multiple-choice questions to test progress. Tutors should provide opportunities to develop simple plans and discuss implementation issues. All students should develop a portfolio of materials based upon two brands from contrasting sectors. The portfolio should contain examples of marketing communications practice and relationship issues that are encountered by the organization. It is through this form of work that effective learning develops.

The Marketing Management in Practice unit will build on the theory and basic skills developed in this unit by practising students in the planning and implementation of communications activities to support marketing and wider business objectives.

Additional resources (Syllabus – Professional Diploma In Marketing)

Introduction

Texts to support the individual units are listed in the syllabus for each unit. This Appendix shows a list of marketing journals, press and websites that tutors and students may find useful in supporting their studies at Professional Diploma.

Marketing journals

Students can keep abreast of developments in the academic field of marketing by reference to the main marketing journals.

- o *Corporate Reputation Review* – Henry Stewart
- o *European Journal of Marketing* – Emerald
- o *Harvard Business Review* – Harvard
- o *International Journal of Advertising* – WARC
- o *International Journal of Corporate Communications* – Emerald
- o *International Journal of Market Research* – WARC

- ○ *Journal of Consumer Behaviour An International Review* – Henry Stewart
- ○ *Journal of the Academy of Marketing Science* – Sage Publications
- ○ *Journal of Marketing* – American Marketing Assoc. Pubs Group
- ○ *Journal of Marketing Communications* – Routledge
- ○ *Journal of Marketing Management* – Westburn Pubs Ltd
- ○ *International Journal of Market Research* – NTC Pubs
- ○ *Journal of Product and Brand Management* – Emerald
- ○ *Journal of Services Marketing* – Emerald
- ○ *Marketing Review* – Westburn Pubs Ltd

Press

Students will be expected to have access to current examples of marketing campaigns and so should be sure to keep up to date with the appropriate marketing and quality daily press, including:

- ○ *Campaign* – Haymarket
- ○ *Internet Business* – Haymarket
- ○ *Marketing* – Haymarket
- ○ *Marketing Business* – Chartered Institute of Marketing
- ○ *Marketing Week* – Centaur
- ○ *Revolution* – Haymarket

Websites

The Chartered Institute of Marketing

www.cim.co.uk	CIM website containing case studies, reports, addresses
www.cim.co.uk/learningzone	Website for CIM students and tutors containing study information, past exam papers and case study examples. Also access to 'the marketer' articles online
www.cimeducator.com	The CIM site for tutors only

Publications on-line

www.revolution.haynet.com	Revolution magazine
www.brandrepublic.com	Marketing magazine
www.FT.com	A wealth of information for cases (now charging)
www.IPA.co.uk	Need to register – communication resources
www.booksites.net	Financial Times Prentice Hall Text websites

Sources of useful information

www.acnielsen.co.uk	AC Nielsen – excellent for research
http://advertising.utexas.edu/world/	Resources for advertising and marketing professionals, students and tutors
www.bized.com	Case studies
www.corporateinformation.com	Worldwide sources listed by country
www.esomar.nl	European Body representing Research Organisations – useful for guidelines on research ethics and approaches
www.dma.org.uk	The Direct Marketing Association
www.eiu.com	The Economist Intelligence Unit
www.euromonitor.com	Euromonitor consumer markets
www.europa.eu.int	The European Commission's extensive range of statistics and reports relating to EU and member countries

www.managementhelp.org/ research/ research.htm	Part of the 'Free Management Library' – explaining research methods
www.marketresearch.org.uk	The MRS site with information and access to learning support for students – useful links on ethics and code of conduct
www.mmc.gov.uk	Summaries of Competition Commission reports
www.oecd.org	OECD statistics and other information relating to member nations including main economic indicators
www.quirks.com	An American source of information on marketing research issues and projects
www.statistics.gov.uk	UK Government statistics
www.un.org	United Nations publish statistics on member nations
www.worldbank.org	World bank economic, social and natural resource indicators for over 200 countries. Includes over 600 indicators covering GNP per capita, growth, economic statistics and so on

Case sites

www.bluelagoon.co.uk	Case – SME website address
www.ebay.com	Online auction – buyer behaviour
www.glenfiddich.com	Interesting site for case and branding
www.interflora.co.uk	e-commerce direct ordering
www.moorcroft.co.uk	Good for relationship marketing
www.ribena.co.uk	Excellent targeting and history of comms

© CIM 2005